Beautiful Swift Fox

NUMBER SEVEN

Tarleton State University
Southwestern Studies in the Humanities

Erna Fergusson (holding hat), her driver, right, *and tourists on the Rito de Los Frijoles, circa 1922. Courtesy Fergusson family*

Beautiful Swift Fox

Erna Fergusson
and the Modern Southwest

BY

ROBERT FRANKLIN GISH

Texas A&M University Press
College Station

Library of Congress Cataloging-in-Publication Data
Gish, Robert.
  Beautiful swift fox : Erna Fergusson and the modern southwest / by
Robert Franklin Gish.—1st ed.
    p.   cm.—(Tarleton State University southwestern studies in
the humanities ; no. 7)
  Includes bibliographical references and index.
  ISBN 0-89096-719-9 (alk. paper)
    1. Fergusson, Erna, 1888–1964.   2. Historians—Southwest, New—
Biography.   3. Authors, American—Southwest, New—Biography.
4. Travelers' writings, American—Southwest, New—History and
criticism.   5. Southwest, New—Biography.   I. Title.   II. Series.
E175.5.F4G57   1996
979'.03'092—dc20
  [B]   96-22471
                                                                  CIP

For Robin, Annabeth & Judy—

new women in a new West

She delighted me with her fine ideals and horse sense.

—CHARLES FLETCHER LUMMIS

Contents

· ·

Preface

. . . .

More than a century after her birth in 1888, Erna Fergusson's accommodating spirit still hovers over much of this account of her Southwestern writings. I felt her presence in a very strong way when I first began to think about her as a literary artist and "first lady" of Southwestern letters. And I felt her penetrating eyes and inscrutable, almost changeling, smile throughout the months when the actual writing took place of what is now *Beautiful Swift Fox: Erna Fergusson and the Modern Southwest.*

In large part Erna Fergusson's presence as person and Southwesterner was very much with me from the start to the finish of this work because everywhere I looked in search of materials, especially in Albuquerque, she was there. She was there in the files of the downtown Albuquerque Public Library. She was there—and startlingly so—in James Wilfred Kerr's portrait which hangs on the wall of the old Edith Street branch of the Albuquerque Public Library, an archive which is now devoted exclusively to rare books and a special Southwest collection. In my long-past years at Albuquerque High School my friends and I met at this old, main library on Tuesday nights to socialize—an activity we euphemistically called studying. But that, too, in its way, was part of Erna Fergusson's modern Southwest—and mine.

Her spirit was also felt in the Huning Highlands, which extend north and south on Edith Street. Even now, a century later, that neighborhood still carries her grandfather's name, and thus her own heritage, into not just the pages of Albuquerque history but into the city's very streets for the later generations who now walk them—shadowed by twin-towered skyscrapers, golden-walled, Cíbola-looking banks, five ancient, dormant volcanoes to the west, and the Sandia and Manzano mountains to the east.

I sensed her presence again while looking through the Huning and Fergusson papers in the Coronado Room at the University of New Mexico's Zimmerman Library. She was in the university's Anderson room as well, a room named for her friend Clinton P. Anderson, favorite son and U.S. representative from New Mexico during the 1940s. And I found her yet again at the Erna Fergusson Library, another branch of the Albuquerque Public Library system, located in the newer northeast heights on San Mateo Boulevard. Here her presence had leaped quadrants of the city, from southwest and southeast to northeast, from *her* valley to *her* heights, a jump indicative of just how truly pervasive her legacy in books is in old and new Albuquerque.

I soon realized with even greater conviction than I had first intuited, when the slightest glimmerings of a book on the Fergusson family was taking shape, that I grew up feeling the same spirit of place which she felt, which her brothers Harvey and Francis felt. In a real sense, I had felt and now reimagined and recreated both her presence and her Southwest. Her spirit was at Castle Huning, her grandfather's spectacular home in Albuquerque's Old Town. I first became aware of it as a school, for as the turns and quirks of history would have it, I attended kindergarten there shortly after World War II. I saw in my teachers something of Fergusson's presence, just as I felt her grandfather Huning's eccentricities in the gazebo where we hid or rested in the shade, or inside the castle where we performed dramatized nursery rhymes, complete with improvised but ingeniously ornate costumes. In my role as Simple Simon going to the fair, and in my schoolyard escapades, I was also running with Erna Fergusson, with a gracious and wise "beautiful swift fox."

Later, in the late 1950s, long after the Huning family sold Huning Castle and shortsighted entrepreneurs decided to demolish it, I would stop at the Dairy Queen malt shop or the Lota Burger drive-in and look across the street at the bleak and deserted lot filled with tumbleweeds and still awaiting "development" and new profits. Rather than the horse-drawn streetcars, which her grandfather sponsored in his own contribution to progress and which Fergusson herself enjoyed riding between Old Town and New Town when she was a child, I would watch the *vatos locos,* the stompers, and various hot-rodders and "squadros" cruise by or peel out, or I would rehearse the tunes and songs of my own rockabilly band, The Drakes, or simply sit and slurp to the car-radio rhythms of Elvis, Tiny Morrie, Ricky Nelson, and the other big-name and local rockers of the day.

Erna Fergusson and her spirit were at Albuquerque High School, too. She had literally walked the same halls I walked, but some half a century earlier. And she was at Manzano Day School on Central Avenue West, not far from Old Town and Castle Huning, where I took my daughter, Robin, for her first two years of elementary school. Fergusson, in fact, had grown up in that same rambling adobe building, known to her as La Glorieta, a school of a different sort. It was the place where her father had committed suicide, haunted by ghosts of depression and perceived failure.

She was present during the interviews I had with some of her friends, friends who had known her at various times during her life—early and late—but who had survived her: Irene Fisher, Peggy Pond Church, Lawrence Clark Powell, Paul Horgan, and T. M. Pearce—all but Powell (at the time of this writing) now deceased but, like Fergusson, very much immortalized in the pages of Southwestern literary history. I could sense she was still very much alive in all of them—as person and woman, yes, but also as spirit—and even in legend as Beautiful Swift Fox, as she was called by certain Pueblo Indians of the region. She was in the letters of the numerous correspondents whom I queried: in the letters of Roland Dickey and Mrs. Alexander Caemmerer Jr., Fergusson's niece and one-time illustrator, Li Browne; in the scores of business and personal letters she left; in the words of her brother, the late Francis Fergusson, and his wife, Peggy, whose fondly remembered hospitality in their New Jersey home and in their supportive letters, knew no limit. Harvey Fergusson II also gave me much needed endorsements and support, as did Honora Neuman.

Above all, Fergusson and her Southwest were in her writings. I had first read some of her Southwestern books as a student of Professor David Remley at about the time he wrote and published the first scholarly monograph on her. Over the years David has remained a friend and a teacher and has introduced me to more than one deserving new book, more than one new insight about the Southwest. In my earliest aspirations to become an author and lead the "literary life," I was unable to write the pamphlet he suggested I contract to do on Mabel Dodge Luhan, strapped as I was with course work and a dissertation to finish. But I did read his Steck-Vaughn pamphlet, *Erna Fergusson*, and I did listen hard when he talked about travel narratives in his colonial American literature class. And on one wild trip from Durango to Albuquerque, through snow and rain, clouds and sun, gazing through the windshield of a Volkswagen Super Bug, we looked west toward the majestic shape and colors of Cabezon Peak (*tse najin*) and knew the same surge of enchantment with space and time, known to Fergusson and found in her writings about the modern Southwest. In a special sense I think of this study of Erna Fergusson's Southwest as a repayment for Remley's confidence in assigning a graduate student such an ambitious project as a work on Mabel Dodge Luhan—and an extension of his own commentary on Fergusson. Much before feminism and regionalism, and a curricular interest in New Journalism and Women's

Studies found their way into the academy as I knew it, Remley recognized and incorporated into his classes his particular perspectives on the new West and the role of new women like Luhan and Fergusson in it.

Like David Remley, the late Professor T. M. (Matt) Pearce always had more than enough time for me and my questions about the Southwest and its literary history. He knew what can only be described as the Southwest renaissance firsthand, edited the *New Mexico Quarterly* in its halcyon days, organized the lecture-under-the-stars series to which Fergusson contributed frequently, knew her as a close friend—simply knew the books and the authors who had made the 1920s, 30s, and 40s such interesting decades for the fine arts in the Southwest.

In addition to knowing what I think of as the "Isleta way," for he had lived on Isleta Road, old Highway 85 between Albuquerque and Isleta Pueblo, when he first arrived in New Mexico, he had also discovered the Southwest in which I was born and started to "discover" some decades later. And so he, too, like Charles Fletcher Lummis, Paul Horgan, and Harvey and Erna Fergusson, led me to new discoveries about the Southwest as *la tierra del alma*. Although decidedly Anglo and ethnocentric in their attitudes, Matt Pearce, Erna Fergusson, and company suspected, and acknowledged, and, of more importance, attempted to understand and interpret the significance of the multicultural and pluralistic thickness of the American West.

Beyond the dedication to my daughters, Robin and Annabeth, and my wife, Judy, who know Erna Fergusson's and their own modern Southwests, I dedicate this study to the memory of Matt Pearce, and to those glorious and enlightening days in David Remley's American Studies courses at the University of New Mexico, and to our convergence as kindred spirits in the dimensions of space and time known to us all—and to Lummis and Fergusson and others from generations earlier—as the "Southwest."

Beautiful Swift Fox is not a biography in any narrow sense of the word—although this study, like all literary studies, has biographical as well as autobiographical dimensions. I do not lay claim to firsthand knowledge of Erna Fergusson or her era. The books on the Fergusson family developed thus—first, a literary biography of Harvey Fergusson called *Frontier's End* (Lincoln: University of Nebraska Press, 1988) and now this volume on Erna Fergusson. *Beautiful Swift Fox*, like my other book in this series, *Nueva Granada: Paul Horgan and the Southwest*, may be read as a kind of companion or "sister" volume.

I take it upon myself—with some apprehension and much empathy for the lives and experiences of women—to write *about* a woman writer, a feminist of her own prototypic mold. Perhaps it is gratuitous, if not problematic, to attest here to the androgynous aspects of all authorship—both Fergusson's and my own. Despite old myths and stereotypes, the old and new West was and is much more than the mythologized "man's world." In my approach to Erna Fergusson's Southwestern writings, I view her, in a certain larger sense, as a significant writer who happened to be a woman and who resisted allowing confinements of stereotyped and prescribed roles to stifle her expansive and adventurous spirit. As a result, her life and activities, her travels and talking-turned-writing introduced other women and men to the expansive geographical and psychological possibilities of the region. She is, as a first lady of modern Southwestern writing, exemplary. Erna Fergusson certainly expanded my own understanding of the womanly West. Male that I am, I seek only to understand and interpret my perceptions of her, sans sexism, to whatever extent possible.

Talking with her younger brother Francis and writing about her other brother, novelist Harvey Fergusson, have brought me closer to knowing Erna Fergusson as a Southwesterner and a kindred spirit, and I admit to a certain nativistic pride in sharing her birthright as a New Mexican. But I do not intend to suggest that I have her special blessings out of the annals and pages of history in my attempt to acknowledge and interpret her Southwestern writings. I do lay claim, though, to being a part of the modern Southwest and thus to her Southwest.

Like her I grew up essentially gringo in the Rio Grande Valley area of Albuquerque—albeit as a *chapito* and several generations behind her. I hope that in my attempt to show how varied and significant Erna Fergusson's talents as a Southwestern writer really were that I capture, perhaps revitalize, a bit of her spirit and her presence and thereby lead present and future readers, Southwesterners and others, back to her books. She was an undisputed regional "first lady," a lover of Southwestern landscapes and lives, a traveler, a historian, and an advocate for greater intercultural understanding—appreciation not just of her Southwest but, in her words, "Our Southwest." It is that special part of America which continues to prove so alluring in the 1990s' Sunbelt migrations, just as it did to past tourists and travelers for whom she wrote and for whom she served as tour guide. We can only wish that she were here for the millennium. Even so, the Southwest of the twenty-first century will carry something of her legacy.

My thanks go to all who have assisted me in this enterprise. Those who provided needed and timely assistance include William A. Koshland, Cathy Henderson, Stella de Sa Rego, Raphael Clancy, Don Berke, Thomas B. Catron III, and Paul W. Robinson. I am also grateful to the estates of Paul Horgan and Alfred A. Knopf for granting permission to use and quote from archival materials. I had the special pleasure of the help of my daughters, Robin Elaine Butzier and Anne Elizabeth Gish, their own new West women. They found their ways around both Manzano Day School and sundry libraries in New Mexico and the Midwest, cordially and efficiently assisting in the research for this book. To Judy and Tim I am ever grateful for their patience over the years with my grumbling when writing time strikes. To the staffs of the Center for Southwest Research at the University of New Mexico Zimmerman Library, the Harry Ransom Humanities Research Center at the University of Texas at Austin, the University of Arizona library, the University of Northern Iowa Donald O. Rod Library, Cal Poly's Robert E. Kennedy Library, and, most especially, the Albuquerque Museum and the Albuquerque Public Library I offer my most sincere thanks.

The National Endowment for the Humanities and Professor Leonard Dinnerstein gave me a summer to first formulate and draft an essay on some of the ideas expressed here. A portion of chapter 2 appeared in a previous version in the *American Indian Quarterly* under the title "Erna Fergusson's Travels toward Exoticism," and is reprinted in *Beyond Bounds: Cross Cultural Essays on Anglo, American Indian, and Chicano Literature,* published by the University of New Mexico Press, 1996.

Tom Pilkington, Mark Busby, Jerry Bradley, and Craig Clifford—who love Texas and the Southwest and communicate that love in their writings and in their encouragements to other writers devoted to the literature and the history of the Southwest—I regard as inspirations, sponsors, and compadres. Warren Baker, Glenn Irvin, Harry Sharp, and Paul Zingg have my gratitude for their encouragement to maintain a commitment to writing and scholarship while launching and directing a new ethnic studies department at Cal Poly.

To my parents and their search as Okies for health and life in the Southwest, and for our Cherokee heritage; for the reverence they instilled in me for the Southwest's flora and fauna, its rivers and streams, mountains and mesas; for the vistas they allowed me on our travels; and for our times and talks in Albuquerque's South Valley—for such a legacy I offer these thoughts on how the Southwest helped determine a person—a traveler, historian, and advocate called variously Erna Fergusson and *Beautiful Swift Fox.*

Beautiful Swift Fox

Chapter 1

Inspiration:
Tierra Encantada

Once in his lifetime a man . . . ought to give himself up
to a particular landscape in his experience, to look at it from as many
angles as he can, to wonder about it, to dwell upon it.

—N. Scott Momaday

During the 1950s and 1960s Erna Mary Fergusson (1888–1964) was generally regarded by the national and certainly the Southwestern "literati" as that region's most prominent living female writer. Outside literary circles she was recognized as a humane and knowledgeable spokesperson for equality among the Southwest's three major cultures: Native American, Hispanic/Latino/Chicano, and Anglo-American.

She was also an Anglo-American and a woman, and these facts are not entirely incidental in her written self-dramatizations. Both as a writer and as a lobbyist for greater understanding in Southwestern intercultural relations, Fergusson was able—through good humor, common sense, determination, and the pervasive written word—to reduce racism, sexism, and cultural misunderstanding between the dominant Anglo-American majority and the cultural and gender minorities represented by Native Americans, Hispanics/Latinos/Chicanos, and women. Many of her attitudes and assumptions, although ethnocentric to some degree, and thereby extensions of Anglo-American social conditioning, were nevertheless tempered by her ability to empathize with "otherness"—to grasp the relativity of cultural and individual differences. Although Fergusson was born into an

illustrious family of some economic and political prominence, that prominence, and her Anglo roots, still needed reconciling with the cultural and
literary dominance of the day which was predominately masculine. Thus,
she identified with the minority status of stereotypical and cultural pre-
scriptions about the role of women. As traveler, guide, and writer, Fergusson sought to reposition herself, and others of her kind, as a new woman
in a new and evolving, expanding modern Southwest.

The purpose of this account is to take a latter-day look at Erna Fergusson's writings about New Mexico and the Southwest. Thus, this study provides an assessment of the nature and extent of her contributions to the
literary and cultural history of that region—a region (particularly the U.S.–
Mexico border) with a past and a future crucially important to the history
of the United States. Fergusson was a tremendously complex and fascinating person, combining keen intelligence and critical mindedness with
personableness, a passion for fairness, and a decidedly humanistic and
pragmatic sensibility. But the variations on her public identity as a Southwestern writer (traveler, historian, and advocate) provide an organizational
means for understanding the measure of her achievement, which in sum
was much greater than any one of these roles, justifying her claim as an
American presence as well as a regional author and civilizing force—a prototypic new woman in a new West.

She studied, talked, and wrote about other places, especially Mexico
and Latin America, and other concerns than those of the American Southwest. But at the heart of her values and attitudes, and her persona as a
modern Anglo-American woman (which she dramatized in her writings,
including her interpretations of Latin American and Hawaiian cultures),
was her identity and birthright as a native-born New Mexican and Southwesterner, and as a granddaughter and daughter of an illustrious pioneer
family that figured prominently in the settlement as well as the statehood
of New Mexico. The effect of a landscape, of an ethnic and cultural environment, on a writer's mind and spirit is no small part of seeking to understand Fergusson's mind, heart, and soul—her style and her subject as a
regional writer.

New Mexico, known as the "land of enchantment," has long cast its
spell over artists of various kinds, most notably writers and painters—so
much so that many such artists think of New Mexico as the heart of the
Southwest. This, of course, is a debatable, if not unresolvable, issue. In any
event, to seek Erna Fergusson is to seek the spirit of place and to appreciate
the significance of regionalism in literature, the importance of setting as
inspiration and theme, process and substance. And this search allows one

to face life, to see it and interpret it as she did—as a woman, an Anglo-American, and a Southwestern writer.

Because Fergusson was so multifaceted as a person and as a writer, her written versions of the Southwest exist in several forms, reflective of her perceptions and activities: travelogue, journalistic report, lyrical description of lives and landscapes, popular history, informative and persuasive essay. Her writing is almost always recognizable as some type of exposition or argumentation, with heavy reliance on two dominant modes of discourse so common to travel writers and writers about "place": narration and description.

Although she aspired to write a novel about Malinche, Cortez's much maligned mistress and lady of many Mexican American/Spanish American myths, she published no fiction, no plays, no poetry in the strictest sense of those literary forms. But her talents as an essayist demonstrate how truly far-reaching and encompassing the potential of nonfiction is in helping both writer and audience to see, to name, and to "know." Her use of the essay form—drawing on the techniques of journalism and historical inquiry—helps us appreciate the flexibility of the essay in expanding the boundaries of nonfiction into what has come to be called "new journalism," among other classifications. Similarly, she helps the reader understand that the distinctions among qualitative, narrative, and descriptive history, that is, history respectively viewed as either social science or as art, are all too often arbitrary and reductive.

In this sense, too, Fergusson's writings are much in the romantic tradition of writing about the West as discovery, as a brave new world, a land inhabited by strange and sublime landscapes and by dark-skinned peoples with alien languages and exotic ways, much in need of explaining (or at least recognizing) by those lighter-skinned travelers who see or imagine that inevitably grandiose region as either settlers or as tourists. They feel compelled to write about it and explain it for the sake of the curiosity, interest, and knowledge of other "explorers" and emigrants. In this context Fergusson's writings offer much commentary about the reciprocal perceptions of East and West. For the point can be made that much of her audience was in fact Eastern, or, at least, was portrayed and projected as such in Fergusson's Southwestern writings.

True to its name and legend as a *tierra encantada*, New Mexico held many enchantments for Fergusson—the person, the citizen, the writer. She was native born to the state. She loved the land, the climate, the people. She loved the Native Americans, Spanish Americans, Mexican Americans, and Anglo-Americans who lived there. Those groups made up what she called, in the subtitle to *New Mexico,* the "pageantry of three peoples," whose histories and cultures mingled with the land and made it what it was: geological, geographical, and historical place; and idea, part of the myth, legend, and lure of the American Southwest.

In the simplest terms Fergusson is a Southwestern writer because she was born there and because she wrote about its lives and its landscapes. But behind such a simple definition of what makes first claims to constitute a regional writer is a more complex network of cause and effect. If she is a New Mexico writer, a Southwestern writer, a Western writer, it is because the region and its enchantments inspired her, motivated her to write, and to write about the very essence of her inspiration and her heritage.

Many writers, amateur and professional, have experienced and tried to explain what can be thought of as the poetics of regionalism, the psychological and aesthetic spell—as impetus and as literary product—of the Southwest and, more particularly for Fergusson's life and profession, of New Mexico. New Mexico has historically been a *tierra encantada* for writers and artists, travelers and questers of all nationalities and cultures: American Indians in search of a harmonious, protected environment for hunting or farming, an appropriate sanctuary, perhaps an alternative version of an Anglo-European Edenic garden in which to prosper; the Spanish in search of Cíbola, the Seven Cities of Gold, of Quivira, of a place of riches, an El Dorado to claim for Christ, king, and wealth; the nineteenth-century *rico,* or the twentieth-century Mexican American and Mexican in quest of the mythical homeland of Aztlán, or simply the more prosperous "good life" north of the border; the Anglo-American looking for commerce and profit, for ostensibly unlimited natural resources to use and sell, for fresh air, sunshine, good health, and wide open spaces, for the progress of town and railroad, of automobile, of settlement, of laboratory for advancing scientific and military technology, the desert sands transformed into a new kind of silicon.

Whether as Nueva Granada, Mexican or U.S. Territory, the modern mecca of the Southwest for tuberculosis and pulmonary patient or tourist, the more recent manifestation of "continental drift" to the Sunbelt—as all of these things and more, New Mexico continues to hold various and sundry enchantments. In many ways, this spell can be viewed as a metaphor— just like the Rio Grande valley itself—for the spell of the entire Southwest, from as far east as Arkansas, Oklahoma, and Kansas, all the way west to California and its ageless dream.

Whether from the vantage point of the native born or the emigrant, the resident or the exile, amid the definitions and explanations, there remain many complex issues associated with the magnetism of the Southwest and New Mexico, the stimulus on and response of Anglo writers to their particular kind of regionalism—as Southwestern, Western, and American writers. The enchantments of New Mexico that Erna Fergusson experienced and wrote about (and helped continue, sustain, and promulgate as "tradition") help her readers piece together the complexities of a cultural, psychological, and aesthetic puzzle associated with a "spirit of place." That "place," known as the "Southwest," thanks in part to Charles F. Lummis's naming it, is also more generally associated with westering—a process of discovery and settlement, old Southwest becoming new Southwest. In such contexts Fergusson helps us realize that the modern Southwest is a hybrid of many previous "southwests."

NEW MEXICO BAROQUE

Not everyone is attracted to the Southwest or things Southwestern. Southwestern and New Mexican art ranges from lowbrow, curio kitsch to highbrow, authentic objects; from the self-consciously stylized to the natural, from the simplicity of functional pioneer and folk art to utterly nonutilitarian abstractions, from primitive to modern, popular to elite. Moreover, within each of these styles of this or that kind are degrees of good and bad quality. Often, the pros and cons, likes and dislikes of individual taste are associated with the biases of East-West.

The explosion of what Erna's brother, Harvey Fergusson, among others, came to think of as a kind of hysterical, if not cultish, worship of the primitive took his own heartfelt love of his homeland to such an extreme that he was compelled to satirize both the movement and some of its principals—for example, such personages as Mabel Dodge Luhan, Witter Bynner, Mary Austin, and even his sister, Erna, in novels like *Footloose McGarnigal* (1930). Similarly Stanley Walker's indictment in the 1950s of what he labeled the "lofty pretentiousness" of "New Mexico baroque" is a classic illustration of objecting to this tendency. Walker, who was born in Texas but moved to the East and joined the staff of the *New York Herald Tribune* in 1940, claimed:

> One either thinks New Mexico baroque is great or one doesn't. An odd thing happens to writers who live in the high country, especially in the mystical stretches along the Rio Grande above El Paso. It happened to poor old D. H. Lawrence, to Mabel Dodge Luhan, and to many others—to a lesser degree to such a sound citizen as Miss Erna Fergusson. They see the mountains, the sand, the stars, the cactus, the wrinkled Indians, and they begin to babble about "time" and "space."

At best, and in moderate doses, this can be fetching literature; at its worst it can be baffling—like something by Dylan Thomas out of Sitting Bull.[1]

The ornate, embellished, "lofty" quality which Walker dislikes in certain New Mexico writers presumably also entails the fundamental reaction—the motivation and inspiration—as well as the style and substance of Anglo writers like Luhan, Lawrence, and "Miss Erna Fergusson" to the exotic, sublime, the peculiarly striking landscapes and cultures of the Southwest: "the mountains, the sand, the stars, the cactus, the wrinkled Indians." More than likely, Walker's rankling is occasioned by passages of lyrical description which amount to the same thing which more favorably disposed contemporary "Western" readers/writers like Lawrence Clark Powell frequently find in Erna Fergusson's writing, passages which Powell regards as moments of "transcendence." Whatever the style and the substance of what Walker labels "New Mexico baroque," it amounts to more than babbling about time and space, as he satirically, but seriously, would have it.

In any event, if Luhan, Lawrence, Fergusson, and "other writers on the Rio Grande above El Paso" share certain stylistic elements of "New Mexico baroque," then certainly they come to it and express it from differing vantage points: Lawrence from England and other world wanderings; Luhan and Horgan from Buffalo, New York; and Fergusson from New Mexico. And they come to it from their values and assumptions as Anglos. If writers as stylistically different as D. H. Lawrence and Erna Fergusson can be mentioned in the same breath, then clearly there is some powerful "spirit of place," some abiding animus at work in their art and in the lure of the Southwest.

Leonard Lutwack documents with considerable erudition the disarmingly simple observation that the "role of place" in literature—as inspiration and as theme—is extensive.[2] Lutwack touches on many individual and national reasons why a consideration of place is essential in literary studies. He also sounds a new note of ecological urgency for such attention: "In so far as the representation of place in literature has an important influence on how people regard individual places and the whole world as a place, it may be concluded that literature must now be seen in terms of the contemporary concern for survival."[3] Certainly the reverse of Lutwack's premise is true as well; how people regard individual places determines the nature of literature and its very creation as a means of survival for the author as much as for the audience. Most literature, when viewed nationally, can ultimately be considered the literature of "place."

Much Southwest/New Mexico literature is the literature of "home." It is expressive of the need for home in all its essences as the very means of a special magic and enchantment known to writers, whether of fiction or of fact—the inspiration to translate that home into words. Charles Fletcher Lummis was one of the earliest modern Anglo writers to consider New Mexico and the Southwest as "enchanting," and thus he was one originator of that tradition. Another New Mexico writer of a later generation and another racial heritage than Lummis and Fergusson, Rudolfo A. Anaya, describes this sense of home and of the compulsion and, indeed, the ability of a writer to write about his or her own particular homeland as "epiphany in landscape."[4] If, as New Mexico poet Peggy Pond Church suggests in "Return to a Landscape: For Mary MacArthur Bryan,"[5] a woman's response to New Mexico is different from a man's, or a poet's sensibility is different than a novelist's, then certainly Anaya's response as a Mexican American novelist to his particular enchanted land, his *tierra del alma*, is different from Fergusson's as an Anglo woman of an earlier time who expressed herself primarily in the humanistic pragmatism of nonfiction Southwestern writings. Ethnicity, class, gender, age, we are coming more to realize, are all variables in the perception of truth—be that truth geographical or cultural/historical.

Nevertheless, general similarities exist in the ability and disposition of New Mexico and the Southwest to cast their enchantments over woman and man, native born, emigrant and visitor alike. In this sense, what Anaya says about New Mexico as epiphany is applicable to Fergusson and to all writing about "West," as is, similarly, what Lummis, Lawrence, Luhan, and even the likes of such diverse individuals and sensibilities as John Collier, Carl Gustav Jung, and Edmund Wilson thought of New Mexico and the larger region as a land of enchantment for writers and artists, bureaucrats, political activists, and psychoanalysts.

When Anaya speaks of landscape he prefers to use the Spanish words *"la tierra"* because they suggest a more profound relationship between person and place, and it is that relationship which brings to landscape the potential for metaphor and epiphany:

> On the one pole of the metaphor stands man, on the other is the raw, majestic and awe-inspiring landscape of the southwest; the epiphany is the natural response to that landscape, a coming together of these two forces. And because I feel a close kinship with my environment I feel constantly in touch with that epiphany which opens me up to receive the power in my landscape. I don't believe a person can be born and raised in the southwest and not be affected by the

land. The landscape changes the man, and the man becomes his land-scape.[6]

Such an epiphany, such finding of magic in the realism of the Southwest, is at the heart of what Stanley Walker finds so incapable of empathizing with.

Fergusson is not a symbolic or metaphorical writer in the main. She is not a poet like Peggy Pond Church. She is not a Western novelist like her brother, Harvey, not a practitioner of what is now generally identifiable as "magic realism" in certain romantic writers—whether American like Hawthorne, Latin American like Gabriel García Márquez, or Chicano like Anaya. She sees the land as a journalist, a reporter, a historian, assuredly. However, she also sees the Southwest and New Mexico as her home and opens up to the revelations of its landscape in ways which can be viewed as transcendent, an epiphany of the realization that there is indeed something special about her relationship with the land as a woman born in and to the Southwest. And, finally, it is this relationship itself about which she writes and, more than likely, the relationship which accounts for her identity as an *aficionada* of Spanish American, Mexican American, and Latin American heritages, not to mention the closeness to the land inherent in the American Indian worldview.

In her various voicings and self-dramatizations, in her various modes and techniques of presenting New Mexico in her life and in her writing, she extends the tradition continued at the end of the nineteenth and the beginning of the twentieth centuries by Lummis, an Anglo traveler from Massachusetts. And she confirms Anaya's categorical Chicano belief, based on his own close relationship with his *tierra*, that a person (by implication any person, regardless of gender or class, race or ethnicity, though inevitably an individual born and reared in the Southwest) must be inspired and "enchanted" by the landscapes and the inhabitants of New Mexico and the larger Southwest.

Anaya goes on to suggest that there is a special healing power—in addition to a creative power—in the ever-potential epiphany waiting in a person's close relationship with Southwestern landscape. For Anaya, like most writers with an indigenous perspective, a person's relationship to landscape has a restorative, curative power, just as "the end of all art is to make us well and to cure our souls."[7] If the writer is separated from his or her sense of place, alienation and frustration set in, or an estrangement from the "redemption of epiphany."

Anaya explains that in the process of composition, though alone at his desk, the writer is always, through memory, seeking the surge of creative energy which comes through an experienced epiphany with landscape—especially in New Mexico, Anaya's personal metaphorical center as a writer. What Anaya says of his own art can also be applied to Fergusson and her attempt to communicate her own sense of New Mexico: "It is our task as writers to convey our landscape to our readers and to work through the harmony of this essential metaphor."[8] Wordsworth, Emerson, Thoreau, and other high Romantics speak of much the same impulse, a similar epiphany of landscape—a perception and a sensibility more sublime than picturesque. It might be argued, however, that what ultimately prevents Erna Fergusson's claim to greatness is her inevitable intuition of the sublime accommodated through filters, if not lenses, of the picturesque.

New Mexico as epiphany, as a special spirit of place, as inspiration and subject for Anaya and before him for Fergusson as another native-born New Mexican, was also experienced—perhaps not as profoundly as Anaya or Lawrence or even Lummis (at least in his photographs)—by Mabel Dodge Luhan in her westering attempt to revive and recover from a life of leisure and ennui in the East. In her newfound sense of purpose to "save the Indians," Luhan said of her arrival in New Mexico and her impetus to publicize the "spiritual qualities" of the place, "For the first time in my life I heard the world singing in the same key in which my life inside me had sometimes lifted and poured itself out."[9]

Mabel Dodge Luhan's celebrated Taos guest, D. H. Lawrence, not only took advantage of Luhan's invitation to visit New Mexico but went far to confirm that she was right in believing that New Mexico would be a "simpatico" place for him. Luhan, after reading some of Lawrence's works, felt that he was the one writer "who can really *see* this Taos country and the Indians, and who can describe it so that it is as much alive between the covers of a book as it is in relation [*sic*]."[10]

Mabel, with the assistance of her Taos Pueblo husband Tony, worked her own brand of enchantments, drew herself into the "core of her being," "leaped through space," and joined herself "to the central core of Lawrence" while he was traveling in Italy, India, Australia, and Ceylon. She finally succeeded, she believed, in willing Lawrence (with his wife Frieda) to New Mexico.[11] Lawrence's stay in New Mexico (1922–23, 1924–25) has been well-chronicled.[12] His real and imagined vista from the ranch where he stayed above Questa, north of Taos, resulted in the revised version of *Studies in Classic American Literature* (1923), *St. Mawr* (1925), and numerous essays, including "Indians and an Englishman," "Taos," and "New Mexico."[13] Fergusson held to the conviction that Lawrence's *Mornings in Mexico* owed its descriptions of Indian dances to his observation of American

Indian dances in New Mexico, and that in his haunting excursion into the exoticism of willed primitive sacrifice, "The Woman Who Rode Away," Lawrence "describes a Pueblo dance as an ancient Aztec rite."[14]

Probably Lawrence's descriptions of Pueblo ceremonial dances and Lummis's own accounts before Lawrence both influenced Fergusson's descriptions of Indian dances in various narrative accounts, including *Dancing Gods* (1931). At least it is enlightening to view her Indian travel and tour narratives within this tradition of exoticism. Even more significant in charting this tradition here is the reciprocal influence of Erna Fergusson's *Dancing Gods* and Harvey Fergusson's chapter on "The Dancing Builders" in *Rio Grande* (1933), his history of the Southwest as manifested in northern New Mexico, not to mention Laura Gilpin's and Paul Horgan's later Southwestern river books, *Rio Grande* (1949) and *Great River* (1954). And, no doubt, Harvey Fergusson's *Rio Grande* and many of his Southwest novels both influenced and were influenced by Erna Fergusson's other Southwestern writings, such as *Our Southwest* (1940), *Albuquerque* (1947), *Murder and Mystery in New Mexico* (1948), and *New Mexico: A Pageant of Three Peoples* (1951). Fergusson and her father and mother, H. B. Fergusson (1848–1915) and Clara Mary Huning Fergusson (1865–1950), made their allusive, veiled, imaginatively "reconstructed" appearances in her brother's novels, just as Harvey is mentioned frequently (as are other family members) in his sister's books. Therein the Fergusson family reemerged as a family of privilege and dominance, as Anglo *ricos*, as a *familia* of the larger Southwest, microcosm become macrocosm and universalized.

Certainly the effect of New Mexico on D. H. Lawrence is implicit in his intuitions about the "deepest self," the "IT" of America in *Studies in Classic American Literature*, and most especially in his opening chapter, "The Spirit of Place," wherein he makes his now familiar assertion that "every continent has its own great spirit of place. Every people is polarized in some particular locality, which is home, the homeland. Different places on the face of the earth have different vital effluence, different vibration, different chemical exhalation, different polarity with different stars: call it what you like. But the spirit of place is a great reality."[15] What he called the center of it all, the "nodality," he found in Taos and New Mexico. He reports that the "Indians say Taos is the heart of the world."[16] And he believed it—to a point. When he arrived in Taos he felt something final, an arrival, an essence that still existed and could be felt by a traveler. William Carlos Williams, much aware of Lawrence's *Studies*, in his own panoramic account of America's "spirit of place," *In the American Grain* (1925), projects a similar exuberance into Columbus and other visitors to the New World.

Lawrence's descriptions of Taos Pueblo, of his arrival in New Mexico, of the Native American presence which struck him with such power provide something of a prototype for Fergusson's travel accounts and her descriptions of landscape and lives, especially *Dancing Gods.* The kinship is not so much in tone or technique but in allegiance to a belief in the nodality, the lasting spirit of place. Not only did she sense what Lawrence calls the nodality of New Mexico (and Anaya its "epiphany"), she also attempted to communicate the mysteries of place and the epiphanic experience of it through her writings.

Lawrence insisted that New Mexico was the "greatest experience from the outside" that he had ever had, that his "touching" of the country changed him forever. In his account one finds the same enchantments of place that prompted Fergusson to write and that provided her with a subject—her clear-eyed journalistic and pragmatic perspective notwithstanding. She was involved in the business of tourism as creator and promoter. But that was not central to her writing. She touched the country, and she wanted her readers to touch it, too, much the same way as the paying Eastern dudes did on the Koshare Tours she led. Lawrence, like Fergusson, knew that beyond the superficialities and stylizations of a place as peculiar and publicized as New Mexico was the power of the Southwest as a *tierra encantada:*

> New Mexico, one of the United States, part of the U.S.A. New Mexico, the picturesque reservation and playground of the eastern states, very romantic, old Spanish, Red Indian, desert mesas, pueblos, cowboys, penitents, all that film-stuff. Very nice, the great Southwest, put on a sombrero and knot a red kerchief round your neck, to go out in the great free spaces!
>
> That is New Mexico wrapped in the absolutely hygienic and shiny mucous-paper of our trite civilization. That is the New Mexico known to most of the Americans who know it at all. But break through the shiny sterilized wrapping, and actually *touch* the country and you will never be the same again.[17]

Lawrence's shift from the ridiculous and the glib to the sublime and the serious, his ability to see greater truths, the silliness of affectation and parody—like Williams's satirical "against the grain" condemnations as well—affords a complex interplay of satire and irony, which Fergusson also uses to great effect in her New Mexico writings. She is never as "mystical" nor as devotedly "vitalistic," not as much the worshipper of the primitive and the "solar plexus" as Lawrence (or numerous others of the eccentric Taos/

Santa Fe crowd of artists in the 1920s and 30s); and certainly she was not deliberately his imitator. But she shares his intolerance for sham and cant and his appreciation for essences. If Lawrencian "blood consciousness" had anything to do with it, it was the blood of birthright, of being part of the nodality of the Southwest by birth. Lawrence observes (the language and imagery echo that of Mabel Dodge Luhan as well, upon remembering her arrival in New Mexico) that "in the magnificent fierce morning of New Mexico one sprang awake, a new part of the soul woke up suddenly, and the old world gave way to a new."[18] For Fergusson that morning was a new century, but one that, thanks to the technological advances of transportation and communication, especially the automobile and the printed page, made the old world of the Native American, Hispanic, and Yankee pioneer past capable of rediscovery and preservation.

Swiss psychoanalyst Carl Jung, on his visit to New Mexico and Taos Pueblo, in an attempt to know not only himself but Europe better from "an outside point," carried on many discussions about Native American religion with Ochwiay Biano (Mountain Lake), "a chief of the Taos pueblos."[19] Jung experienced his own kind of epiphany concerning people, culture, and landscape, the symbolism of mountain and water in the religion of Taos Pueblo. For the first time in his life he saw "the real white man," saw through the superficialities about which Lawrence speaks, actually "touched" the place and its truths about others and self: "For the first time in my life, so it seemed to me, someone had drawn for me a picture of the real white man. It was as though until now I had seen nothing but sentimental, prettified color prints. This Indian had struck our vulnerable spot, unveiled a truth to which we are blind. I felt rising within me like a shapeless mist something unknown and yet deeply familiar."[20] With what he calls "a secret stab," Jung realizes, in a panoramic mental flash of history, the barbarous aspects of imperialism—from Caesar, to Charlemagne, to the Crusades, to Columbus, to Cortez, and other "conquistadors."

Beyond his conversations with the disarmingly simplistic Ochwiay Biano, who concludes that while the whites "think with their heads. . . . [w]e think that they are mad," Jung's epiphany is affected by and mixed with the surroundings of his discussions. In a sense, the tremendous effect of the landscape and its moods places Jung's observations quite correctly under the chapter heading of "Travels" and within the conventions of travel narrative as also practiced by Erna Fergusson.

As Jung talks with Ochwiay Biano on the roof of the pueblo—a structure he compares with modern skyscrapers—the directionality of height and ascent reinforces the mood of revelation and recognition upward from the pueblo to its sacred mountain, the sky and the sun:

At frequent intervals figures of other Indians could be seen on the roofs, wrapped in their woolen blankets, sunk in contemplation of the wandering sun that daily rose into a clear sky. Around us were grouped the low-built square buildings of air-dried brick (adobe), with the characteristic ladders that reach from the ground to the roof, or from roof to roof of the higher stories. . . . Before us the rolling plateau of Taos (about seven thousand feet above sea level) stretched to the horizon, where several conical peaks (ancient volcanoes) rose to over twelve thousand feet. Behind us a clear stream purled past the houses, and on its opposite bank stood a second pueblo of reddish adobe houses, built one atop the other toward the center of the settlement, thus strangely anticipating the perspective of an American metropolis with its skyscrapers at the center. Perhaps half an hour's journey upriver rose a mighty isolated mountain, *the* mountain, which has no name. The story goes that on days when the mountain is wrapped in clouds the men vanish in that direction to perform mysterious rites.[21]

Jung's epiphany brings him to the realization that the lives of the Taos Indians, as "sons of the sun, a people who live on the roof of the world" and assist the sun daily in its rising, are much more cosmologically meaningful than the lives ("our lives," as he addresses an Anglo-European audience) of non–Native Americans: "Knowledge does not enrich us; it removes us more and more from the mythic world in which we were once at home by right of birth."[22] In Jung's epiphany, his own kind of "New Mexico baroque" effulgence of expression, he acknowledges the "enviable serenity" of the Pueblo Indian: "Such a man is in the fullest sense of the word in his proper place."[23]

Anaya, Luhan, Lawrence, and Jung—like Lummis, Harvey Fergusson, Paul Horgan, and other contemporary Anglo-American writers, including John Nichols, Tony Hillerman, Max Evans, Norman Zollinger, and countless others in the broader tradition of Southwest "enchantment" literature of place—all give testimony in their own unique ways to the impetus and inspiration which New Mexico gave Fergusson in her writing. She, too, was at once in her proper place as a privileged Anglo and, estranged from its mythic, aboriginal essences, knew it, and chose to share her knowing yet ambivalent "enchantment" with others in her actions and books. In a certain fascinating way, all respective historical sojourners amid the sublime landforms and vistas of the Southwest, visitors among the "curious" indigenous cultures, whether native or foreign born, are essentially tourists.

NATIVE BORN

Erna Fergusson was born in Old Albuquerque, January 10, 1888, in her grandfather's wondrous Castle Huning, located east on Railroad Avenue toward New Town. The mansion had been inspired by Huning's recollections of his boyhood in Germany. Franz Huning (1827–1905) had emigrated to New Mexico in 1849 as a bullwhacker along the Santa Fe Trail. He worked for a time in Santa Fe and then moved south a few miles to Albuquerque. There, in partnership with his brother Charles (1832–94), who had accompanied Franz to America, he established a store fronting on the northwest corner of the Old Town plaza on property sold to the Huning brothers in 1863 by Archbishop Jean Baptiste Lamy's fellow cleric and ally in Albuquerque, Joseph Machebeuf.

Two other Huning brothers, Louis (1834–1901) and Henry (1838–?), four years younger than Louis, joined Franz and Charles in settling in the American Southwest. While Franz and Charles concentrated their business efforts in Albuquerque, Louis and Henry established a mercantile business a few miles south of Albuquerque at Los Lunas. In 1888 that partnership ended, and after selling Louis his share of the enterprise, Henry moved to Arizona and played a role in the settlement of the town of Showlow. Louis's store in Los Lunas eventually became the Huning Mercantile Company which still is a viable business, now in association with the Ace hardware chain. Louis Huning ran the Huning Mercantile Company until his death December 23, 1901, in Los Lunas. He was also one of the charter owners of the First National Bank of Albuquerque. His descendants, starting with his son, Fred D. Huning, and extending through the fourth generation into the 1980s to Louis's namesake and recent mayor of Los Lunas, figure prominently in the history of Los Lunas, Belen, and all of Valencia County and Rio Abajo.

According to family history, as well as the Valencia County and Albuquerque municipal papers, Louis Huning arrived in Los Lunas with forty-five dollars to his name. After buying the mercantile business in Los Lunas, he purchased another one in Belen. In partnership with Henry he formed the firm of L. and H. Huning and in addition to the mercantile business at one time had sixty thousand sheep and eight thousand head of cattle. In 1870 Louis and Henry built one of the most efficient flour mills in New Mexico Territory, according to sources reported by Franz Huning's granddaughter, Lina Fergusson Browne, in her notes accompanying her published account of Franz Huning's memoir, *Trader on the Santa Fe Trail*.[24]

As impressive as the holdings of Louis and Henry Huning were, their elder brothers, Franz and Charles, were equally well positioned in a city destined to become a merchandising and business metropolis, thanks to the arrival of the railroad in the 1880s. Charles gave up his partnership with Franz in 1875 and returned to Germany, leaving Franz to represent the Huning name in the history of Albuquerque's New Town railroad development. By the time of Erna Fergusson's birth in 1888, "Grospa" Franz had given up his store on the plaza, which had kept him freighting on the plains between Santa Fe and Saint Louis during the Civil War and into the 1870s, before the coming of the railroad. He was also operating his beloved flour mill, Molino de Glorieta, enjoying the profits of his real estate and other investments, and the esteem of his family and the local citizenry. Perhaps, most of all, he marveled, like others in town, at the creation of his eccentric but beautiful castle, its grounds, and orchards.

Castle Huning, as it came to be called, was built in 1883, just five years before Fergusson's birth. Huning's first real home after his settlement in Albuquerque, besides the quarters his Old Town mercantile business offered, had been an ancient adobe hacienda known as La Glorieta, located just a mile or so east of the Old Town plaza. It was to La Glorieta that he took his wife, Ernestine Franke (1837–1923), after their marriage in 1864—the same year he built Molino de Glorieta. And it was at La Glorieta that Huning raised his four children—Arno, Lina, Elly (who died at the age of six), and Clara Mary, Fergusson's mother. But by 1883 Huning needed a dwelling befitting his prosperity, and one that would take the shape of his nostalgic yearnings for Germany. Construction began in 1881, and for three years Albuquerque watched Huning's eccentricities and European imaginings take material shape. Upon its completion, and until it was razed in the 1950s for real estate speculation and development, Huning's castle was not only an architectural marvel but the stuff of myth. Both the razing of Castle Huning and of the great Fred Harvey stop, the Alvarado Hotel, on First Street, along with other historic cultural treasures, such as the El Fidel Hotel, bespeak a tragic phase in Albuquerque's shortsighted rush toward commercial progress, wherein tradition was viewed as an obstacle in the way of the future.

Although it was built from earthen bricks, called *terrones*, which had been dug from nearby fields and marshes, the castle was designed by Huning to resemble the stone constructions of his European memories. In part this was possible by erecting walls which were two and, in some places, three feet thick. The exterior was veneered in wood. At least two towers balanced two stories and a kitchen wing extending to the east. The main interior hallway ran sixty feet—the full length of the first floor.

Paul Horgan, in "A Castle in New Spain," (from *Figures in a Landscape*), captures in fiction the myth and mood of Huning's castle in this word picture:

> The castle was white, with lacelike shadows all across its faces from the carved wooden ornament that clung to every possible ledge, arch, cranny and corner. It had been set among trees already old, so that it had an ancient look. There were terraces and cascades; peacocks yelled among the rosebushes; there was a long rose walk covered by lattice; there was a sundial set in the turf as pavement. There were meandering streams with miniature bridges, and in one corner of an artificial hill miniature Bavarian trolls in brightly painted carved wood lived among miniature caves, chalets, forges and crags. The tangle garden was a melancholy and languishing setting for any black-cloaked figure to be discovered in, sobbing under the shadow of the Gothic ruins where a large plaster owl made a gloomy silhouette on the yellow sky above the river. (169)

It was into this "enchanted" setting, surrounded by the larger enchantments of Albuquerque, New Mexico Territory, and the New Spain of the Southwest, that Erna Fergusson was born.

Her mother, Clara Mary, who prided herself on being one of the first blue-eyed babies in the town, had married Harvey B. Fergusson, who had come from Alabama. After receiving a B.A., M.A., and a law degree from Washington College (later Washington and Lee University) in Lexington, Virginia, he had been sent by a Virginia law firm to White Oaks, New Mexico, to handle the mining litigation of the firm's clients. H. B. Fergusson made a name for himself as an attorney in White Oaks and met soon-to-be influential New Mexicans, including Emerson Hough, Albert B. Fall, and William C. MacDonald, later governor of New Mexico. During his White Oaks years, a good many of H. B.'s cases were tried in the historic Lincoln County courthouse—the venue of Billy the Kid and Pat Garrett, among other outlaws and lawmen. H. B.'s career as an attorney during territorial and early statehood days inspired Fergusson to write *Murder and Mystery in New Mexico* (1948) and to dedicate that book to the memory of her father, a man who "believed in law and order." The famous Colonel Albert J. Fountain murder trial held in Doña Ana County in 1898, which found H. B. and his colleague, Albert B. Fall, as defense attorneys for rancher Oliver Lee and his cowboys, James Gilliland and William McNue, provided the material, many years later, for one of Erna Fergusson's best narratives in *Murder and Mystery in New Mexico*. H. B. Fergusson moved to Albuquerque in 1883 where he met and became friends with Franz Huning (when construction of his castle was just under way), and prospered further through that connection. H. B. Fergusson was destined to play a leading part in the development of New Mexico Territory, where he served in the state constitutional convention and in the U.S. Congress as a delegate from the territory and as representative from the state.[25]

Huning—for a wedding present in the spring of 1887—gave his daughter, Clara Mary, and his son-in-law, H. B., his former home, La Glorieta, located across from Castle Huning. It was in La Glorieta that Erna grew up, along with her brother Harvey, only two years younger, and her sister Lina. When her father went to Washington, Erna spent part of her formative years in the nation's capital as well. And her brother Harvey began his writing career there as a newspaper man, entitling one of his earliest novels *Capitol Hill* (1923). Fergusson's other brother, Francis, was several years younger and thus knew a different childhood and an even more modern Albuquerque than did Erna.

She grew with the town, attended public and private schools in Albuquerque, and the Girls' Collegiate Preparatory School in Los Angeles. After graduating from the University of New Mexico she took a master's degree in history from Columbia. Her historian perspective is everywhere apparent in her writings. She first taught at Chatham Hall in Virginia, and then returned to Albuquerque and taught for a time in the public schools, worked on an Albuquerque newspaper, the *Herald,* at the society desk (under the editorship of Albuquerque pioneer newsman H. B. Henning), and during World War II traveled the entire state as supervisor in the Home Service Department of the Red Cross. In part, she was hired by the Red Cross because she could speak Spanish and did not really mind the rugged trips into remote areas of the state. This experience, she said, "gave me my first wide contact with New Mexico and my first realization that it was a very wonderful state to belong to. This enthusiasm and a desire to share it led to the establishment of the Koshare Tours with Miss Ethel Hickey."[26] The Koshare Tours took tourists to virtually all of New Mexico's pueblos to experience their dances, as well as to Navajo country and on to Hopi country for the famed snake dance, which affected D. H. Lawrence, among others, so strongly when he witnessed it. With Ethel Hickey, Fergusson was hailed as one of the first dude wranglers, and when Fred Harvey established his Indian Detour (organized auto tours through "Indian country"), he chose her to inaugurate his "courier" service and train the women couriers.

After the Koshare Tours and the Fred Harvey Detours, Fergusson made other attempts at dude ranching—including an abortive venture with Mabel Dodge Luhan in the late 1920s whereby Fergusson was retained to turn Mabel's spacious Taos adobe into a deluxe guest house.[27] Through her friendship with poet and Santa Fe personality Witter Bynner and both his and her brother Harvey's connections with publisher Alfred A. Knopf, she wrote and then published *Dancing Gods,* a book on New Mexico Native American dances, which she felt was so very much needed. That led her to other encouragements by Knopf and a trip to Mexico, where she wrote and became a member of the faculty of the Mexican Seminar conducted by the Committee on Cultural Relations with Latin America. That association led more directly to later books on Guatemala and Venezuela (and subsequently to other books on Latin America, and Cuba, and again on Mexico). She returned to New Mexico in 1939 for a year's intensive work which resulted in *Our Southwest* in 1940.

During World War I Fergusson worked in Washington for the Office of the Coordinator of Inter-American Affairs, with, among others, Frank Waters. During the 1940s and 1950s—particularly prolific years for her—she published seven more books, bringing her total number of published books (including her *Mexican Cookbook*) to thirteen. In her later years she planned a definitive biography of Albuquerque mayor and New Mexico governor, Clyde Tingley, and his colorful wife, Carrie Wooster Tingley. Illness and age prevented Fergusson from completing and publishing that project. And a long-planned novel on Cortez's mistress, Malinche, about which she conferred off and on with Haniel Long, Harvey Fergusson, Paul Horgan, and others, never took shape.

Her sometimes fellow traveler, Dorothy Woodward, writing in the *New Mexico Quarterly,* summed up Fergusson's native-born talents as a writer about the Southwestern scene: "She but views the world about her with an appraising eye, always alert to the human element. She visits with the influential rich and the exploited poor, the educated and the illiterate. She sees objectively and writes clearly. Her world is a kaleidoscope of people, and her courage, friendliness, humor and intelligence make her a woman who has successfully pioneered."[28]

If the autobiographical and biographical material which accompanied Fergusson's writings for publicity purposes is to be believed, her first recorded "epiphany in landscape," as Anaya would call it, was experienced while she worked for the Red Cross, traveling far and wide across New Mexico. She is quoted as saying that those travels gave her the "first realization that [New Mexico] was a wonderful state to belong to." She later described with characteristic wryness those World War I Red Cross days in New Mexico to H. L. Mencken (who introduced her to readers of his new journal, *American Mercury,* as "a sister to Harvey Fergusson" and whose writings, including a serialized version of *Rio Grande,* appeared frequently in the *Mercury*): ". . . we had a war and I ran around all over the State fixing things up for Mexican soldiers who had enlisted under a couple of names, for mothers who asked me what the ocean was, and for wives who had forgotten to marry."[29]

No doubt she did enjoy a new awareness, did come closer to the lives and landscapes of her native state and Southwest during those times and travels. However, her childhood in the Old Town portion of Albuquerque, and her perceptions of the transitions of New Town, and the boom occasioned by the railroad in 1880, less than a decade before her birth, and the Albuquerque ambiance of ubiquitous mesas, picturesque and historic river, extinct volcanoes to the west and the Sandia and Manzano mountains to the east, all colored her perceptions and shaped her personality. She was, if anything, not just a Southwesterner, a New Mexican, but an Albuquerquean. She was born in Albuquerque. And it was in Albuquerque—more than any other place in South or North America or New Mexico—where she chose to reside and which she claimed as her own.

ALBUQUERQUE AND THE TINGLEYS

Fergusson's impressions of Albuquerque no doubt first took shape around Old Town, her grandfather's Castle Huning where she was born, and her parents' gift hacienda, La Glorieta. She played there and in Castle Huning and explored the grounds around them to the extent that a girl expected to act like a lady could. Although much of her schooling was in Albuquerque—where she finished high school at Albuquerque High in 1906, and later the University of New Mexico, where she took a Bachelor of Pedagogy degree—she also traveled. She went west to Los Angeles for school, she briefly knew the Washington, D.C., of her father, and she lived in New York while attending Columbia.

World War I brought her the travels which were part of her Red Cross job—and her realization that New Mexico was a special place. Even after her wide-ranging trips throughout the American Southwest, Mexico, and Latin America, Albuquerque remained the center of her perceptions of what New Mexico and the Southwest meant. And it was Albuquerque which allowed her to develop as a journalist and to turn her perceptions into words. Albuquerque remained both an inspiration and a compelling subject throughout her writing career, leading to newspaper columns, encyclopedia articles, lectures-under-the-stars at the University of New Mexico, chapters in others' books, a book of her own, and a long manuscript (never published) on mayor Tingley.

About the same time she was teaching history at Albuquerque High School, she took a job with the *Albuquerque Herald* during 1922 and 1923 and wrote a feature entitled "Old Albuquerque, Do You Remember?" In 1926 she wrote two essays for *Century Magazine* after its editor, Hewett Howland, heard some of her tales and commissioned her to write what turned out to be "Redskins to Railroads" and "From Rodeo to Rotary."[30] Many of those *Herald* articles, such as "Do You Remember the First Street Car?" and "Do You Remember the First Train?" (and twenty-eight shorter tales) in addition to her two *Century* pieces, found their way in revised form into *Erna Fergusson's Albuquerque*, a book she decided to finance and publish (both write and underwrite) in association with the regional partisan and designer of fine books, Merle Armitage, a one-time editor with *Look* magazine. Her niece, Li Browne, daughter of Lina Fergusson Browne and C. Spencer Browne, after having proven effective as an illustrator for the *Mexican Cookbook*, was enlisted to do the drawings for *Albuquerque*. Although published after World War II, the essays in *Albuquerque*—along with representative articles written by Fergusson in the late twenties for the *Albuquerque State Tribune*, and an early essay on Albuquerque for the *Encyclopaedia Britannica*, reveal not only her developing feeling for "place," which infused all her writing, but also show her early, characteristic style as an essayist and hybrid journalist/historian/storyteller—a budding "new journalist."

The *Century* essays, *Herald* articles, and *Tribune* feature, "See New Mexico First," are readable, informative, entertaining—and filled with hints of Fergusson's even greater potential as a writer. In these "texts" she found not only her persona, style, and subject matter but, behind that, her motive for writing—her increasingly conscious and expressed regard for her region, her home.

Fergusson attributes much of her finding of her own voice and style to Southwestern writer/editor Kyle Crichton, author of such works as *Law and Order, Ltd.* (1928), to whom she showed some of her earliest drafts of her essays for *Century*. As she records Crichton's role in her metamorphosis from fumbler to writer, she turned over two examples of "overstrained and wordy prose" to Crichton, who praised the material but damned the style (*EFA*, 23). "Telling was easier than writing," exclaimed Fergusson out of frustration and anger at Crichton's criticism. That truism led to a discovery of method which she claimed from then on.

David Remley observes that although the "Do You Remember?" series is sometimes dull and awkward, it is important because it shows two techniques Fergusson mastered later in her books: "the interview and the informal, almost conversational prose style"; and it also reveals "an attempt at that characteristic technique of American humor, exaggeration."[31] Whether such things are matters of technique or tone or style is perhaps a moot point. Remley is right in his identification of interview and exaggeration and anecdote as characteristic of Fergusson's writing method—stemming from, no doubt, her gregarious personality and her early conversation with Crichton about her writing.

Her overall persona—early and late—is that of a good-natured but critically minded woman who is open for new experiences, has an adventuresome and independent spirit, and shows tolerance for individual, cultural, and geographical differences—but, like D. H. Lawrence and other iconoclasts of place as idea, when meeting the enchantments of the Southwest as epiphany, has little tolerance for cant or sham or snobbery in the face of such giant forces of culture and geography. Thus, not only her identity as a tolerant and open-minded "new woman" of social conscience, independence, and daring comes through in her style, but also her disposition for satire is established early in her writing. If she does point to certain follies and foibles of "small" institutions and individuals and closed ways of perceiving culture and region, she is never misanthropic or cynical. She accepts tourists, greenhorns, and nonentities into the places or times or cultures she has knowledge of, just as she accepts her own inadequacies: it is an acceptance mixed with an ambivalent pioneer pride of an Anglo confronting the bafflements of time, space, and culture. In a sense, too, it is an acceptance which bespeaks part of Fergusson's New Mexico baroque "loftiness," as criticized by Stanley Walker, or parodied as the worship of the primitive by Harvey Fergusson in some of his Southwestern comedies of manners, such as *Footloose McGarnigal* or *Hot Saturday* (1926).

One is constantly struck by the fact that in her life and in her writings, Southwestern and Latin American, Fergusson does not let stereotypical notions of gender, most notably the notion that a woman's place is in the home or behind her man, hamper her. Fergusson strikes out in a kind of tough-woman, gracious-woman, confident-woman assertiveness which claims nothing of the audacious, rather which assumes the matter-of-factness of her self-reliance. It is, moreover, apparent that many of her heroes are indeed heroines, and she features both famous and obscure women throughout her historical, anecdotal, and advocacy accounts. Very much in the spirit and the vanguard of liberation for all peoples, Erna Fergusson lived and advocated the role of a liberated, self-confident woman—mature, intelligent, and self-sufficient. Perhaps she was merely an extension or a culmination of her own mother's adventurous spirit and the pioneer spirit of her "explorer-settler" heritage, maternal and paternal. Perhaps she anticipated much of what now is thought of, not always clearly, as a feminist.

Probably she was both. She stood under no intimidation or doubt of male dominance. She traveled boldly under no shadows of men or of what women could or could not do because of their gender. Thus her stature as a "new woman" was predicated on long-nourished pioneer virtues. She was educated, urbane, witty, and willful. And these qualities add to the enjoyment of her writing today at century's turning. Albuquerque allowed her to grow up with it and to reflect on that maturation of city and citizen.

Paul Horgan, when he reviewed *Erna Fergusson's Albuquerque* in the *Albuquerque Tribune* in 1947, called the book and its style "Breezy, Wise and Immensely Readable."[32] Horgan wrote not only as a friend but as a boyhood citizen of the town and one-time Albuquerque journalist, who in his cub days for the *Albuquerque Morning Journal* in the summer of 1922 shocked more than one society matron by his outrageous descriptions of weddings and parties. He also wrote as a librarian who appreciated quality examples of the bookmaker's trade. About her depiction of Albuquerque Horgan says, "No other American city is more interesting, as our author makes clear by the very evidence she has collected, and no other city has been more fortunate in its biographer. . . . No one is better qualified than she to sketch the history, habits and atmosphere of her town."[33]

Erna Fergusson's Albuquerque survives as a kind of compendium of her many writings about Albuquerque. It does have a fragmentary quality about it, evidencing the original separateness of the essays it collects, and it does reflect another characteristic of its author: to save and revise, reuse and recycle previous work. The collection, however, is much more than a rehashing of old material and can be seen more accurately as a characteristic outgrowth of Fergusson's lifelong endeavor to rethink her allegiance to place and give it vital new shape. In just eighty-seven pages and seven chapters, *Albuquerque,* as volume and as evidence of Fergusson's fascination with the city as subject, finds its reflections, too, in such essays as the one she wrote for the *Encyclopaedia Britannica* (updated and reprinted as late as the 1973 edition), in chapters published in such fine regional works (and trend-setting formats) of the day as *Rocky Mountain Cities* (1949), edited by Ray B. West Jr., and with an introduction by Carey McWilliams, and other chapters by such noted Western authors as Walter Van Tilburg Clark and Haniel Long, on Reno and Santa Fe, respectively.[34] Moreover, strong echoes of it are found in both *Our Southwest* and *New Mexico.*

Albuquerque gains its unity from its chronological organization—the history of Albuquerque "Now," "Then," and "Whither"—and by its illustrations and overall book design. In her opening chapter, "Albuquerque Now," she begins with an aerial point of view—the city and the surrounding landscape from the vantage point of a plane. Such an elevated, if not omniscient, positioning is used frequently, especially to great advantage in *New Mexico* where the narrator does not fly over the city but is nevertheless similarly elevated atop the Sandia mountains to the east of the city. In that particular instance the viewer is ancient Sandia Man; whereas, in *Albuquerque* the viewer is modern, progressive, a flier (not, insignificantly, first from the east, and then, alternately, from the west) across vast portions of time and space—one who is "dazzled" by what is seen of the landscape:

> Planes come sweeping into Albuquerque across arid wastes that seem from above to be pocked and pitted with rocks and scarred by waterless stream beds. Coming from the East, your plane clears the Sandia range at 10,000 feet and you look down into Tijeras Canyon's tumbled rocks with patches of cedar and pine. Then you are out over a valley whose vastness seems not to end with a silver peak against the sky, but only to spread out beyond it. From the west you pass that peak, Mount Taylor, and fly over the villages of Acomita and Laguna like beds of pine needles among the lava flows left over from Mount Taylor's active life. Northbound and southbound you have seen hints of the Rio Grande cutting a swathe of green through a greenless land. However you approach Albuquerque your eye will be dazzled by the contrast between that leafy valley, looking as lush as the Nile, and the desert. As your pilot comes in for a landing you see how that verdure has drowned a town, leaving only reaching tips of a couple of tall buildings and smoke stacks, and how it is spreading among houses out across the arid mesas. (*EFA*, 1)

With these descriptions of geography and landscape, Fergusson characteristically begins her accounts of travel as arrival into a wondrous and sublime vista of forms—natural and human-built phenomena, either blending into or intruding on each other. She takes up a transcendent, cosmic, "geological" perspective, not a "baroque" style, and never fails to share her impressions of the marvel and wonderment, the enchantment of place and how it teases the perceiver—narrator and accompanying voyager, reader— into both aesthetic and metaphysical inquiry.

Just as characteristic of her aerial, transcendent attitude and descriptive point of view is her transposition, or modulation, to a more practical, oftentimes literally down-to-earth, look at the details not so much of landscape in the cosmos as landscape on earth, "geography" and topography intersecting with "geology" and human history. In *Albuquerque* Fergusson makes this modulation simply but effectively: from arrival by plane, to arrival by train. It is not difficult to anticipate the next step in the sequence: from flying, to riding in both train and car, to walking. Given the psychology of correspondence between sublime landscape and sublime thoughts, her transcendent moments are entirely appropriate. Given her occupation as tour guide for first the Koshare enterprise and then Fred Harvey, and given her times, it is only natural that train and car predominate as vantage points from which her descriptions and perceptions follow. Seldom does she carry her point of view or her stylistic choices atavistically back further in evolutionary sequence to travel by either horseback or walking. When she does, it is, significantly, in observation of Native American, Spanish, or Mexican American interludes.

At whatever stage in the sequence of her diverse positionings and shifting perspectives, the point to be made is that *Albuquerque* is representative of what these modulations reveal about Fergusson's attitudes and relationships to landscape—and the lives which cross it. The changes in her vantage point in the opening essay, "Albuquerque Now," follow the formula precisely—from plane, to train, to car. From the mountains and rivers, to the outlying villages, to the highways, such as Route 66 and Highway 85, which approach the city, and the streets of outlying settlement, to Central Avenue downtown, then West Central, and the Old Town plaza, she zeroes in on her destination. Note the progression:

> Come in by train. Quite as smoothly as a plane landing, the Santa Fe's Super-Chief or El Capitan slides in alongside the old Alvarado. When the Santo Domingo Indians first watched the Super-Chief passing their pueblo they made a song about the Silver Snake; and so it looks, at rest with Diesel engines potent in their quietude. (*EFA*, 2)

> Come in by motor and Albuquerque will welcome you miles out with hundreds of tourist camps; more elegantly called courts. (*EFA*, 3)

> Route 66, named for Will Rogers and popular also in song, takes Tijeras Canyon's dangerous curves through the mountains and comes out on an aerial view of the volcanoes across the valley with Mount Taylor beyond. (*EFA*, 3)

> Along Highway 85, connecting Canada with South America along the Pan-American, you see the worst the motor age can do. (*EFA*, 4)

> Beyond the little parks, West Central is monopolized by motorists, rushing through like driven refugees. A few fine old adobe houses have been lost under neon signs or pushed back by jerrybuilt hamburger joints, bars, Flying Chicken, 'last chance for gas with no city tax,' and stands selling fruit and quick lunch goods. The mob passes

all unaware of the old plaza, laid out in 1706 by a Spanish Governor, and the fine adobe church planned by a Franciscan friar. (*EFA*, 6)

It is impossible to illustrate fully all of her transpositions and descriptions, but the direction of her narrative is significant and characteristic. Fergusson has seen and wants to communicate greater truths than the insensitive mob has seen or will see unless they listen and look. The land and its history—betwixt and between the hustle and bustle of a burgeoning town in a frenetic moment in history—afford the real satisfaction and solace.

Albuquerque as place is thus, like so many things, both imaginary and real, superficial and authentic. And it is Fergusson's job, as she sees it and works it, to slow things down, point things out, relish the commonplace enchantments of history and nature, the Lawrencian nodality of a small but significant spot in New Mexico, the Southwest, the West, the United States, North America, the world, the cosmos. The marvel of the equation, the modulations, is that the cosmic and the earthly are reciprocally awesome, more than worthy of seeing and knowing and codifying in words and writing.

The Sandia mountains to the east of Albuquerque, as part of the Sangre de Cristo, southern extension of the Rocky Mountains, remain as the most distinctive landmark of Albuquerque—complemented by the enchantments of the Rio Grande, which provides a kind of western border to Old Town, and the low-lying volcanoes and their extending plateaus on the western horizon. Mountains have always been the subject of travel writers, especially from the time of their discovery as tourist sites by such eighteenth-century British instigators of the picturesque, the sublime, and the beautiful as Joseph Addison and Edmund Burke, to the more recent writings of American nature and travel writers John McPhee, Barry Lopez, Terry Tempest Williams, and Frederick Turner III. Addison, in his commentaries on "The Pleasures of the Imagination," explains the aesthetic of responding to sublimity in landscape:

> By *greatness* I do not mean the bulk of any single object, but the largeness of a whole view, considered as one entire piece. Such are the prospects of an open champaign country [of flat fields], a vast uncultivated desert, of huge heaps of mountains, high rocks and precipices, or a wide expanse of waters, where we are not struck with the novelty or beauty of the sight, but with that rude kind of magnificence which appears in many of these stupendous works of nature. Our imagination loves to be filled with an object, or to grasp at anything that is too big for its capacity. We are flung into a pleasing astonish-

ment at such unbounded views and feel a delightful stillness and amazement in the soul at the apprehension of them.[35]

Addison's sense of "greatness," Burke's sense of the "sublime and the beautiful," "the images of vastness, of sudden rise and fall, of dark obscurity or blazing light," the landscape moods of British poets of the 1740s such as William Collins, Thomas Gray, and James Thomson are not all that distant from the geological wonderments of the Rockies, as described perhaps most recently by John McPhee, or the enchantments of the Sangre de Cristo range which so permeated the consciousness of Fergusson.[36]

The Sandias, their presence, shape, color, mood, and grandeur, drew Fergusson's attention just as they do the attention—whether conscious or unconscious—of all those who live in or pass through Albuquerque. In *Albuquerque* Fergusson proffers a description of the Sandia mountains, a description with enough beauty and grandeur in it (in the object being described and in the description) to trivialize Stanley Walker's condemnation of "New Mexico baroque":

> From Albuquerque the Sandia [*sic*] shows a true mountain blue by day with silvery rock slides and purplish patches where evergreens grow. Evening light brings on the show that a native daughter backs against the world. Then daytime blue shading in and out of all the purples is swallowed by rose and gold from the sunset sky. Leaping the valley in long shafts of light they inundate the mountains with color, rising from mesa to peak, and go off before the brain can quite register what it saw. The mountains are blue again, but an azure deepening into midnight blue and leaving the sky to stage the real show. Stars and stardust are near, planets close, and when the moon sails out above the city fathers cannily douse the electric street lights as mere impertinences.
>
> This grandeur of nature so near is not without influence in the town. (*EFA*, 9)

The "evening light" which "brings on the show that a native daughter backs against the world," the gold and rose of the sunset leaping the valley with long shafts of light, the startled brain of the viewer, the stars, stardust, planets, and moon—all this "grandeur of nature" as described by Fergusson confirms that her Southwest, her home, her Albuquerque is, in her thinking and feeling, quite a spectacular place. For her, Albuquerque is all the more marvelous for its timelessness of landscape, accelerated sense of history, and cultural heritage mixed together on its streets: "Age of the horse-drawn. Age of engines on the ground. Age of engines in the air. And, now and again, the flash of an untried and fearful age in the sky" (*EFA*, 11). It is this sense of grandeur and surprise, mixed with the ostensibly "ordinary" routine of just being amidst it all that so infuses her writing with its own special Emersonian sense of pleasure in "seeing," as he advances in "Nature" with his metaphor of person as eyeball, and links her to a long tradition of transcendental "discovery" literature. Her grandfather, Franz Huning, speaks much in the same terms in his journal, *Trader on the Santa Fe Trail*, of his 1849 trip to the Southwest along the Santa Fe Trail.

In the chapters on the founding of Albuquerque, on Spanish coloniza-tion and Mexican settlement, on military, social, and political history across three centuries, on Albuquerque as a health resort and tourist attraction, on the town's developing organizations and institutions, and on the old tales and anecdotes about the place's sundry citizens from 1718 to 1947, *Erna Fergusson's Albuquerque* is indeed a testimonial to one woman's, a new and enduring woman's, *tierra encantada*. The text reveals how her writing—persona, voice, and style—was shaped by that place, and how she became a woman, native born, who "assumes the right to poke a little fun at her honorable home." According to her, the book is "one woman's picture of the town she knows and likes so well that she has never seen another where she would rather live" (*EFA*, 85).

The pride which Fergusson took in being a new "historic" and signifi-cant woman native born to the Southwest, an heir to a legacy given by her own family's early settlement of Albuquerque, is made apparent by her careful selection of events and places to describe when space is limited. Thus, she begins her *Encyclopaedia Britannica* article with not just the iden-tification of the geographical landmarks—the ford in the Rio Grande, the pass between the Sandia and the Manzano mountains to the east—or of the Hispanic founders, the thirty-six Spanish families who settled there in 1760. Rather, into this historical background she weaves an account of her own grandfather Huning's era and how the railroad enabled him to build his castle and make his fortune as Old Town became New Town. What results is a veiled tribute not only to the town or to her grandfather but to her own heritage, her own familial relationship and familiarity with the places, persons, and dates about which she, as one might mistakenly first guess, "objectively" writes:

> The original plaza was the town's center until 1880 when the Atlantic and Pacific railroad (later the Atchison, Topeka and Santa Fe) laid its tracks one mile east of the plaza. The town quickly closed the gap with a streetcar line and began to spread eastward. By the time the "new town" was organized as a town (1885) the first "r" had been

dropped from the name. Albuquerque was incorporated as a city in 1890 and adopted the commission-manager form of government in 1917. The characteristically Spanish "old town" of Albuquerque and the mission church of San Felipe de Neri (1706) still survive.[37]

The railroad, the streetcar line, the old plaza, and new town not only figured in the lives of her ancestors but in her own life—from girlhood when she played on the horse-drawn trolley, through adulthood when she worked the Fred Harvey Detours.

That same persona carries over from her first journalistic feature, "Do You Remember?", incorporated in *Albuquerque* from another of her newspaper features, the "See New Mexico First" series which ran in the *New Mexico State Tribune* in 1929. Most of those articles appeared in the spring and summer months of that year and include such titles as "The Pajarito Plateau," "Bernalillo County," "Mesa Verde Cliffs," "Back Tracking the Santa Fe Trail," "The Jemez Mountains," "Spilling the Beans on Fishing Places," "Cities That Died of Fear," "The Snake Dances and the Hopi Mesa," "Zuni, Ice Cave, Inscription Rock," and "San Juan Days."[38]

One of these articles in particular shows again how central and crucial Albuquerque was to Fergusson's sense of self and self-reliance, how emblematic of her relationship to New Mexico and the Southwest as extensions of, but different in their dawning from, the old frontier. In "Bernalillo County" she recommends some close-to-town automobile tours that can be taken safely, even more conveniently, during the rainy month of August. After some general and humorous pointers on touring New Mexico in the rainy season, and a report on road conditions according to the state highway department, she plots some more specific routes for the courageous souls who refuse to take her advice to "arrange a series of porch parties."

She takes the opportunity in her preliminary banter to poke fun at the unreliability of the highway department in providing any real assistance to stranded motorists if their chains break or if the "strong right arm" of a young gentleman rescuer fails to get a stuck car out of the rain-soaked, muddy roads. Much of the charm of this satirical banter is dependent on the two anecdotes she relates, complete with dialogue. The highway department spokesman: "Well, if I wanted to go, I'd take chains." Fergusson's repartee: "It appeared later that he did not want to go, for when we were stuck hub-deep in mushy mud and looked about for that representative of the highway department, he was not there." The strong, young rescuer: "Women never ought to travel alone. They are fine in towns, but they certainly ought not to travel alone." Her response: she simply takes her reader along on a sight-seeing jaunt within a twenty-mile radius of Albuquerque.

Her first tour is across the Barelas bridge from Old Town to the village of Atrisco. Once across the bridge, she and her reader are in another world, the world of "as quaint a Mexican village as any in New Mexico." She describes the church and plaza, the rambling old houses, the doors, windows, *zaguanes,* and *vigas*—the long portals representative of "the best type of Mexican architecture." It is, she says, representative of what Albuquerque was back in time, before the gringos opened stores on the Old Town plaza. The activity then prescribed—with the help of a little Spanish—is an hour's chat with one of Atrisco's residents. Such a chat, she conjectures, will take one back to the dreadful days when *los Tejanos* romped through the area to capture Albuquerque and to try to hold it for the Confederacy. The past, she suggests, still lives just across Albuquerque's Barelas bridge.

North from Atrisco on the road along the buttes above the Rio Grande, Fergusson takes her reader to another "Mexican" village—that of Corrales. That road has its special enchantments: "It is interesting to get that slant on Albuquerque. The wide chocolate brown Rio Grande makes an alluring foreground for a town that is a bower of trees with one or two tall buildings, a few spires, and towering mountains to the east. Given such views and such a drive in some parts of the world and they would be known far and wide. It is about 12 miles from Atrisco to the Corrales bridge."[39]

Once in Corrales the reader is taken back to the time when that village was known for its light claret, its *vino del país* and its grape brandy. The recommended activity: "No better way to spend a late August afternoon than tasting grapes in a Corrales vineyard." On the trip home to Albuquerque she takes a right turn across the river, down the River road (Rio Grande Boulevard, the very road and region where Fergusson lived for a time), past a Penitente *morada,* or ceremonial sanctuary with a cross still standing in front of it, past "great old cottonwood trees," filled with tales of their own if they could talk—tales her own grandfather, Franz Huning, had told her: "Tradition has it that these were the trees on which Albuquerque's earliest citizens hung their undesirable neighbors." Once back to the Old Town plaza by this route she suggests another route—from Barelas bridge out to the volcanoes on the West Mesa. The directions are neighborly and simple: through Five Points and on to Goff's house, located in the middle of the road, then left on the Laguna cutoff, then right at the top of the mesa. Once at the extinct volcanoes: "Visitors with imagination can find hot rocks and one very imaginative soul is reported to have cooked an egg." And on such a clichéd but "climatic" note she ends her own real but imaginative tour of Albuquerque's Bernalillo County. The native daughter has found, and pointed out, and, in so doing, recreated herself in and through the special enchantments in her own backyard.

Fergusson summarized much of the point she tried to make in her *New Mexico State Tribune* feature, "See New Mexico First," when, in the spring of 1940, she talked to the Tourist School conducted by the New Mexico Department of Vocational Education in cooperation with the New Mexico State Tourist Bureau, the Albuquerque Public Schools, and Chamber of Commerce. She reminded her audience that

> We in Albuquerque are apt to forget that we are in the midst of New Mexico's greatest wealth of attractions for the tourist who can linger a minute, or who can be taught that only by moving slowly can he profit by what we have. The pueblo of Jemez is within a leisurely couple of hours, and on that trip are three other pueblos—Santa Ana, Zia, and Sandia. Beyond Jemez pueblo is a wonderland of forest crossed by fine roads. One may go over the Valle Grande and into Santa Fe by the Pajarito Plateau. One may skim by the Valle Grande and drop down from the Jemez range to Cochiti and back into Albuquerque by way of Santo Domingo and San Felipe. Beyond Jemez pueblo is Jemez Springs and beyond that whatever the fisherman and the hunter yearns for. And, in the course of a year, these villages put on some of the finest and most highly artistic pageantry and dance that can be seen anywhere.[40]

That locale, that pageantry led most directly to the writing of *Dancing Gods,* her first and best book-length travel narrative, and provided the impetus for the histories and travel books to follow.

An early example of Fergusson's interest in the geography surrounding Albuquerque and Bernalillo County and her perceptions, as an automobile traveler, of how culture merges with place includes her "See New Mexico First" piece on "The Jemez Mountains," another travelogue that also ran in 1929. In her instructions to would-be trip takers on how to cross one of the Southwest's, if not the world's, largest extinct volcanic crater at twelve miles across—the Valle Grande—Fergusson makes clear from the beginning that not only are the Jemez mountains and the Valle Grande ageless, their perception by humans is part of the "history" of place. New roads across the Valle Grande are not new at all: "As usual when we start something new in New Mexico we find that it was done long since by our aboriginal predecessors or by those pioneering Spanish or Gringo adventurers."[41] Furthermore, where the "new" road will lead is to the annual— that is to say, historic if not ageless—July 12 Corn Dance at Cochiti Pueblo, or the mining ghost town of Bland, two places which offer historical counterpoint to the mineral water resort of Jemez Springs or the growing mountain town of Cuba. Indian dances, frontier ghost towns, good fishing in streams such as the *Rio Las Vacas*, beautiful scenery, and the excitement of motoring on mountain roads—all of these things are described in a good-humored tone, which presumably made Fergusson's own auto tours so attractive: "The road . . . has other matters in mind [than fishing] as it has got to go up about the steepest two miles known to man, making numberless hairpin and hairbreadth and breathless turns. Fine for tourists. Marvelous views. The greatest country probably accessible anywhere by motor and if you have confidence in your driver, your brakes, and your fate, not to be missed on any terms."[42] The proximity of such sights to Albuquerque made Fergusson's plea throughout the years for a beautiful and livable Albuquerque that would not violate its landscape, ecology, and history all the more forceful.

Fergusson's Albuquerque friend and fellow journalist, the late Irene Fisher, remembered (at the age of eighty-six, and just a few years before her own death in 1984) that when she arrived in Albuquerque in 1920 she found that Fergusson was "the focus of all the people who were interested in writing and painting . . . here in Albuquerque."[43] Through her writing and in her participation in projects of civic pride and restoration, she helped shape Albuquerque's future by rediscovering its past. Fisher met Fergusson through contacts on the *Albuquerque Herald* and subsequently became part of both Fergusson's "entourage" in Albuquerque and Witter Bynner's and Robert Hunt's group in Santa Fe. Fisher recalled: "She was an independent person in every way: in her thinking, in her approach to people. She was quite independent. And like a lot of independent people she liked a lot of people stringing along behind her. And I was one of them. That was one of her characteristics. She made life interesting; there's no contradiction to that. She was respected. The family was respected. . . . [She] was a very highly respected person, because of herself and her family."

Fergusson and Fisher knew the charm of Albuquerque in the 1920s and 1930s: the Alvarado Hotel, the Franciscan Hotel, the Masonic Hall, and the red sandstone buildings—the Commercial Club and the Grand Central Hotel. In later years Fergusson tried to get the populace of the city interested in preserving some of the old buildings and ambiance of the city. And Fisher did much to restore and preserve the Old Town plaza. She relates that Fergusson was one of the founders who, along with Dick Bennett, Nelda Sewell, and a few others, formed the Albuquerque Historical Society in 1942 or 1943. One of their first civic-minded projects was to "rediscover" the Old Town plaza. Through the hard work of Fergusson, Fisher, and others the huge redstone wall, erected in W.P.A. days and which went all around the plaza and cut off all the view, was demolished in 1948, and the plaza opened up again. What had taken fifty thousand dollars and three months to build during the W.P.A. period took "three days and no money at all to tear down. And it . . . made the place much more attractive. That was during the period Erna was active in the historical society."[44]

Beyond *Erna Fergusson's Albuquerque* and the founding of the Albuquerque Historical Society, part of Fergusson's civic involvement and interest in her hometown took the shape of a family history of Albuquerque's mayor (and later governor of New Mexico) Clyde Tingley and his wife, Carrie. That project (intended for publication by Fergusson's friend, Roland Dickey, at the University of New Mexico Press and titled *The Tingleys of New Mexico*), though she labored over it many years and did finish several chapters of the projected thirteen-chapter manuscript, was never published. Based on the Tingleys' recollection of their forty years in Albuquerque, it amounts to a history of Albuquerque as much as a history of Tingley; but it is written in a flat and all too matter-of-fact manner, with none of the sparkle and wit of her earlier New Mexico writings.

Fergusson's attorney and lifelong friend, W. A. Keleher, recommended her to Tingley as his biographer. In 1955 Keleher wrote to Tingley:

> I have thought over the field of possibilities, and always come back to the proposition that Miss Erna Fergusson will be the ideal candidate for such a place. I believe that you should employ her at a compensation that is agreed upon between you, to come to your house every day, for five days each week, for two hours during which she could talk to you and Mrs. Tingley together, and get your recollections. Then she could shape these recollections up into a continuity which would be interesting and valuable. While you are at it you should not only tell of the years of your official service in Albuquerque, but you should also give her the facts on your four years in the Governor's mansion.[45]

By the middle of February, 1955, the whole enterprise was on the footing of a "sound business-like basis": for the consideration of $3,900 Fergusson would interview the Tingleys three mornings each week and work up her notes two mornings. In a formal agreement drawn up by Keleher, Fergusson agreed in return "to do a complete job of the contemplated narrative, although she may spend more than 52 weeks in the performance of that obligation."[46] Perhaps such routine, methodical arrangements contributed to the lifelessness of the written product as Fergusson struggled through her many accumulated notes to bring them the "continuity" about which Keleher speaks.

Despite the lack of "snap" in the manuscript, *The Tingleys of New Mexico* confirms yet again that from the beginning of Fergusson's career as a journalist through her more or less final writing project on the Tingley history, Albuquerque remained her own Southwest, her *tierra encantada*. If the Tingley family history ultimately proved disappointing as material for a book, it was not because of Fergusson's conception of how the book might take shape, of what she saw in and through the Tingleys' lives in the Southwest and their telling of those lives to her as testimonials to enchanted lands. She was troubled by a severely painful arthritic hip and was unable to fully carry out, in work and writing, all that she saw and was still inspired to write about her beloved hometown and its place in the history and story of the modern Southwest.

Chapter 2

. . . .

Travel:
Beautiful Swift Fox

But the unforgettable glory of it all!
—Charles F. Lummis (in memory of tramping the Rito
and the Tyuonyi, Los Alamitos, New Mexico)

Erna Fergusson's works were not only in the vanguard of travel narratives and the promotional literature of tourism (brochures, pamphlets, essays, and letters) that surged westward in the first quarter of the twentieth century, when railroads and automobiles made the landscapes, lives, myths, and mystique of the West accessible and relatively inexpensive and convenient for sight/site-seers. Her writings also placed her in a long tradition of Southwestern travel writers. Fergusson is associated more closely with the literature of tourism—given her founding of the Koshare Tours and her subsequent involvement with the Fred Harvey Detours, both of which contributed to the writing of her most well-known Southwestern book, *Dancing Gods,* and given her self-proclaimed identity and persona of a dude wrangler. But even so, she is also part of the tradition of discovery and travel narratives begun by such early Spanish travelers to the Southwest as Cabeza de Vaca, Juan de Oñate, and New Mexico's earliest recognized travel writer, Gaspar Pérez de Villagrá.

Linking Fergusson to the likes of Villagrá is admittedly based on a broad conception of tourism. But all explorers of new lands, new sites and sights, are, in a sense, tourists. And, given these boundaries, Fergusson may be placed in a narrative tradition that encompasses both an oral and a classical heritage, a mythic-legendary tradition which goes much beyond Anglo-European and Anglo-American sources to include the tellings of Native Americans and Mexican Americans about the journeys of the larger Southwest, and especially the Rio Grande valley.[1] In this sense, too, much of the literature and history written in response to finding and seeing the West/Southwest is the literature of "tourists" as explorers, health and wealth seekers, social scientists, artists, sightseers, and settlers. The concern of this chapter is with only one portion of Fergusson's role as Southwestern writer and woman, although she wrote equally as much about Hispanics and Anglo-Americans as she did about American Indians.

Fergusson's identity as a traveler—both in her life and in the personae of her Southwestern writing—takes on special interest. She was native born and a new woman in the New West—an independent woman who prided herself on going solo into the far and exotic reaches of not just the American Southwest but Latin America and Hawaii. She was a woman of certain daring if not "heroic" proportions who experienced an especially fascinating period of social history related to the changes brought by railroads and automobiles, of the progress of westering and modernism, of convergence of old and new, male and female, and androgynous aspects of male in female, female in male. Fergusson contributed substantially to the nature of some of those changes and to the social, geographical, and ideational directions they took in the Southwest.

Broad or narrow definitions of discovery and travel narratives notwithstanding, it is virtually impossible to think of the Southwest, especially as represented by New Mexico—in either geography, history, or art—without thinking of travel and the travelers who have entered into its enchantments and mystiques. For example, one of the most famous symbols of the Southwest as place and process is El Morro, or Inscription Rock, which Fergusson metaphorically refers to as the region's "great stone autograph album."[2] Don Juan de Oñate's 1605 inscription, *Pasó por aquí,* (I passed through here) on his return from discovering the South Sea (i.e., the Gulf of California) gave theme and focus to the already numerous stone-etched petroglyphs. Fergusson's own grandfather, Franz Huning, scribbled his name on El Morro during his own youthful explorations of western New Mexico and Arizona (then one territory), shortly after his arrival in 1849 via the Santa Fe Trail. Her brother Harvey wrote about Huning's New Mexico–Arizona exploits in the fictionalized version of Huning's life, *In Those Days* (1929), among others of his Southwestern fictions. And Fergusson, through her early Red Cross travels, her trips as a tour guide, and her wanderings in search of her Southwest (she liked to refer to it as "our" Southwest, a possessive indicative of her characteristic self-portrayal and persona as guide) lends added claim to the rock, to the emblem of El Morro, and the list of illustrious and ordinary names who "passed and are passing through" the Southwest.

The importance of travel as exploration, settlement, profit, and tourism to the identity of the Southwest and other regions of the West has long been recognized, documented, and interpreted. Travel literature has generally been regarded as a relatively inferior artistic form and thereby held in less esteem by many literary critics and historians. But more recently geographers, historians, and other social scientists—not to mention new generations of travel writers—are beginning to reevaluate its potential and product as artifact and art. Conspicuously absent in many such discussions is Fergusson and her role as Southwestern traveler. Not only should she be noticed in historical context as one who "passed through" and interpreted that region, her travel writings merit serious analysis and evaluation. Although *Dancing Gods* and *Murder and Mystery in New Mexico* bear the distinction of remaining in print, others of her books are available only in libraries. No doubt, more of her books will soon enjoy much needed reprinting.

The more travel literature enjoys an ascendancy, the more likely we are to see a renewed interest in Fergusson's work as a modern progenitor of the genre. One of the earliest and most valued studies of modern tourism in the American West, Earl Pomeroy's *In Search of the Golden West* (1957), makes no mention of Fergusson. Pomeroy's subject is, admittedly, the Far West, California and the Pacific Northwest. He claims to have "examined sources of Western history that included . . . practically every extant volume of Western memoirs, travel, and description, and every magazine published in a Far Western territory or state."[3] Pomeroy does allude to the Southwest several times in his account of tourism in the West; he mentions Charles F. Lummis repeatedly and Mabel Dodge Luhan. But in spite of his discussion of Fred Harvey's Indian Detours, and in spite of sharing the same publisher (Alfred A. Knopf) as Fergusson, Pomeroy neglects to include her in even so much as a footnote. Pomeroy, then, becomes prototypic of both the neglect and the potential rediscovery of Erna Fergusson as travel writer and as female travel writer. One cannot help but wonder if, for example, male historians and critics blipped over her, perhaps because of their own unconscious or conscious domination, *because* of gender? Perhaps because of her alleged "baroque" style—her tendency toward lyricism, her seeming enrapture by desert scenes and indigenous cultures? If ever there was a context for Pomeroy to mention Fergusson's contribution to tourism in western America, for example, this is it:

Enthusiasts for the Hopi and Navajo country held out the spell (1920) of a "vacation that is different from any that you have ever had; or if you are seeking something new—an unexplored land where white men seldom go and where you will meet unknown dangers—then go to the desert. . . ." Yet the Santa Fe's Indian detours did not draw many patrons until Packard sedans with courier-hostesses replaced the mules in the twenties. The drivers were cowboys skilled in singing around the campfire and in appealing to ladies "of uncertain age but certain bank accounts."[4]

Leaving aside Pomeroy's insensitive attribution of motives, the absence of any presentation of accurate background information on the preparation of the couriers and Fergusson's innovations is telling.

A later updating of Pomeroy's subject is John A. Jackle's *The Tourist: Travel in Twentieth-Century North America* (1985). Jackle, a professor of geography, takes all of the United States as his domain but devotes a chapter to tourism and "The American West as Region." Jackle, like Pomeroy, has culled through many sources, including the writings of amateurs and professionals, but he, too, neglects to mention Fergusson. He discusses the sublimity of mountains and deserts in the Southwest and cites more than one anonymous or obscure tourist's response to them. He recounts the descriptions of one Melville Ferguson and his drive through the "opaque pall" of a New Mexico dust storm to reach Albuquerque "full of grit."[5] Although Jackle alludes to Fergusson's fellow Albuquerquean, Ernie Pyle, not a sentence is devoted to Erna Fergusson. This is doubly ironic in that she, perhaps more than any other twentieth-century Southwestern travel writer, spread the very word Jackle sees the West holding for tourists:

> The West surprised, amazed, disturbed, and disappointed tourists. It was many things to many people. However, whatever the images, the West was always attractive to tourists. It was the region that popular sentiment said was most worth visiting. Travelers first had to find it. Where did the West begin? Where did it end? Then they had to ascertain its true character. Expectations were validated, or invalidated. Although the West changed throughout the early twentieth century, the prevailing touristic images remained remarkably consistent. The West was vast. Its scenery was superlative. Its cities were progressive. Its people were unhurried, friendly, happy. The West was a place both of opportunity and of contentment. The West was not as refined as the East, since frontier conditions lingered there, but the

future belonged to the West. The West was North America's promised land.[6]

Although the arguments Pomeroy and Jackle make for the importance of tourism and travel writing might be made stronger by some consideration of Fergusson, their sympathies are admittedly with the significance of tourism and travel writing in general. Be that as it may, Fergusson's Southwest travel writings confirm much of what present-day writers are asserting about the West and travel as important aspects of American social and literary history.

Janis P. Stout's *The Journey Narrative in American Literature* (1983) and Leonard Lutwack's *The Role of Place in Literature* (1984) afford further consideration of how truly wide-ranging and significant the "placeness" of America is, as are the journeys—to, in, and from it—in our national literature.[7] For Stout the journey narrative (whether as water voyage or westering trek or open road) is the dominant form in American literature. She also makes the credible points that the patterns which American journey narratives take are numerous (whether as escape, quest, exploration, colonization, or aimless wandering) and that the patterns (whether from the known to the unknown, from restriction to freedom, from East to West, from "social" to "presocial," future to past, or the reverse) are not mutually exclusive but may exist in any given work either in combination or in series. Of all journey narratives, Stout insists, "The Western, that most American of fictions, also appears in several contexts because it is actually a composite form, utilizing more than one type of journey."[8]

Stout's taxonomy of patterns also assumes that these patterns have a chronological or historical basis: exploration, escape, and "home founding" are early patterns, while "aimless wandering" is more closely associated with the twentieth century. This chronology of patterns is, furthermore, complemented by certain respective tonalities: the satiric, associated with the traveler's "lie," the "mock journey," or the picaresque; the eschatological, associated with the epic migration; the tragic or exultation narrative, associated with home founding; acceptance of the status quo, associated with homecoming; and either the high comedic or high tragic is associated with the heroic quest or night journey.[9]

Although Stout speaks mainly about fiction and, to a lesser extent, poetry, her generalizations are equally applicable to Fergusson's travel writing. Whether her travels are regarded literally, as they must be, or figuratively, as they can be, her travels, like her life as a traveler and tour guide, were something of a reward in and of themselves. Life as journey/process, and not the destination/end—the journey as traveler's telling—was both the aspiration and the prize.

In his chapter on "Place and National Literature: The American and His Land," Lutwack—like Stout, but from a somewhat different vantage point—insists that "no national literature ever generated more faith in the influence of geography on art than . . . American literature."[10] And where geography is such a great factor, space and time and travel become intrinsic—as Emerson, Thoreau, Melville, among the great Romantic writers, and Frederick Jackson Turner, among American historians, have observed. Lutwack, in accounting for the responses of historians and literary critics to land and how the "West," in space and time, has been perceived, singles out Turner's "Significance of the Frontier in American History," Henry Nash Smith's *Virgin Land,* and Leo Marx's *The Machine in the Garden* as representative commentaries—each author establishing a different paradigm: "The relation of people to land is finally a product of the interaction of three factors: the basic physical nature of the environment, the preconceptions with which it is approached by its inhabitants, and the changes man makes in it. Turner addressed himself to the first of these, Smith to the second, and Marx to the last."[11]

While Turner thought the West as geographical area was the most significant determinant, Smith thought its conception as "the garden of the world" was more influential, while Marx demonstrates how the garden was destroyed by a passion for industrial progress. In Lutwack's adaptations, then, America, and especially the West, is best viewed variously as El Dorado, garden, and wilderness. Fergusson, in her way, and with much greater attention to the collision of Anglo-Americans' ethnocentric assumptions with Native American and Hispanic and Mexican history and culture, confronts all of these determiners and influences as they coalesced around her travels in the modern Southwest.

ITEROLOGY AND THE SOUTHWEST
AS WONDERMENT

The consideration of Fergusson as a Southwestern traveler assumes in part the important link between travel writing and westering. It can be argued, clearly, that the literature of the American Southwest is as much a part— perhaps even more so—of American literature of discovery and wonderment (and, thus, of travel) as is the regional literature of New England or the South. The Southwestern identity is a composite identity of travelers: individuals and groups. Moreover, the Southwestern identity is impossible to contemplate apart from the travels of early exploration and settlement, and later in the tourism, health seeking, and "continental drift" south to the Sunbelt. And if one considers the implications of immigration and emigration, and of the processes of assimilation and Americanization, the "travels" implicit in such processes, such "stories," are apparent. But if the literature of the Southwest is the literature of travel, it is also the literature of biography and autobiography. William Butler Yeats writes, "We may come to think that nothing exists but a stream of souls, that all knowledge is biography."[12] One senses that stream of souls in Fergusson's inclination to interview countless individuals wherever she traveled. Thus, she turns not only her sense of history, or time, into biography but thinks of geography, or space, in terms of biography as well. To say that all knowledge is biography or that all literature is travel is surely a distortion of the ordinary, accepted boundaries of literary form and historiography. Such distortion, however, is not without some usefulness since narrow definitions of genre, travel narrative or otherwise, as of historical "knowledge" and truth, at times result in the obfuscation of the universal and the obvious.

For the earliest Anglo-European discoverers and explorers to the Southwest, for sensitive tourists, and for life-or-death health seekers, the Southwest, like America itself, was and still is often viewed as commensurate with humanity's capacity for wonderment. William Carlos Williams's *In the American Grain* dramatizes this feature of the American landscape in his accounts of Columbus, Hernán Cortez, Cabeza de Vaca, de Soto, Champlain, and others, just as that more modern discoverer, Nick Carraway, and with him F. Scott Fitzgerald speculate in the concluding scene of *The Great Gatsby*. Surely, to travel, to see, to name, and to tell are almost inevitable actions in writing. And these actions were just as essential to the early Dutch immigrants with whom Carraway identifies, to the conquistadors (or with the Indians, the discovered seeing the discoverers) imagined by Williams, and to later Anglo-Americans who came West (or in the case of the Spanish, who went north) for religious and economic conquest and settlement as they were to Fergusson. Indeed, Fergusson was a native-born granddaughter of a Santa Fe trader, daughter of a frontier attorney and territorial representative to Congress, a "native" Anglo-American observer and commentator who came to be known among certain Indian peoples as Beautiful Swift Fox. It is perhaps sufficient to say that all American Southwestering is replete with the wonderment of travel and its oral and written telling. N. Scott Momaday calls the spaces of this vastness of West a "house made of dawn," and Ivan Doig terms it a "house of sky." The wonderment of West in all its directionality is never-ceasing and constantly experienced by those who pass along its ways and make written note of it.

As novelist Michel Butor would have it, to live is to travel: travel is writing, writing is travel.[13] Coining a term, "iterology," for the new science tied to literature but concerned with all human travel, Butor (more metaphorically and extensively than others) classifies all the various types of travel he can think of, all the various kinds of trips, as analogous to kinds of reading and writing which take shape in what he chooses to call the *récit de voyage:* reading as escape; reading as the filling of the whiteness on the page; travel one-way or round-trip; travel as wandering or nomadism, as settlement and exodus, as leaving one home for another, as business trip or vacation, as exotic, alien experience (i.e., stranger in a strange land), as a return home, as pilgrimage, as either horizontal or vertical motion (one-dimensional or multidimensional), over distances which stretch out, head up or down, or which penetrate. To explicate the intrigues of travel writing, Butor claims that Gérard de Nerval's *Le Voyage en Orient,* because of its circuitous and multidimensional structure, in effect, proves history "false," while a book like Chateaubriand's *L'Itineraire de Paris à Jerusalem* in its traditional, one-dimensional structure, which follows an itinerary from one principal town to another and is hence a linear trip, proves history "true."[14]

Fergusson's Southwestern travel writings, on first look, seem to fall in the category of Chateaubriand's book, proving history "true." Even so, a text like *Dancing Gods* also veers away, into the teasings of myth and ceremony, outside of history. In his attempts to relate actual, physical travel to books about travel, Butor explains what he calls the "degree of literariness" contained in any given journey. There are romantic voyages which are invariably "bookish," being either about books or precipitated by books; or, in Butor's words: "The travellers read books during their journeys, they write them, usually keeping a journal, and they always produce a book upon their return. . . . They travel in order to write, they travel while writing, because, for them, travel is writing."[15] In addition, there are voyages of "signature" which dwell on paths cleared, landmarks identified, tombs inscribed, and registers signed. Conversely, too, there are voyages in which travelers avoid at all costs leaving any kind of disturbing signatures and pass over the landscape or through it as an "invisible intruder" leaving his mark only on the recitation of his travel, in his travel book.

In Butor's iterological sense, then, Fergusson's travel writing has a greater degree of "literariness" than anyone has yet observed. Her Southwestern writings generally point more to the "signature" type of work, primarily because of their tourism origins, than to the work of the "invisible intruder." However, much of her respect and appreciation for what she describes stems from her desire to be an accepting and acceptable intruder, if not an entirely invisible one.

Travel writing, says Butor, is often motivated by the desire to create a "representative object," be it map or book (or both in one), in which words become the very landmarks linking one traveler to another.[16] By implication, Butor's "science" of iterology become art involves the act of travel as an end in itself; thus, travel is the autobiographical itinerary of one's life. It is a similar paradox involving literature into life, life into literature, which Stout also finds in journey narratives and motifs. The conundrum is clear. Speaking for himself, but with ramifications for interpreting Fergusson's presence in and reaction to her Southwest, Butor says, "I have always felt the intense bond that exists between my travels and my writing; I travel in order to write—not only to find subject matter, topics or events . . . but because to travel is to read, and to write is to travel.[17]

The autobiographical dimensions, the relationships between Fergusson's travels as she lived them and as she wrote them, are quite close, for although she indulges in metaphor and transcendent description (Walker's "New Mexico baroque"), her travel writing is not about imaginary journeys, not fiction. Rather, it is the journey as record. She captures and invites such literature/life correspondences in the assumptions, tones, and narrative structures of her writing through her voice and dramatic stance as a modern, Anglo-American, native-born Southwesterner, a Beautiful Swift Fox with the greatest of inclinations and empathies for the "otherness" of time, of culture, and of place. In this sense, Fergusson's beauty, especially her bearing and temperament, extends the beauty of her historical presence and her name.

Moreover, the imagining exists on the part of the reader, the prospective and perspicacious traveler who, during the "journey" of the reading, accompanies Fergusson as author/guide. Moreover, after the reading, the traveler/reader may both imagine what a visit to such a spot, or such an event, might really be like and actually visit it, imagining what it might have been like not to have first read and traveled, and then traveled, experienced, and remembered what was read. For Fergusson the traveler/writer and her traveler/reader—the real and the vicarious—fuse, mix, and enrich each other.

Paradoxes and conundrums of the real and the illusory, life and literature, travel as word and as actual physical movement and sensory experience notwithstanding, Butor's essay illustrates the obvious. That is, he shows how important travel is in everyone's life, underscoring the by now trite but true metaphor of "the journey of life" and its "passages," as Gail Sheehy, Robert Bly, and Sam Keen, commentators both clichéd and archetypal in their interpretations, have illuminated it. But Butor also generalizes about why travel matters to the writer and to writing and, still more intriguingly, to the reader and to reading. His categories of travel as reading and writing provide interesting mappings through which one can locate Fergusson, like Thoreau, as a home traveler, discovering newness and regeneration, not just for herself but for those who accompany or follow her. The guide, although knowing more about the places, sites, and sights described, nevertheless finds novelty, surprise, and a new degree of the unknown in the known.

Pomeroy, Jackle, Stout, Lutwack, William Carlos Williams, ecological travelers Rick Bass and Barry Lopez, "erotic" travelers such as Terry Tempest Williams, and "intelligent" travel theorists such as Marta Weigle, Sylvia Rodríguez, Donald Horne, and Michel Butor all offer what might be regarded as revisionist views of travel writing, focusing on structure, narrative, motif, utility, and the relativity of cultural perspectives rather than seeing travel writing as strictly a linear, solely a one-dimensional departure/ arrival recording. They are merely part of a larger chorus of critics who, although they seldom discuss Fergusson, nevertheless provide a broadening base, a more encompassing "vocabulary" by which her Southwestern travel writings may be discussed and assessed. For example, in the early 1960s Columbia University's English Institute was devoted to the topic of literature as travel. Out of those sessions came a noteworthy group of early modern essays which also provide a greater understanding of travel writing as type and mode and its overall expansiveness and inclusiveness: "The traveller's interest may be concentrated chiefly on commerce, or geography, or archaeology, or natural history, or sociology, or anthropology, or linguistics. He may be at heart a historian, by profession a diplomat or political observer."[18]

The West and Southwest as the occasion for travel writing are dealt with even more theoretically in the writings of two other recent and especially insightful critics, Wayne Franklin and Stephen Fender.[19] They, too, provide broader background for a consideration of Fergusson as Southwestern "traveler." Although Franklin's speculations may seem overly weighty when applied to the writings of a "popularizer" like Fergusson, they do invite relevant applications. Franklin is concerned with the disparities that can exist in travel writing between fact and fiction, between physical realities and the naming of them, between things and words, between the perception of reality and its expression in language. He points out that travel books are particularly determined by the limits of expository and descriptive language, "the [intractability] discovered when words and things fall asunder" ("S&T," 19). Franklin takes the travel narratives of New World discoverers such as Columbus, Hernán Cortez, John Winthrop, John Lawson, and Alvar Nuñez Cabeza de Vaca, and—acting as a kind of scholar/discoverer himself—explores "the problem of inexpressibility," saying: "Wherever they went, New World travelers were agreed about the inexpressible quality of their visual, social, and . . . their spiritual life on this side of the Atlantic. Things, people and experiences all taxed the lexical equipment of these travelers, and they reacted to the challenge thus given them in similar, and highly interesting, ways" ("S&T," 19). Fergusson faces the intractability and frustrations of trying to "express" the reality she observes, and linguistically, at least, of not only the English language but of Pueblo, Navajo, Hopi, Apache, and other Native American languages, and of Spanish.

Even in the twentieth century the landforms and the peoples were defiant of complete description and expression. Furthermore, the "rhetoric" of the problem—how to describe, explain, and, in many cases, argue what was observed—was, for Fergusson, complicated by the centuries of diverse histories from diverse cultural perspectives of Native American, Hispanic, and Anglo assumptions and accounts of the cultural and geographical laminations and convergences which had transpired over, at the minimum, three centuries.

Franklin contends that the central rhetorical issue in American travel accounts is the need to bridge New World experiences with Old World audiences. With certain twentieth-century adaptations, this is precisely Fergusson's need: to bridge any number of differences, now/then, East/West, male/female—to explain the wonderment of the at-once historic and timeless Southwest, to interpret its exotic yet indigenous peoples and cultures to various "tourists" who either aspire to see it or are trying to see and cannot comprehend what they are seeing, or who are careless to the point of breezing by all that surrounds them in a blur of mechanized oblivion.

In the rhetorical flourishes of Cortez and in the accounts of many other Spanish explorers, Franklin finds the bedrock of a nagging recognition which is fundamental to all American travel writing:

> And that recognition, altered as it may become by later centuries of "converting" the American scene through word and deed—strewing the names and institutions of Europe over it—that recognition continues to exist at the center of the American travel book. It typifies the psychological shock of Westward discovery, and this points ahead to that sense of alienation which Octavio Paz has described in *The Labyrinth of Solitude,* and for which Philip Slater has provided Northern analogues in *The Pursuit of Loneliness.* ("S&T," 21)

Insofar as Franklin is correct about the difficulties of American travelers to truly express America, then Fergusson, some five centuries later, as a modern Southwestern traveler, faced, at least to some degree, the same lexical and rhetorical wonder and challenge of expression. Perhaps she even felt a special shock of solitude and alienation as an Anglo-American at "home" among Native American and Hispanic culture (present and past) and startling, picturesque/sublime landforms and vistas. (One is reminded here, again, of Nick Carraway, somehow sensing across the centuries the "capacity of wonder" felt by early Dutch explorers in the new world of America. And Ivan Doig, in his now classic rendering of the Big Sky of his immigrant father and his own Montana youth, carries forth a similar sense of West wonderment.)

Fergusson, too, had to query—"How to express it all?"—not, to be sure, to European audiences but to other Anglo-Americans inherently "distanced," if not lost, in the exoticism and strangeness, the marvel of the Southwest as presence in time. She attempted to lessen their own estrangement in a strange land, through the comforts, reassurances, and camaraderie of tours, and detours—be they in high-powered Packard or Franklin touring cars with strong cowboy drivers and uniformed, charming couriers, or in books with fine Borzoi or Armitage designs containing in the bite of ink on paper wondrous descriptions, explanations, definitions, and illustrations.

For the likes of Cortez, Cabeza de Vaca, or, one might add, Fergusson, American Indian and Hispanic cultural, linguistic, and social "phenomena" posed major challenges of exposition. The business—literally and figuratively—of being a traveler was no simple matter, especially if the traveler recast the travels in words. According to Franklin, "Far from enjoying the simple position of an eyewitness, the traveler becomes an interpreter as well; and as his roles diversify, his task as writer becomes more difficult. Added to the failures of close observation are the failures of cultural misunderstanding. More 'foreign' at times than American objects, the native words which describe them may interpose another barrier between self and world" ("S&T," 22). Analogical naming was a typical way around such a problem, as in the case of Magellan referring to bananas as "figs a foot long" ("S&T," 23).

Similarly, there is something significant in Fergusson's choosing to name her guide service the Koshare Tours and drawing in her promotional brochures the implicit analogy between her role as a "delight maker" and the Pueblo *koshare* figure—a figure adapted as well by the famous Southwestern ethnologist and traveler Adolf Bandelier in his "novel" *The Delight Makers* (1890). Or is Fergusson priding herself on being given such friendly appellations for her physical abilities among the Hopi as Shi-kya-wa-nim (Beautiful Swift Fox)? Whether apocryphal or actual, Fergusson's perpetuation of this appellation is its own significance. Franklin emphasizes that the failure of Anglo-Americans today to understand empathetically the roles and functions of native leaders, who were frequently, and all too glibly, stereotyped in the popular media as "chief," points to the dangers of seemingly simple cultural/lexical misnamings and misunderstandings ("S&T," 24).

Fergusson, as both Shi-kya-wa-nim and the Anglo-American writer "Miss Fergusson," knew, too, that to call the Shalako and other American Indian ceremonial figures "dancing gods" involved a big lexical and metaphorical leap, because "dancing" and "gods" in the Anglo lexicon are not necessarily the same thing to Pueblo, Navajo, Hopi, and Apache cultures. It is no real wonder, then, that in addition to attempting to translate various words in her text and to transvaluate their meanings, she resorted to appending glossaries for the aid of her uninitiated readers—a fact with obvious, at times patronizing, but, nevertheless, significant rhetorical and expository implications.

In addition to analogical naming, Franklin sees the act of patterning, which is involved in lists and catalogues and is so often resorted to by American travelers, as an essential part of the aesthetics of travel writing. In place of naming a single object or role, "catalogers and collectors begin to create a grammar, principles of subordination and coordination, or of relation and difference" ("S&T," 25). And it is from such cataloging that promotional tracts take form—those travel accounts so common to early America which were used to invite and induce immigration rather than contemplation: "Hard and clear in its details, a catalogue conveys the sense of a world touched, and a world inviting our own touch in return" ("S&T," 29). But if cataloging invites touch it does not, reminds Franklin, accomplish one other important aspect of travel writing: inviting the reader to "feel" what is described as "complete landscapes, multidimensional and complex. . . [an aspect stressed by Butor as well]" ("S&T," 29). The insidious inadequacy of cataloging, its static failure, is due to its suggesting relationships between things and, more completely, other aspects of any given place: "American things are named in the catalogue merely as objects for our own desire, as passive subjects yielding all to their imported beneficiaries. Almost never do the objects interact with each other; even less rarely do they acquire the power of aggressive action over those who have named them and have set out to appropriate their virtues" ("S&T," 31).

As in Fergusson's best moments, only when travel writings shift the reader's attention away from surface details and expository formulas of analogy and cataloging, thereby allowing vastness and complexity beyond the merely picturesque (the ultimate inexpressibility of silence, of relationships between the persons and the things being described, whereby the teller somehow merges with the objects of description and simultaneously transcends them), is the true literary potential of travel writing realized. Thus, the less narrative distance of author from subject, the higher the odds of successful expository, nonfiction artistry. Fergusson's humanness, the humor of her characteristic anecdotes and interviews, make her moments of stylistic loftiness and ethereal transcendence all the more noticeable—to her, seemingly, and to the reader/companion.

In Franklin's view Cabeza de Vaca's *La Relación* is representative of a text wherein the author is utterly absorbed in and awestruck by the environment, in a sense similar to Joseph Conrad's Mr. Kurtz, another sojourner in strangeness. Kurtz's utterance—"The horror! the horror!"—in *Heart of Darkness* offers a literary landmark of the traveler's occupational sense of inexpressibility and wonderment when finally grasping the magnitude of self-involvement, mortality, eternity, oblivion—whatever the nature of Kurtz's comprehension and failure to comprehend, to express or not express, whatever the basis of his motivation to account for awesomeness in words. Strangely enough, Fergusson's humor, her exaggerations, her satirical quips, her sense of, on the one hand, the silliness and fun of what she sees and, on the other, the practicality, if not the profundity, of it is omnipresent in her attempt to "write" the sights and the sites just as she "rides" them in her various touring cars—all functioning as another means by which she attempts to express the inexpressible.

PLOTTING PLACE

In his study of the relationships between American literature and westering, Stephen Fender holds that "the more plotless the landscape, the more plotted the writing."[20] Assuming that the West did not express itself, Fender stresses that it was in the main described by Eastern travelers for other Easterners who remained at home and that it was the American writer's own stereotypical sense of reality which was imposed on the otherwise external reality of "West":

> The traveler's concern at leaving behind what he takes to be his cultural center prompts a more-than-ever rigorous observance of whatever forms he thinks distinguishes [sic] him from the foreign culture in which he finds himself. And these outward conventions must not be covert, subtle and recognized by only a small elite within his society; they must be the lowest common denominator of Englishness, or

Americanness, or whatever nationality they represent—so much so that they have become almost music-hall jokes by the time they are employed.[21]

If this line of thinking is applied to Fergusson's travel writings, it is her Anglo-Americanness and her femaleness which most motivate and prompt her observances. Problematic as gender and perspective are, Fergusson's femaleness, her manly-hearted womanly pride, and her independence as a caring, compassionate advocate and spokesperson (at least as seen in her own mind's eye and assumed and projected through her rhetorical and stylistic stances and voicings) must be acknowledged, stereotyping pitfalls notwithstanding. And her *grande dame* bearing does indeed inform both the occasion and the presentation of her "visits," her "tours," her attempts at understanding and explaining the "otherness" about her. Older sister, commiserating maiden aunt, even natural-born nurturing mother, Fergusson's "woman writer" identity informs her authorial dramatizations and identifications—both explicit and implicit, as an advocate or nurturer of peoples and countries either relatively estranged or alienated, youthful or dependent, or developing. Her reliable and compassionate female presence is a consistent perspective throughout both the Southwestern and the Latin American travel accounts as friend among friends, albeit often portrayed as a stranger in a strange land.

It is not improbable, then, in such a context, to see part of Fergusson's contribution to Southwestern travel writing as obscuring, distorting, even foiling, certainly softening what Sylvia Rodríguez and other feminist travel critics pose as the "male gaze" (implicit in some of the pronouncements of Walker, Pomeroy, et al.), one of the key posited processes for signifying the Southwest during the early part of the twentieth century. Rodríguez notes: "Feminist deconstruction of the male gaze as an instrument of sex-gender hegemony points to several interrelated aspects of the system: physical dominion and control, material ownership, appropriation of services, and above all the power of symbolic representation. Although the role of eroticism in the tourist and male gazes may differ, the two are nevertheless comparable in these specific respects."[22] Fergusson's androgyny, or double vision, (woman dressed as Indian Detour guide, in high-laced boots, riding pants, military-style jacket, and trooper hat) in her role as female guide (something of an oxymoron to some male-dominant perceptions) is significant in its complexity, for while she softened the dominance of the male gaze of tourism, she assumed the vantage point of heretofore pervasive and dominant, "typical" male guides. And in this sense Fergusson, like Mabel Dodge Luhan, Georgia O'Keeffe, Mary Colter, Irene Fisher, and other illustrious modern Southwestern women, helped invert the hierarchy and systems of stratification previously in operation in the nineteenth century —thus contributing to her role as a modern and as a proponent and interpreter of the modern Southwest. As Rodríguez points out in relation to the systems of ethnic stratifications established as tourism to the Southwest began to pick up and either create or recreate the spirit and the perceptions of the locale, Indians, Mexicans, and cowboys set forth the respective reperceived order of importance.[23] Female tour guide, travel writer, and interpreter should also be added to this new order, encompassing the role of new woman within older expectations of "nourisher," aunt, godmother, cousin, even, by association, comforter, compatriot, nurse, and "mother."

Fergusson is, however, at the same time a native-born New Mexican who is attempting most of all to point out the authenticity of what she sees and where she goes to nonnative-born travelers who, presumably, although Anglo-Americans too, have less sensitivity and sensibility than she does as indigenous guide (guide to the indigenous), the offspring of earlier, pioneer newcomers.

Fender, moreover, poses the intriguing possibility that the greater the distance the travel writer is from his or her cultural center, the greater the likelihood for melodramatic enhancement, for thicker plotting, and the use of literary romance formulas. When Fergusson is considered in such a context, her Southwestern travel writing, although not heavily "plotted" in the ordinary sense of the term and although not especially melodramatic or cast in the formulas of romance, is nevertheless enhanced by her capacity for wonderment in face of landscape, laminated cultures, and history. Her at times transcendent "style" and attempts at dramatizing or staging a scene alternate, in their leanings to romance and melodrama, with a hardheaded realism and sense of utilitarian urgency to carry on with basic human values of equality and respect. Fergusson's Southwestern travel accounts are characterized by an at-once austere, unselfconscious or unobtrusive presence and by a contrived, conscious "inventiveness" or "stylization." *Dancing Gods* and *Murder and Mystery in New Mexico* are relatively more melodramatic than *New Mexico, Our Southwest,* or *Albuquerque.*

The comparative remoteness of "Indian" detours, departures into exotic Native American lands and dwelling places, or of bizarre or grotesque murders and crimes doubtlessly account, as in Fender's model, at least in part, for the degrees of melodrama which do exist. Her travel writings, however, also move toward satire and humor in the form of mild sarcasm and poking fun—at tourist observers and at herself, though she presents herself as the opposite of the greenhorn. She keeps to the tradition of pioneer humor, albeit communicated from a sophisticated rather than simple folktale stance. All of which transforms what otherwise might be thought of as the crudeness of the folksy, frontier, practical joke, of kidding and pulling the leg of the newcomer, into a more urbane kind of wit. But the greater portions of plotting in Fergusson's Southwestern travel writing are inherent in the landscape and in the ceremonies and overall "historicity" of place.

In Fender's scheme the explosion of travel accounts during the great trek to the California gold fields was but a realization of Tocqueville's and Emerson's prophecies that conventional fictions would, in effect, fall away in the face of the capacity of the American landscape to create wonderment. Faced with the sublimity of landscape and the comparative strangeness of the flora and fauna in the West, the American travel writer would be regenerated, reborn, although somewhat anxiously, out of the kind of wilderness adventure, the kind of primitivism which America offered. In terms of Fender's theories about plotting the West, later nineteenth- and twentieth-century travelers (presumably the artists who flocked to Taos and Santa Fe, the tourists who rode the Santa Fe and Southern Pacific, the "lungers" who sought the restorative powers of bright sun and clear air, and of native-born travelers like Fergusson who awaited their arrival and took them to the exotic places they had heard rumored) collectively and individually experienced a double anxiety: "For once the twin polarities of American unease, the fear of underplotting and the surfeit of overplotting, were experienced not in turn but simultaneously. The wilderness was manifestly devoid of 'culture' in any sense: empty, unplanted, largely uninhabited; yet it had been described, even inscribed, and there were ample texts, from widely circulated books to names carved on lonely, distant rocks to attest to that inescapable fact."[24]

Certainly the "anxieties" which faced Fergusson as a travel writer at mid-twentieth century were not identical to the pressures of either the original guides or their followers to the Far West. She had been a close part of her grandparents' and parents' attempts to establish the civilities not only of the East and South but of Europe in the sleepy Spanish/Mexican/Anglo river town of Albuquerque. And yet the sense of primitiveness and wilderness existed all about her—in the pueblos, on the reservations, across the arid distances of mesas and the timber-lined heights of mountains. Her duty was to bridge the two worlds—frontier past and modern present, to bring comfort and understanding and acceptance of the Native American and Hispanic to the Anglo. Why she chose to write travel books and histories rather than novels is understandable in that the scene unfolding before her, as she was growing up in and touring the modern Southwest and showing it to others from car and book tours, was a "plot" in and of itself—a sequence of actions and motives revealing itself in the cavalcade of events common to her time: a process inevitable to succumb to life as plotted autobiography, travel narratives revealing her own personhood as a native-born Southwesterner.

It is against this complex and fabulous network of forces, individual and societal, which shaped and were shaped by travel as writing and by writing as travel in American literature and history, that Fergusson's Southwestern travels and her identity as a traveler can best be appraised. Her travels and travel writing are the mappings of one attempting, with charm, tolerance, and common sense, to accomplish two ends—to civilize (in the sense of trying to understand and explain and marvel at rather than blindly or naively ignoring or rejecting) and to reconcile the convergence of Native American and Hispanic cultures with the strange but intrinsic otherness of Anglo-American industrial icon and motive riding the rails and the highways of her time.

THE KOSHARE TOURS

As the Atchison, Topeka, and Santa Fe's speedy transcontinental train, the California Limited, increased the number of passengers traveling the Santa Fe route across New Mexico and the Southwest, and as the automobile improved its performance, and national highways like U.S. 85 and U.S. 66 (Main Street America) made travel to the Southwest even easier, Fergusson turned her knowledge of the Southwest to commercial ends. With her friend, Ethel Hickey, she formed a business devoted to scheduling, outfitting, and guiding short trips of either one day's or several days' duration to key points of landscape, history, and culture. As Fergusson describes it: "When the war [World War I] ended I began to dude-wrangle. I dragged tourists all over New Mexico, Southern Colorado, and Arizona to see Indians and Indian ceremonials. They blamed me bitterly for almost everything, but some of them liked it and came again."[25] Fergusson and Hickey called their "dude-wrangling" business the Koshare Tours after the Pueblo dancers who, as emissaries of the gods, were called the "delight makers" by Bandelier. One of the early Koshare promotional brochures—almost as interesting for its advertisements as for its timetables and descriptions—announced to prospective customers the purpose of the company as envisioned by these two Southwestern entrepreneurs: "Koshare Tours were created to reveal to you the delights of a land as yet but little known to the traveler, to invite you to get away from the railroad and shake hands with a thousand years."[26] The emphasis of the metaphor (and odds are that Fergusson herself conceived it) is clearly on hospitality as much as on history.

By implication, hospitality would be welcomed in an exotic land, "as yet little known to the traveler." *The Koshare Book* advertised on its cover (in bold, stylized Art Deco lettering) both "fascinating motor trips from Albuquerque" and information about New Mexico and Albuquerque, "The Hub of the Indian Land." The sights included "Mountains and Mesas; Indian Dances, Indian Towns, Cliff Dwellings and Ancient Ruins; Sleepy Mexican Villages; A City in the Sky; A City of Seven Terraces."

Fergusson and Hickey, who took it upon themselves to show the uninitiated the exoticism of Indian country, also acted as cultural buffers between the cultures and races. For example, *Sunset Magazine* and *Women's Citizen* featured Fergusson as an "Interesting Westerner," a "Woman Dude Wrangler" and a "Feminine Van Manager," and she was profiled by her friend Louise Lowbar Cassidy not only as a shrewd businesswoman but also as a cultural emissary, a "civilizing" force in what was projected as the rather stereotypical lost land where a friendly, "diplomatic," knowledgeable Anglo guide (one of the reader's own ethnic, if not exclusively gender, kind) wins (for herself and the accompanying traveler) the acceptance and trust of the "natives":

> Miss Fergusson . . . is perfectly at home in the remotest Mexican village or with the most diffident Indian tribe. Her knowledge of Spanish, the diplomatic language of the Southwest, and her cordial sympathy with the natives insure her a welcome in any community. She knows that a can of tobacco presented as a gift between friends will win a bit of genuine Indian hospitality for her guests, and perhaps some extra entertainment in the way of ceremonial songs and dances. The Koshare party is not infrequently permitted to witness religious ceremonies from which less respectful whites are barred.[27]

Cassidy's profile of "Miss Fergusson" and her Koshare Tours, although well-intended, is noticeably ethnocentric and patronizing toward the "natives." Intended as a testimonial to the credibility, effectiveness, and goodwill of Fergusson, the effect of the piece is now ironic. And yet, in its day, it was presumably an innocent compliment to Fergusson and, as the basis of a persona and legend of the trusty tour guide, enticing to the would-be tourist.

According to a legend, which came to surround Fergusson as head of the Koshare Tours (a legend no doubt encouraged for commercial reasons, since the image was no doubt helpful in advertising the services and personnel of the tours), Fergusson came to be known (and promoted) as Shi-kya-wa-nim, or Beautiful Swift Fox—a name presumably *earned* and deserved by winning a "footrace over a group of Indian girls following the annual Snake Dance" of the Hopi.[28] Again, the treatment of such an accomplishment now seems to suggest motivation by commercialism or presumption as much as by concern for cultural harmony. Nevertheless, Cassidy's intent, and presumably Fergusson's consent in the promotion, has an air of naïveté and innocence about it. Such picturesque credentials as these, this christening by the Indians as Beautiful Swift Fox, whether true or utterly apocryphal, and the publicity of being an "accepted" and "respectful" Anglo-American guide among the "natives" in association with her unique role as a "woman dude wrangler" contributed to the success of the Koshare Tours. They also prepared Fergusson to assume the more authoritative role of an author who had firsthand experience, a native-born woman who had "been there" and participated in certain lesser ceremonies and was privileged to be allowed to witness certain more private ceremonies.

The stereotype of an assimilated, accepted blood-brother compatriot out West runs from the earliest of Anglo-European and Anglo-American literature of the Puritans through that of the mountain men, and the Western, up to latter-day films such as *The Outlaw Josey Wales* and *Dances with Wolves*. Seldom is a woman so assimilated and accepted as a "blood sister." Rather, as in D. H. Lawrence's archetypal story, "The Woman Who Rode Away," women were assimilated—Aztec fashion—into the maw of volcanoes, as virginal sacrifices, occurrences of potential apotheosis. Not quite deified, Fergusson's promulgated persona as Beautiful Swift Fox functioned as a kind of pantheistic icon of trial and test, of bestiary, fable, and ethos.

As contemplated by Rodríguez, Marta Weigle, and other commentators on Southwestern tourism, the entrepreneurial roles of travel become tourism, become aspects of promotion, publicity, public relations, of seeing and showing and "selling" the place and its people, landscapes, and cultures, soon became inextricably connected with capitalistic commercialization and "commodification." Such connections are not necessarily complete—or essentially evil or unethical—in their putative compromises and corruptions. Weigle's apt positing of the evolving corruptions of the Santa Fe style and "coyote art"[29] provide a basis for tempting, although too easily concluded and clichéd, analogies and convincing extrapolations of how Fergusson's iconographic fox might be viewed as part of the commercial and cultural corruptions of bandanna-bedecked, polka-dotted, silhouetted, plywood, New Age–curios coyotes in every Taos and Tucson, Scottsdale and Santa Fe store window. Although Fergusson's self-promotion—her adoption, appropriation, or, many would say, misappropriation of an Indian name and Indian ways, albeit as a player of games and runner of races with young girls—might today be viewed as totally exploitative, she was herself no doubt sincere in her dramatized identifications with the Indian and the Southwest as budding commodity. Indians, too, could capitalize on this new influx of train-riding, money-spending whites. Their cultures, their ways, and their wares were indeed salable—but what the harm? Who could see the far end of such business? Indian accounts, either on-the-spot or oral tellings, of that special running and consequent naming have presumably evaporated as swiftly and as finally as the panting breaths and excited exclamations, the fleet and fleeting footsteps of the event—and of the reputed honor, reverence, and respect involved in her Shi-kya-wa-nim christening.

According to Cassidy, and to most others who knew Fergusson, her warm and human personality also contributed to her acceptance by Native Americans, Mexican Americans, and Anglo tourists as a "delight maker": "It is this talent for entertainment in Miss Fergusson which makes her so eminently successful as a tourist guide. A person of unusual wit, she has the faculty of seeing the amusing side of every situation and of making it appear so to her guests—a true 'delight maker.'"[30] But as Fergusson explained it to Cassidy, the whole "delightful" enterprise took considerable planning and work: "I have been accused of making a living out of what I most like to do [travel the Southwest], with the implication that it is therefore no work. . . . But that's not half of it. When we arrive at your door in a big car with a spade on behind for possible mud, a lunch kit for the inevitable famine, huge thermoses for probable thirst, a strong man for emergencies and an expectant group of tourists in the back seat, don't get the idea that it just happened."[31]

Between trips, Fergusson taught for a time in the Albuquerque public schools, worked on the *New Mexico Tribune* at the society desk, and wrote her columns about "seeing New Mexico first." Her travels led to the writing; her writing led to the travels. Both occupations helped in the planning. When the trips finally came for the tourists, she relieved them of all responsibility. Cassidy outlines Fergusson's duties for her customers: "She . . . provides them every night with the best bed available, at a hotel if there is one within striking distance, on an air mattress under the sky or perhaps in an Indian home or a remote rancho; feeds them iced cantaloupe and crisp salads in the middle of the blistering desert in summer, and hot tea and sandwiches in late winter afternoons when dinner is several chilly hours further up the highway. And she tells them more than they can possibly remember about the history, folk lore and customs of the people and places they visit."[32]

Fergusson's role in reconciling Anglo-American, Native American, and

Hispanic worlds through her Koshare Tours is reflected too in the uniforms that she and her female guides wore, and which later she helped design for the couriers in Fred Harvey's Indian Detours. As one guide recalls, "The uniform couriers wore was in excellent taste—neutral tan suits, special material, well tailored. Hats, too, were especially ordered—a modified Stetson, narrow brim. As I remember, we had a choice of three types of brown oxfords. Purses, too, were brown leather. Velvet Navajo blouses could be any color, belts were woven of silver conchos and we all went wild with Indian necklaces, bracelets, rings, pins, earrings."[33] Such a combination of spiffy forest ranger or highway patrolman attire with American Indian ornamentation—the classic and subdued with the wildly romantic, the masculine blending with the feminine—to some might seem an excessive, contradictory stylization. Aspects of cultural and gender appropriation notwithstanding, with hats, blouses, belts, necklaces, bracelets, rings, pins, earrings—uniform and jewelry—two worlds are combined through all of the messages and emblems a uniform can convey: Anglo-American institutionalized power and Native American adornment. Where some might see such Indian imitation as a well-intended form of flattery and assimilation, the Koshare and Harvey couriers underscored cultural separation as well. By extension Fergusson's *Dancing Gods* and her other Southwestern travel writings represent a similar attempt, ambivalent or even "misguided" as it may strike one in retrospect, at cultural blending and reconciliation.

Harvey Fergusson wrote the lead essay on New Mexico in *The Koshare Book* and attempted to picture, in as inviting a manner as possible, the role of his sister and her cadre of women couriers and "strong men for emergencies" on a typical tour. Cassidy, in her *Sunset* essay on Fergusson as an "interesting westerner," relies heavily on this lead essay of Harvey Fergusson's, and it is worth noting that the picturesque tone of Harvey Fergusson's words are also indicative of Anglo, ethnocentric assumptions about Southwestern types. Novelist turned travel agent, he writes of his sister and her customers: "She takes you out in a high-powered car with an expert driver, she serves you luncheon and afternoon tea, arranges for your accommodations in advance, and introduces you to artists, cowboys and Indians."[34] All in all, Harvey Fergusson's essay is a portrait of what he regarded—not as cynically as in other writings—as the worship of the primitive. Nevertheless, he was a native son too and has high praise for the "experience" of the Southwest and how his sister's tour brings one closer to the truth of the place. In his praise he resorts to a kind of "New Mexico baroque" style of his own, a style which one is capable of finding in his extended history of northern New Mexico, *Rio Grande* (1933):

New Mexico is the great unknown of American travel. To thousands who go west annually in search of health and recreation, it has always been a vast expanse that one crosses on the way to California. This was inevitable. One must leave the railroad to discover the real New Mexico.

That discovery by the public has just begun. The pioneers were artists. A few years ago some of them explored the Southwest and found in New Mexico a hidden treasure of wild beauty and primitive life. There are now large colonies of painters in Santa Fe and Taos. These colonies are growing and the artists are being followed by the enterprising tourist who likes to turn aside from the well-worn roads in search of the strange and the new.

It is a fact which has become almost a tradition that those who visit New Mexico once almost always return if they can. Beyond a doubt it is one of those regions that captivate the imaginations of men. It exerts a fascination that is more easily felt than described.[35]

Here once again is a mixture of civility and primitivism. The real land is beautiful and remote and fascinating. Tea, a high-powered car, a driver, a waitress, all mingling with artists and all the eccentricities they possess, enough to make them almost one with the potential and real ruffian "romance" of cowboys and Indians. Though Harvey Fergusson, in this and some of his other writings, clearly loves and respects the landscape and the indigenous peoples, there is more than a bit of sarcasm in some of his language, at least if one recognizes his satirical thrusts at the kind of people who surface as the implied audience of *The Koshare Book,* or in some of his portrayals of artists and tourists at one point or another in novels like *Footloose McGarnigal.* And although Erna Fergusson, too, from time to time, disdains tourists, at least the insensitive ones, she never entirely abandons her tour guide persona when addressing the implied, uninitiated audience of her travel writing.

It is a natural consequence of a business aimed at not only initiating but also "civilizing" and sensitizing tourists and informing more serious travelers. And it is much in the same manner that British immigrant and big-time entrepreneur Fred Harvey and his network of Harvey Houses and Harvey Girls (complete with palatable food served and Indian artifacts to see and buy) made travel all along the route of the Santa Fe much more comfortable after 1876, when the first Harvey Eating House opened in Topeka, Kansas. And it is no great surprise that the Koshare Tours were soon incorporated into the larger scheme of Harvey Detours to the even more sublime spectacles of the Southwest, such as the Grand Canyon.[36]

Fergusson's influence on the Harvey Detours has never been fully appreciated, for in many respects Harvey simply expanded what Fergusson and Ethel Hickey had already set in place. Fred Harvey was, in turn, not only tremendously successful but also a significant cultural force in the Southwest. Keith Bryant overlooks contributions by Harvey's predecessors like Fergusson when he says, "Before the coming of Fred Harvey, the traveler in the West suffered grievously."[37] In this view Harvey gets perhaps more credit than is his due, although credit is also shared with his "managers and waitresses": "Harvey, his managers and waitresses 'civilized the West,'" claims Bryant, "providing railroad passengers and local residents with wholesome good food served in a graceful style."[38]

The qualities described in Fred Harvey's advertisements—"attractive and intelligent young women of good character" to work in his system in the West—were no doubt not only met by Fergusson herself but also coincided with her own Koshare Tours' standards and criteria as well.[39] She devotes an entire chapter to Fred Harvey, "Civilizer," in *Our Southwest*, tracing his biography and business from Harvey's arrival in New York in 1850, through the founding of the first eating house in Topeka, Kansas, in 1876, to the establishment and succession of his whole business empire to his sons. Fergusson says nothing about her own involvement with the Detours but respectfully observes, "The Harvey System is a fascinating study in meeting new conditions without sacrificing old character."[40] But Fergusson was very much a part of that process, especially in regard to the confrontation of the "new" with the "old" of Southwestern Native American culture. Richard H. Frost generalizes about this process and time (with no specific mention of Fergusson):

> The 1920s and early 1930s represent the full flowering of the Pueblo's romantic appeal. . . . The luxury hotels of the Fred Harvey system promoted Indian arts and crafts, as did curio shops and trading posts. The "Harvey Detours" out of Santa Fe provided limousine tours of the Pueblos and archaeological highlights, guided by a corps of two dozen attractive young women who had been trained in local archaeology and ethnology. Thanks to newly graded highways in the Southwest, this was a decade in which auto tourism thrived; the Indians were easier than ever to reach, and their exotic appeal was not jaded from overexposure.[41]

Fergusson, moreover, as "the woman behind a service of Girl Couriers in the Indian Country," as Frances Drewry McMullen called her in her January, 1927, *Woman's Citizen* article, "Ask Miss Fergusson," struck a blow for the emergent woman of the 1920s, proving with congenial good fun that a "dude wrangler queen" could outdo her male counterparts. McMullen made her own preference as a modern traveler clear. She much preferred Miss Fergusson:

> Out on the sun-baked mesas of New Mexico, a daughter of pioneers is developing a new profession for women. On most sight-seeing trips in the world, the man-with-the-megaphone conducts you. In the Indian country of the Southwest, a soft-spoken girl courier is your guide. When you meet first one, then the other, on your travels, you will realize that they are not the same thing. One merely shows strangers the sights. The other plays hostess to friends. (26)

Fergusson's participation in this segment of American history is documented in a much-neglected travel book, an oversight made all the more significant in that it is Fergusson's first and best book, *Dancing Gods*—a book which turned her experiences as Miss Fergusson, as Beautiful Swift Fox, and as the "dude wrangler queen" of the Southwest into lasting literature.

DANCING GODS

Encouraged by the popularity of the Koshare Tours and their promotion through brochures and by a visible, "uniformed" presence in tourist circles, Fergusson combined tourism and travel, dude wrangling and journalism in a book. During these various activities she discovered her voice and style, her method and subject as a writer—all motivated by the "baiting" comments of her journalist friend, Kyle Crichton, who advised that she should try to write the same way she talked. Through such advice and her experience as a local journalist, Fergusson successfully adapted her style to her material. Central to life becoming art was her persona as a traveler/writer and the process and result of riding/writing *Dancing Gods*.

Fergusson hoped that her book, like her tours, would serve to initiate non–Native Americans into the exoticism of Southwest culture and place. The reception of *Dancing Gods* was generally favorable and confirmed in her mind that future books about her native land might meet with similar acceptance. Reviewers were receptive—like eastern readers in general—to a book about Native American ritual and ceremony. The reviewer for the *New Republic* pointed to the treatment of the winter Shalako ceremonies at Zuni Pueblo as the most impressive part of the book and judged it "at once an excellent guidebook and a valuable piece of reporting," saying, "Miss Fergusson manages to supply us with a good deal of general information and at the same time keep up throughout the freshness and realism of personal experience."[42] Concerning the author's overall tone, the same reviewer said, "She is close to the New Mexico earth in which this poetry and beauty has flourished, and far from the hysterical mysticism with which the admirers of the Indian have sometimes beclouded his outline."[43] In short, *Dancing Gods* was judged a first-rate "popular" book written by a woman who could communicate the wonders of the Southwest through words: "the sunlight, the landscape, the bright colors, the masks, feathers and blankets, the faces and movements of the Indians, and the people who come to watch them as well, all come to life in her pages."[44] The reviewer's notation of Fergusson's descriptions of the "people who come to watch" is astute enough, though made more or less casually in passing and thus in need of more analysis. Implicitly, the one who came to watch, the one who is most completely described, is Fergusson herself.

In the first reviews of *Dancing Gods*, although Fergusson is credited for "visiting" the pueblos discussed, little direct attention is given to her as a traveler. Writing in the *American Journal of Sociology*, Leslie A. White observed that Fergusson "writes from the point of view of the artist rather than an ethnologist, but she is well informed and treats her subject intelligently and with sympathy."[45] The result, said White, is that "the author has supplied much ethnological and historical information that is necessary for an understanding of these dances and ceremonies; one cannot only 'see' them in this book, but understand them as well."[46] The *New Mexico Quarterly* described her "viewpoint" as that of a journalist (choosing not to stress her role as traveler as a complementary one) but offered the rather impressionistic thought that "[t]hrough Miss Ferguson's [*sic*] book runs the rhythm of the Indian dance, and starkness of the Pueblo land, the feel of vast expanses in land and in time."[47] Another reviewer, Fred T. Marsh, himself writing in the vein of Fergusson's implied "respectful" non–Native American author and reader, said, "It is a fascinating volume about peoples whose Americanism antedates those of the bluest or red-white-and-blue American blood; peoples whose culture, though savage and uncivilized, was far from negligible."[48]

By 1958, nearly thirty years after its publication, *Dancing Gods* had attained the status of a Southwest classic, recognized as a readable, albeit "popularized," account of Indian ceremonials, written in lay language for the lay reader, and judged significant enough as a seller that Roland Dickey, Fergusson's friend and then-director of the University of New Mexico Press, reprinted it in a larger format with newly designed opening pages. Reviewers of that reissued edition not only found the text of lasting importance but also commented favorably on the sixteen photographs of masterful paintings by northern New Mexico painters (e.g., Robert Henri, Howard Patterson, Walter Ufer, Grace Ravlin, E. L. Blumenschein, Gerald Cassidy, John Sloan, T. Van Soelen, Will Shuster, M. Wright Gill, Andrew Dasburg, Frank Applegate, Olive Rush, Nils Hogner, and Victor Higgins). Maurice Fink criticized the author's lack of scholarly documentation but commented, "As it stands it has great value as a readable and informative guide for the tourist and the layman who enjoy watching the dances . . . and would like to have some understanding of them."[49]

In his notable reconsideration of *Dancing Gods* half a century after its first publication, Lawrence Clark Powell (Southwestern author and Fergusson's friend in the later years of her life) sees Fergusson as surpassing in her very first book the writings of such illustrious writers as Charles F. Lummis, Mary Austin, and D. H. Lawrence on the subject of American Indian ceremonials.[50] One of the few who speak in specific terms about the literary qualities of the book, Powell writes:

> That Erna Fergusson's prose is the best ever written about the Indian ceremonials—Pueblo, Navajo, Apache—is because it is perceptive and simple, reverent and lucid, and is also infused with qualities of character and style which remain in solution, so that the writer's personal idiosyncrasies and anthropological theories do not muddy the flow of clear prose. The result is deceptively simple, a language like crystal through which the reader sees the subjects free from the distractions of self-conscious personality.[51]

Powell is correct in admiring Fergusson's prose style; however, there is more of Fergusson's self-consciousness—as a teller and a traveler—in her rendering of her subject than Powell allows. To be sure, *Dancing Gods* is not a psychological novel with an assigned and prominent first-person narrator, but Fergusson is very much *in* her descriptions (in choices and perceptions and ethnological assumptions) of the various ceremonials and of her own and other's on-the-spot reactions to them. Thus, her books, although written as tours, are of some interest, as is most travel literature, for certain autobiographical anecdotes.

In most ways, *Dancing Gods* was never surpassed by Fergusson in its harmonizing of author, narrative voice, subject, and form. Even though she repeated the narrative and descriptive techniques of the book in later works, she would never again be as vibrantly present, as close to her reader as she is in this, her prototypic first travel book. In later travel books, as she took on larger geographical subjects—the Southwests of Texas and Arizona, her "history" of the state of New Mexico—more and more she objectified and distanced herself from her respective subjects, downplaying first-person narration and personal anecdote. But her travels and her tellings are indistinguishable in *Dancing Gods*, a book which, taken all in all, is the one work she seemed most destined to write and the one major achievement which was to influence all others.[52]

In *Dancing Gods* Fergusson's fascination with the Southwest, New Mexico, and Native American ceremonialism is seen in considerable variety and descriptive detail. As a result, *Dancing Gods* is the masterwork among Fergusson's Southwest travel books, books which after *Dancing Gods* she often seems to replicate, although she wrote for the larger ends of defining an entire region (in *Our Southwest*)—or for the more focused purpose of accounting for the "history" of her homeland (in *Albuquerque, Murder and Mystery in New Mexico,* and *New Mexico*). She wrote again and again about her Southwestern travels, her sense of place as landscape and history, and her liberal, democratic views as an advocate of Native American and Spanish/Mexican American cultural and civil rights. But "travel" in these latter works—exclusive of *Our Southwest*—is more incidental than it is in *Dancing Gods,* the work which best captures the kind of travel book she was suited, by temperament and experience, to write, the kind of book which allowed her the opportunity for her own kind of "dancing" as author/tour guide.

The effect which Fergusson's first book had on no less a mind and literary sensibility than Edmund Wilson is one salient instance which helps illustrate Fergusson's enduring role and influence as author/guide. Wilson, self-consciously identifying himself as an Easterner and as a journalist, attributes his traveling in 1947 to Zuni Pueblo to see the Shalako ceremony to his reading of *Dancing Gods.*[53] Wilson's account of his trip to this famous New Mexico pueblo—in its own right an exemplary piece of travel writing—offers good evidence as to just what kind of ideal audience Fergusson had in mind when writing *Dancing Gods:* someone appreciative of powers of description, a person of intelligence, respectful sensitivity, and curiosity, who is also desirous of making the journey in person to see the primitive and the exotic, experience it, seek to know it, and perhaps write about it in turn. Just as Fergusson relies on numerous scholarly resources (e.g., anthropological studies, interviews, and the like), so too does Wilson rely on Fergusson's book as his primary written source, the author remaining as explorer/guide/traveler/translator. That Wilson relies on Fergusson as more than mere motive in his seeking the wonders of the Shalako is obvious enough insofar as he quotes extensively from *Dancing Gods* in his attempt to explain (and understand) part of the colorful and, to him, bizarre ceremony.

One can only guess that Fergusson appreciated Wilson's essay and the mutually shared sense of what Wilson calls the "spectacular," the difficulties which he describes in getting to Zuni—the remote, relatively unknown, and exotic "pueblo"—and the wonderment, as an Anglo traveler, of finally seeing such an alien phenomenon which he considered in danger of complete obliteration. Like Jung's epiphany of culture and landscape at Taos, part of Wilson's experience of the Shalako is made more urgent by the recent effects of totalitarianism and world war. In his words, "the journalist like myself, who has reported many hateful and destructive events, wants to get a good look at the Shalako birds, bringers of happy abundance, before they shall have ceased to come, and before the bad liquor of the white man and the worship, perhaps, of some white Führer shall, even for the Zunis, have taken their place."[54] That such destructive forces are at work not just in war-racked Europe and Asia but nearby in the American Southwest is apparent in Wilson's description of his jumping-off place, Gallup: "The town of Gallup in northwestern New Mexico is one of the most forbidding stops on the Santa Fe railroad. It is a trading post and coal-mining town of the dismal and grimy kind, and the place to which the Indians resort to buy the liquor they are not supposed to have. They get drunk, have their wallets stolen, and come to in the morning in jail."[55]

Wilson shares Fergusson's sense that in traveling to the Pueblo country, in contrast to the squalor of Gallup, where things have gone amok, they are experiencing something wondrous and worth recording from their Anglo-American perspective—for the enlightenment and enjoyment of other Anglo-American readers to be sure and, maybe, given Wilson's picture of Gallup, for certain Americanized or dulled Native Americans unaware of the "happy abundance of the Shalako birds." Although Fergusson romanticizes her subject more than Wilson does, both of their Zuni travel pieces reflect a certain journalistic tough-mindedness, in addition to a satirical edge. This kinship in personae, as well as some degree of epiphany in landscape, must have attracted Wilson to *Dancing Gods* in the first place. And as Wilson's essay on Zuni suggests, Fergusson was, in her earlier written tour of Zuni, "on the road" to something significant for American culture generally and for the larger world civilization in need of something as beautiful and restorative, something as old, enduring, and strange, as the Shalako birds.

Fergusson was profoundly aware, by the time she came to write *New Mexico* in the early 1950s, of the ironies of Pueblo culture in conflict with the "culture" of the atomic bomb: Los Alamos, the Manhattan Project, Trinity Site, myth and science colliding in the modern Southwest. When she wrote *Dancing Gods* nearly two decades before Wilson traveled to Zuni—that is, before World War II—that a collision of worldviews and cultural forces was already much in the making. She saw a need to at least try to account for the world as embodied in Native American ceremonialism. And perhaps in confronting it she somehow hoped to preserve it in the face of differing Anglo assumptions about "civilization." In a very personal way she sought to see the distant gods of certain Southwestern Native American peoples for herself and describe what she saw so that others might see them. If she was a "popularizer" she was not a trivial one. She offered her purpose of watching her "dancing gods," or "dancing builders," as her brother Harvey referred to them, in the most forthright terms:

> This book attempts to give a description of the principal southwestern Indian dances, based upon observation, and an account of their significance, based upon all available sources of information. It is not an exhaustive study, for several reasons, the most important of which is that the material available is not exhaustive. A few scientists have made detailed studies of a few of the southwestern Indian dances. I have consulted those authorities, I have seen most of the dances which are open to the outsider, I have talked with many people, both whites and Indians, and I have concluded that nobody knows all about Indian dances, not even Indians.[56]

Fergusson presents herself as an outsider, comparatively, but she is a resourceful and reflective one. She presents herself, too, as something of a trailblazer, the Koshare Tours guide, the Fred Harvey courier, the *Albuquerque Herald* and *New Mexico Tribune* reporter, a personal observer in pursuit of something combining social science with art and entertainment, scholarly consensus of the time with individual subjectivity and impressionism and enjoyment. She does not presume that she knows more, as an enlightened, "pioneer" Anglo, than the American Indians know about their own dances and ceremonies, but she suggests that she knows something special about the dances—at least as much as she is able to discover in her own non-Indian way of knowing. Dancing, for the gods and with the gods, is one thing; explaining in words is something else. As traveler and writer she seeks to keep these two humbling facts in the forefront. If American Indians do not "know" all about their dances in an analytical, intellectualized way, then an Anglo writer can only hope to approximate meanings and significance through words.

Definition of terms is an important expository tool in her inquiry—as Wayne Franklin insists it is for all travel writers. And in her initial definition of terms Fergusson stipulates that "[an] Indian dance . . . is a ceremonial, a symbolic representation, a prayer" (*DG*, xv–xvi). Drawing attention to religious dramas throughout history—from Hebraic, to Greek, to early Christian, to medieval and modern ceremonies—she emphasizes that the Zuni dance, like all the other dances she describes, is both dramatic and religious. Reflecting the liberal attitudes and assumptions of her writer and artist friends and fellow Democrats in New Mexico during that era, especially concerning their advocacy of American Indian art and culture (considered in chapter 4 of this book), Fergusson suggests that part of her role as traveler and writer is to help preserve Indian dances as an art form in the midst of the separation she sees taking place between the religious and artistic aspects of the ceremonies. "In time," she writes, "as Indians are weaned from their ancient faiths, it is likely that all their ceremonies will lose meaning. . . , and it is important that interested white people should help them to preserve their dances as an art form when they no longer serve as a religious form" (*DG*, xxviii).

The assumptions here seem decidedly ethnocentric. Ostensibly, American Indian ceremonialism had relatively little personal religious significance for Fergusson. Its significance to her personally was primarily aesthetic, for she believed that American Indians would be "weaned from their ancient faiths" and that their dances would one day possess mainly "artistic" significance. Moreover, the assumptions behind her dichotomy of functions is decidedly Anglo. Whether or not American Indians should want to maintain an organically religious ceremony only as "art" (however defined in Anglo terms) is problematic. In the worst light, her assertion that American Indian ceremonialism be continued for its artistic aspects implies performance as theater for Anglo entertainment.

In a better light, the American Indian dances Fergusson describes are seen as having aesthetic significance for the performers as well as the assumed Anglo audiences. Her intentions are kindly, albeit somewhat patronizing. Francis Drewry McMullen boasts of the fact, in 1927: "Miss Fergusson might request a pueblo to get up a dance for the benefit of visitors; but she never offends them by asking for dances that have religious significance, and she does not pay for their services. Instead, she delights their childlike hearts with gifts of feathers and handkerchiefs."[57] In any event, whether understood in its context or rejected a half-century later by either Anglo or American Indian readers, *Dancing Gods* is in part the outgrowth of Anglo-American assumptions and values of the time. It is, however, made all the more interesting as a "text" for study and as a cultural artifact because of that very fact.

Fergusson organizes *Dancing Gods* around the dances—seasonal in their purpose and occasions—of the Pueblos, the Hopis, the Navajos, and the Apaches. After a few background pages dealing with the history and the religion of these cultures, she describes thirty or so major dances which non-Indian tourists are allowed to see. Her intent is to recreate as closely as possible the sensations of the experience to the audiences of the dances and of the book itself. She is aided in this attempt by the various illustrations: sixteen paintings of pueblos, persons, and landscapes by well-known New Mexico artists named earlier.

Of the thirteen seasonal Pueblo dances which Fergusson details (e.g., the Deer-dance at Taos, the Buffalo and Deer-dance at San Felipe, the Parrot-dance at Santo Domingo, the Turtle- or Evergreen-dance at Isleta, the Eagle-dance at Tesuque, the Corn-dance at Santo Domingo, the Rainbow-dance at Santa Clara, the Pecos Bull at Jemez, the Sword-swallowers dance, Summer Rain-dance, and Doll-dance at Zuni), the Zuni dances, as Edmund Wilson testifies, are the most meaningful to her. Of these, the Shalako is by far the most sublime, the finest spectacle, the most "beautiful." Just why she regards the Zuni Shalako dance as the finest is in part due to the nature of the masks (in addition to the sublime visage, conformation, and size of the Shalako figures). Her criteria are fundamentally aesthetic: "The distinctive feature of Zuni dances is the masks, which are more elaborate, more varied, and in every way more highly developed than any made by other American Indians" (DG, 71). She regards the Zunis as the world's best artists in the making of such masks.

As in her descriptions of other dances—Hopi, Navajo, and Apache included—much of what makes her descriptions so believable is her staging of the scene in quite personal, diarylike terms. The reader soon is convinced that the author is no mere tourist-voyeur; rather, Fergusson is a determined, persistent artist in her own right, waiting to stay the extra day or awaken before dawn to experience all the preparations from the best possible vantage point—much as a photographer would wait for the best light, the best angle. For example, preparing herself, she also prepares her reader, a silent but enthralled traveling companion, for the fifth day of the Sword-swallowers dance: "Waiting to see the very beginning of the big day, we got up before dawn and went to the sacred plaza. Crossing the village was an eerie walk. It was cold. Lights in only a few houses. No sound at all. Occasionally a blanketed figure slipped from a door and melted into the shadows, not seeing us. We made ourselves as comfortable as we could with many blankets in a corner of the deserted plaza and waited" (DG, 79).

The short sentences with their fragmented effect give the obvious impression of the actual walk, the silence, and the cold. The anticipation is heightened by a certain kind of reverence in recognition of the sacredness of the plaza and the event, combined with the curiosity of a visitor from a different culture. Certainly, too, there is a Gothic element in her descriptions: the eerie walk, the cold and dark, the blanketed figures, the shadows. Such techniques heighten not only the drama and suspense but also add to the "fun." It is a serious event—and an enjoyable one—at once sacred and secular. But her sustained descriptions of the marvels of the Sword-swallowers dance, effective and exciting as they are, fall short of her report on the marvels of the Shalako ceremony.

Fergusson notes that the Shalako ceremony does not have a definite date but always takes place between late November and late December. And she gives a comprehensive explanation of the preliminaries, the ceremony itself, and its aftermath—making clear that all of the stages are related and that, as the greatest Zuni festival of them all, it marks the culmination of the ceremonial year and functions as a prayer for continued blessings of fertility and harvest. Commemorative of the winter solstice, preparations continue throughout each year. Forty-nine days before the ceremony, preparations begin with persons designated to represent Sayatasha, a rain god, and the leader of the Mudheads (jesters of sorts)—each person responsible for counting down the days until the Shalako come. Fergusson is deliberate in not immediately identifying and defining the Shalako dancers, their giant, birdlike costumes, or the exact meaning of the term "Shalako," a word and a sound adding to the mystery of the correlative events it designates. Rather, she builds—small detail by small detail, ritualized step by ritualized step—a composite picture of these special dancing gods, the atmosphere in which they come, the overall meaning of their appearance insofar as it can be expressed in words, insofar as the gestalt of the extravaganza can be captured in words. M. Wright Gill's magnificent painting of the Shalako figure appears strategically in the center of the narrative, serving to coincide with the arrival of the six Shalako birds and Fergusson's attempt to describe them and their actions.

In preparation for the gods' arrival, special Shalako hosts are selected, and houses are chosen with special rooms, a minimum of sixty feet long, both made ready to greet the Shalako and entertain them. Focusing her descriptions on the last day and the great event itself, Fergusson heightens the sense of wonderment by the use of such words and phrases of inexpressibility as "women do unmentionable things to . . . [the] insides" of sacrificial sheep, and "odors of fresh bread and freshly killed meat and cedar fires and close rooms are indescribable" (DG, 94). Precisely because these sights and smells are "unmentionable" and "indescribable," the point is made and the effect achieved: the ceremony is inexpressible in words, impossible to name—the historic dilemma of travelers into strange lands. Adding to the suspense and the spectacle of it all, Fergusson adeptly describes the motley "audience" gathered on the "great day." Again, the emphasis seems to be on the aesthetic potential, the fashion and sociability of the event (at least for the visitors), rather than on the religious meaning:

During the last day everything is finished. . . . Everything has been swept, food is ready, and people begin to appear in their best clothes. All day visitors drift in—long-legged Navajos on ponies, the women sitting astride in their voluminous skirts, the men wearing beaver-skin caps; Indians from the Rio Grande pueblos with turquoise to trade; Hopis with ceremonial garments; and a complete assortment of white-man types, from families of Mormons from the near-by towns to the Greenwich Village aesthete and Eastern tourists in stiff city clothes. (*DG,* 96)

As author and guide Fergusson herself is both above and among such visitors, ready for the happening. In this instance she knows more, not all but more, than the other visitors in their "stiff city clothes," more too than the reader. The reader—as actual, rather than vicarious, visitor—will become more nearly initiated into the ceremony as a result of book travel, the reading of *Dancing Gods.* A half century after the recording of this idealized ceremony (the composite of many of Fergusson's visits), the Shalako still live, as one Southwestern travel writer signified it—print becoming its own reality, words becoming picture. Any current non-Indian experience, real or virtual, of the Shalako owes an immense debt to Fergusson's perceptions of the dance.

The actual entry of the council of gods, who prepares the houses for the visit of the Shalako, is all that Fergusson's suspense (the visitors' and the reader's anticipation finally merging with her own) has made the reader hope for. What Wayne Franklin calls the traveler's confrontation with inexpressibility, or Michel Butor the complexities of "iterology," or F. Scott Fitzgerald our "capacity for wonder" is addressed directly by Fergusson's use of anecdote in relation to the meaning of the key word in the title of her book and half the focus of her attention in her descriptions: the word "gods." Fergusson cites anthropologist Matilda Stevenson's adoption of the term "gods" for the Shalako in 1879, and then Fergusson—relying on an interview—recounts the insistence of a Zuni woman that they are not gods at all but something entirely, lexically, different:

"They are not gods," said she; "that word is wrong. The Zunis have no gods; they are Ko-Ko."

"Just so," said I, expectant pencil poised, "and what is the English word for Ko-Ko?"

"There is no English word for Ko-Ko. I do not know. It is something different. I cannot tell you how it is to the Zuni, but they are not gods." (*DG,* 98)

Through such a dialogue, such a dramatization of herself as traveler/interviewer/journalist, and in her continued "explanations" of the unexplainable, Fergusson succeeds in throwing into ironic relief her own ethos and credibility as an "authority," and the title of her very book. What she is describing are not dancing gods at all. To speak of dancing gods is to speak of the wrong thing; something too inscrutable, be it Ko-Ko or gods or something else, some other word. On the one hand, the rather ambivalent, anthropomorphicized notion of dancing gods allows for greater attention to the dance rather than the theology and may imply the basis of her assumption that at least Native American dances must be preserved on aesthetic grounds. Here is how Fergusson faces up to such a realization—accepted rather too readily straight from an authoritative Indian source, albeit one woman:

> So there it is, as inexplicable as everything Indian must always be to the white man. They are not gods; they are Ko-Ko, and for Ko-Ko there is no English word, and presumably no English idea. It seems likely, from many similar conversations and a sincere effort to get the Indian point of view, that the Indian has no anthropomorphic gods. Yet such creatures as these of the Zunis impersonate something divine: possibly merely an aspect of the great hidden spirit, which in one manifestation is so brilliant that the sun is a shield to hide it. (*DG*, 98)

Only after this mystery of word and ritual, of language and custom, is confronted by Fergusson the traveler and recounted for the reader/traveler is the spectacular entrance of the Shalako described, another experience heightened by its inexpressibility. Fergusson's pacing and arrangement is a masterful instance of the artistry of narration, one which brings the Shalako episode to its own kind of verbalized, composed climax. Nothing in *Dancing Gods*, or for that matter in all of her Southwest travel writing, is as startling and dramatic as her pages on the Shalako ceremony, most notably the actual appearance of the "giant" dancers on one of a ritualized sequence of ceremonial Zuni evenings. The description is "New Mexico baroque" at its best, tempered by a not altogether successful attempt to muster the age-old willing suspension of disbelief:

> In a breathless moment of the swift winter dusk the Shalako appear. They come into sight round the shoulder of a hill, looming, as it were, on the far side of that deep impassable gulf which forever separates the mind of the Indian from the mind of the white. The six magnificent figures tower above their attendants; the eagle-feathers

of their fantastic head-dresses raying like the sun, their flat turquoise faces and upper bodies swaying, their feet looking incredibly tiny under the hoop skirts of the double Hopi kirtles. They are about nine feet high, the tallest masks recorded. . . . The turquoise face is matched by a breast piece, and the white and blue are accentuated by a ruff of shining raven's feathers and by long, black hair. The mask is carried on a long pole hidden under the draperies and steadied by a man who also manipulates strings which roll the great bulging eyes and clack the wooden beak as the figure moves. (*DG*, 100)

Clearly, for Fergusson, these are not gods; they are stagings, puppetry. Yet they are wonderful in their artifice and motive.

After what she describes as much precarious swooping and dipping of these giants, and after they cross the causeway constructed across the river to their sacred resting place, she follows them into the houses which have been fashioned for them to await their reemergence at midnight when sustained dancing begins. Fergusson's description of the close quarters in the Koyemshi house is presumably intended to provide a kind of "comic" relief to the majesty of the Shalako's entrance. The ways of gods and men and men as gods are contrasted in ways that are, by today's standards, overly ethnocentric. The Navajo guests are portrayed as unwashed and greedily hungry. Trying, perhaps, to dramatize the incongruity involved in this meeting of two worlds—Native American and Anglo-American—Fergusson describes the effect of the Navajos on the non-Indians in these fastidious, "modern," ethnocentric, if not racially demeaning, terms:

Nowadays only the most intrepid white, or one well protected by smelling-salts, can bear it long. Generally white visitors drift in and out; in when the cold without seems unbearable, out when the thickness of the indoor air forces them to face the cold again. . . . But aside from this movement near the doors, the audience sits all night, quiet and attentive. By midnight many of the restless whites have left and deterioration has begun to attack those who remain. Ladies' city hats are riding at queer angles, figures which started alert and trim have settled awkwardly among the aborigines, men in proper clothes and spats are huddled into the welcome warmth of borrowed blankets. (*DG*, 103)

The brunt of the satire—such as it is—is the Anglo-American aesthete in city clothes, far removed from the comforts of "civilization." The worship of the primitive has its price. The "deterioration" in dress and demeanor which "attacks" the see-it-to-the-end "whites" who remain suggests the contagiousness of primitivism as somehow inevitable after prolonged experience "among the aborigines." For today's readers such passages—although partially effective in personalizing the event—tend to backfire in their satirical intent. Is the condescension that of the Easterner toward the Navajo, or that of the author toward the Easterner, or even the Navajo? Ironically, although a staunch partisan of things "Indian," Fergusson was, apparently at times, oblivious to the unkind implications of her own deeply ingrained Anglo ethnocentrism.

Luckily, such moments are few in Fergusson's recounting of the Shalako ceremony. In her summation of the event, as it extends over five more days of festivity and the offering of mounds of food and clothing and trinkets given to the Koyemshi for their hospitable part in the ceremony, the pleasurableness of the experience is restored. The visitors leave and are long since gone into the history of tourism. But the purpose of the Shalako ceremony endures, as known to the Zunis in their yearly rituals (now closed to tourists and spectators) and in the amazing pages of an Anglo woman's attempt to record her impressions in the enchanting pages of *Dancing Gods*.

FINE IDEALS AND HORSE SENSE

To see just how adept an artist and how charismatic and unique a persona/person Fergusson was as a traveler and travel writer, one need only read *Footloose McGarnigal,* the seventh novel of her younger brother and collaborator on the Koshare Tour booklet, or *Rio Grande,* his history of New Mexico, to see the tremendous effect Erna Fergusson had on his writing. *McGarnigal* was published in 1930, just one year before *Dancing Gods*. A roman á clef and a novel of manners which deals satirically with the worship of the primitive by the Anglo artists of Santa Fe and Taos in the late 1920s, *McGarnigal* is sprinkled with characterizations of Mabel Dodge Luhan (Mrs. Whitehorse), her Taos Pueblo husband Tony, Witter Bynner (Rynder) and his entourage, and a host of other transparently obvious characters (including a near replica of Erna Fergusson) and lengthy descriptions of their "tours" to pueblos to see the "dancing gods." *McGarnigal,* in all its picaresque plotting and open-road theme, is, however, a novel and not a travel narrative in the strict sense of the term. It offers its own kind of sociological insight into the issues and the ambiance of the Southwest and New Mexico of that time, and the numerous artists and tourists and health seekers who headed there—a fictionalized version of what Erna Fergusson attempts, through nonfiction, in *Dancing Gods*. Surely Harvey Fergusson utilizes in *McGarnigal,* in some of his other novels, and in *Rio Grande* much of what his sister and her Koshare Tour experience told him, and, of course, what he had experienced firsthand growing up in New Mexico and on his many trips back to northern New Mexico after he moved East, and then, after 1931, when he moved to California.

Harvey Fergusson's version of the Shalako ceremony—utilizing one character's point of view—insists that true understanding, even description, of the Shalako is next to impossible and destined to end in frustration for white observers:

> Man, I went to the Shalako dance at Zuni last winter, and that's where I learned how Indians really feel. Those Indians get nothing from the whites. They don't have to put up with us. . . . Their Shalako is a sort of housewarming, honeymooning ceremony. I wandered all over the pueblo and everywhere there were little groups of men, all dressed up, whispering and peering at the girls that went by, standing outside the doors of houses where women were cooking huge feasts over open fires in two-gallon kettles. Man, it was something to paint if you could catch it—red firelight on brown skin and red wool and silver and turquoise, and blue steam coming out of the cauldrons and the black crowding silhouettes of the boys in the doorways—well, I can't do it in words, but anyway, I walked around among those groups for hours and I tried to talk to them. They not only wouldn't answer me, they wouldn't even look at me. They wouldn't acknowledge I was there. They lived in a world where I didn't belong and they simply denied my existence. I felt like a ghost walking among the living. I tell you, after a while I felt funny. I went back to the car and took a drink and kissed a girl, just to feel there was something I could connect with. . . .[58]

The reality of the Southwest for Harms is not Indian ceremonialism but landscape, mountains. Although there is more of Harvey Fergusson in Alec McGarnigal than in Harms, as a novelist he was unable to penetrate Indian ceremonialism to the extent that his sister did as a "travel" writer. Where he turned to the characterizations of fiction and satires of "the Indian question," she turned to journalistic description and the "cause" of preserving Native American culture and reconciling it with Anglo-American encroachments.

Although his novelistic accounts of touring New Mexico's Indian pueblos are not without meaningful local color and satiric success in portraying the more fatuous aspects of Anglo "worship of the primitive," *McGarnigal* falls short of *Dancing Gods* in its descriptions of and assumptions about Indian ceremonialism. *Rio Grande* is another matter and although its focus on American Indians is limited, essentially, to one chapter, it is a more comprehensive and artistically successful account of Southwest-

ern lives and landscapes than *Dancing Gods*. For here history, novel, autobiography, and travelogue converge in the most convincing ways. There is
a panorama in *Rio Grande* which *Dancing Gods* does not really intend to
portray—at least not beyond the first chapter on the "Pueblo People." And
there is in that panorama a narrative and novelistic flair seldom achieved
by Erna Fergusson. Writing from the perspective of a traveler down the
Rio Grande by boat, Harvey Fergusson offers a sense of what history had
in store for the Pueblo cultures: "Along the Rio Grande these men who
had learned how to build and dance were holding their own against
drought and savage invasion but doom was closing in upon them. From the
south and from the east a race of men such as they had never known was
moving upon their valley of last resort—men who fought with lightning
and thunderbolts and rode on strange swift animals, men whom no walls
could withstand, preaching of a God no dance could propitiate."[59]

Comparisons of travel book, novel, and history aside, both Fergussons,
brother and sister, demonstrated considerable and reciprocal talents as
"travelers" in capturing their era's conceptions of the dancing gods and
dancing builders of the Southwest—those attitudes and perceptions which
characterized the Anglo literary and cultural history of the Southwest in
the 1930s. Not to be faulted for narrowness of scope, Erna Fergusson soon
attempted her own comprehensive, panoramic history of the Southwest in
both *Our Southwest* and *New Mexico*. Her travel books and her brother's
novels ultimately strive to say much the same thing: what they knew and
loved of their Southwest.

Some few who knew her personally, as well as through her writing, saw
the essential Southwestern spokesperson of her time in "Miss Fergusson."
Charles F. Lummis, who knew the Southwest as well as any Anglo-
American of his era, knew her only as an acquaintance. But he, too, recognized the potential belle of Southwestern belles lettres. Describing their
first meeting and his first impressions after a Santa Fe encounter, Lummis
said plainly, "She delighted me with her fine ideals and horse sense."[60] The
full significance of her "fine ideals and horse sense" might be measured
today rather more fully against the implications of what Robert Sayre says
about the interrelationships between autobiography and travel writing in
American literary history generally: "Travel books, in which the writer had
the opportunity to define himself as an American against the backgrounds
of Europe, the sea, and the American West, were continued by Dana,
Irving, Margaret Fuller, Parkman, and many later writers, famous and
obscure."[61]

In such a national context it is regrettable that Erna Fergusson, a relatively obscure regional writer in most minds but a premier personality in

Southwestern literary history, is not more recognized by literary and cultural critics at large, just as it is regrettable that travel writing remains a relatively neglected literary form. Fergusson's Southwestern travel books allowed her to define herself "autobiographically" against the background of the inexpressible wonderments of the American Southwest and its cultural mixes. But today they enable readers to define just how they are or might become "fellow travelers," positioned, through "guide" books like *Dancing Gods,* to experience what Charles F. Lummis, with his own invigorated wonderment of discovery, called "the unforgettable glory of it all."

Chapter 3

. . . .

History:
Clio at the Wheel

Calliope and Clio are not identical twins, but they are sisters.
—Wallace Stegner

Erna Fergusson's Southwestern travel writings may be read for their strong spirit of place, for Fergusson's fascination with ambiance and local color, for her evocation of the Southwest as a *tierra encantada,* and for her journalistic reporting on the exoticism of Native American ceremonial dances. Certainly her Southwestern travel writings also contain an autobiographical element which allows them to be read not only for what they tell us about Fergusson but for what they also tell us about the larger landscape and panorama of events. But they contain, as well, elements of biography, of history as personality, as much as of place and event. Considered from these perspectives Fergusson's "travel" writings may be read as history because of what they tell us about the events and people who passed through and across the Southwest over the past several centuries. And, as will be discussed in chapter 4, she writes as an advocate for cultural diversity, civil rights, and recognition, while also presenting herself as part of a vast, complicated network of cultural and ecological forces not fathomable to the categories of travel or historical meaning. Much of how she reconciles such ostensibly diverse and irreconcilable approaches, how and why she assumes numerous personae and rhetorical stances, is a function of her ability to use the rich potential of creative nonfiction. In all of her roles she is consistently a narrator, a voice dependent on chronological orderings, of "history" conceived of and related not so much as social science but as the tales and tellings of an artist.

She was trained as a historian at Columbia University. Her narrative skills were honed as a journalist. And although she is consistently regarded as both an amateur historian/journalist and a popularizer, she was very much the professional. Her Southwestern writings, emphasizing tourism, placeness, cultural interrelations, and minority advocacy, join the tradition of great Anglo-American narrative historians of the West, such as Francis Parkman, Bernard DeVoto, J. Frank Dobie, Paul Horgan, and Wallace Stegner. Like the writings of these illustrious regional historians, all labeled popularizers at one time or another by historians more centrally placed in the academy, Fergusson's Southwestern writings, clichéd as it may sound, truly make history come alive, rendering it understandable and significant for the general reader. She knew firsthand the places about which she wrote; she probed the memories of local inhabitants in interview after interview, much taken as she was with the ways of an oral historian; she read vast numbers of monographs and articles, and she was always able to synthesize her research so that her final product was well made and functional, never trivial or pretentious.

Like *New Mexico: A Guide to the Colorful State,* a useful compilation of the Writers' Program of the Work Projects Administration and first published by the Coronado Cuarto Centennial Commission in 1940, Fergusson's "histories" can all be taken along and read either in transit or on arrival just as readily as at home in an easy chair.[1] Travel and history were closely linked in her mind and turn up that way in Fergusson's writing; her journeying through New Mexico and the Southwest is as much a trip through time as through space.

To be a tour guide was to inform. And to be a tourist was patiently to be informed—to slow down enough to see and learn the history which was all-surrounding and ever-present. Fergusson found New Mexico especially conducive to such living history:

> New Mexico, glory of scenery, marvel of climate, ease of travel and good living can offer something that is found in few parts of the world. Our whole history is here, now, living, going on, in the immediate present. Old Charles F. Lummis summed it up better than anybody has since when he said, "In New Mexico you catch your archaeology alive." In New Mexico, the trick now seems to be to catch your tourist alive; or if he is pretty deadened by life in dull places or by driving too fast, to bring him to life and show him how beautiful

life may be if it moves at a leisurely pace. Poco tiempo! Poco tiempo! And the best day of all in Mañana![2]

All of Fergusson's Southwestern writings implicitly contain this assumption of the close relationship between travel and history, complemented by the belief that, in New Mexico especially, history is part of the living, immediate present, "here, now . . . going on."

Fergusson set the stage for such assumptions about travel and living history—along with various kinds of cultural and political advocacy—in *Dancing Gods,* in her travel essays about Pueblo ceremonialism which grew out of *Dancing Gods,* and in her later histories, *Our Southwest, Murder and Mystery in New Mexico,* and *New Mexico: A Pageant of Three Peoples.* Her Latin American travel books are also consistent with such reciprocal travel/history and advocacy assumptions.

LAUGHING PRIESTS: CEREMONIAL DANCES OF THE PUEBLOS

In "Ceremonial Dances of the Pueblos," written for *Travel* magazine and published in the December, 1931, issue, and in "Laughing Priests," part of a special summer issue of *Theatre Arts Monthly* devoted to the dramatic arts of the American Indian, Fergusson found it possible to describe Pueblo ceremonialism only in the context of the seventeenth-century Spanish presence in New Mexico, and the lingering effects of Catholic missionaries and their attempts (successes and failures) to convert the Pueblos.[3] Her historical explanation of how Christian and pagan ceremonies do or do not coincide helps the inquisitive tourist understand why, among other things, certain dances are open to tourists and other dances are closed:

> Even in New Mexico the church takes part in such incongruous rites only because it is well known now that Indian converts can be held in no other way. The monks tried, in the seventeenth century, to stamp out all evidences of barbarism but with so little success that they finally yielded in the matter of certain dances. They countenance the Corn Dance, which is given in all the Rio Grande pueblos on Saints' days, a few pleasure dances, and, in a few places, the winter solstice dance which is given in the church. The more sacred dances, in which masked men personify the true spirits, were prohibited as witchcraft. As a result, many such dances are given now only in secret and no white man sees them, except in the pueblos unaffected by missionary activities. . . .[4]

Fergusson knows, however, and wisely states that the explanation of Pueblo secrecy and privacy was not a simple matter of Spanish imperialism: "White people, even the most observant, get only hints of these secret rites. . . . Why has no white man's faith supplanted, or even seriously threatened, these ancient nature faiths? No white man knows, and the Indian, the enigmatic, secretive Indian, powerful in the dignity of his faith, will not tell."[5] Moreover, according to Fergusson's assumptions, the Anglo-American concept of history, specifically considered as the history of the Church in New Spain, or of historiography as a quantification of time and the past, of dates and centuries, is not adequate to explain such exotic phenomena as the cultures underlying Southwestern Pueblo dances.

Although Fergusson's main purpose in *Dancing Gods* is to describe and attempt to account for Pueblo dances, her travels to the various pueblos and her reports are presented within a historical context—as both her introduction and her opening chapter on "The Pueblo People" demonstrate. In her subsequent books Southwestern history would take on even more prominence, shift from contextual background to foreground, while still allowing room for matters of placeness, travel, and minority advocacy.[6] In her attempt to answer the essential question—who are they?—Fergusson goes much beyond the Spanish who named the peoples they found in New Mexico "Pueblos," or "town people." Indeed she provides a broader accounting of early cliff dwellers. She follows the chronology of the intrusion of "the white man," focusing on the Pueblo rebellion of 1680, and continues into the nineteenth- and twentieth-century relationships of "the Pueblo Indian and the American." That paradigm—Native American, Spanish/Mexican, and Anglo-American—provides not only a model of the panorama of New Mexico history but the overall chronological structure and theme of Fergusson's attempts to account for the mysteries of the convergence of lives and landscapes which are signified by all that is merely designated, in Anglo-American historiography, by the word "Southwest." Thus the opening chapter of *Dancing Gods* works as a twenty-four-page condensation of New Mexico's history as a panorama of three peoples, at once displacing and assimilating the other—a historiographical construct which Fergusson works constantly to probe and develop in her subsequent Southwestern writings.

As is characteristic of her method, she begins with a description of people and place—as she finds them and sees them in her presence as a traveler. And from that description she seeks to "narrate," by means of chronological expositions, anecdotes, interviews, and interpolated "stories" and "histories," a full account of how the present moment of her own personal convergence with the past was preceded by larger events, bigger questions. Before she can give a fuller accounting of "The Pueblo People" in relation to their own past convergences with Spanish, Mexican, and Anglos, she begins with her own word picture, mentioning objects, materials, and conditions which eventually will generate a "historical" explanation:

> Sun-drenched and quiet stand the Pueblos of New Mexico and Arizona, queerly withdrawn from the modern life about them. Usually built of the soil on which they stand, they appear to have grown out of it, and their color is the same. There are few trees in the villages, but they are surrounded by cultivated fields, and cottonwoods and willows grow along the water-courses. The houses huddle in solid blocks of adobe like slightly battered apartment houses. Irregular ladder-poles rise sharply here and there and protruding beams drop deep black shadows against the walls. Always there is a mission church, carrying the cross aloft on weather-worn adobe towers, and a government building whose machine-made angularities are an insult to the softly molded contours of the adobe. Drifting in and out are the people, brown-skinned and enigmatic, with sloe-black eyes, sliding walk, and flashes of vivid color in blanket, sash, or head-band. (DG, 3)

The colors, the textures, the imagery, the metaphors—all take on significance in relation to "history," which becomes a theme in and of itself. The pueblos—as "past"—are withdrawn from but surrounded by "modern life"; the softly molded contours of the adobe pueblos are compared to a cluster of modern, "battered" apartment houses; the government buildings, made by and suggestive of machines and modernity, stand in contrast to— and insult—the scene. The awareness of time, of history, and the enigmatic movements and colors of the Pueblo people and their presence in such a place tease Fergusson into the fundamental question: who are they? where do they come from? She seeks to answer this question in terms of both story and history, by asking the Pueblos themselves for their own explanations, their own kind of telling and accounting, whether by older methods of myth or gesture or dance—the markings of "Indian tradition"— and by more modern, scientific, "historical," (as well as anthropological, archaeological, ethnological) explanations. In both instances, "narrative" affords the framework for the queries and the responses.

Fergusson's historical "method" is to seek accommodation between myth and science, between, for example, multiple "traditions": the Isleta Pueblo "tradition" that explains its peoples' origins in the north and their crossings of a sea where a rock could be tossed across it (i.e., the familiar account of Native American migration across the Bering Strait and then south); the Taos Pueblo "tradition" of the journey north in pursuit of a bird until the Pueblos settled at the foot of their sacred mountain (i.e., the hypothesis that certain Pueblo Indians originated among the Aztecs and came north from Mexico); the Hopi legend of the building of a great temple, left unfinished because of a sudden confusion of tongues—a Hopi Babel—and a departure to the present Hopi villages to the south (i.e., the unfinished Sun Temple excavated at Mesa Verde). What Fergusson repeatedly calls "Indian tradition" is played off against "scientific investigation" as both a stimulus and a check.

Fergusson traces, in turn, how archaeologists have learned about prehistoric life by attempting to confirm the stories and legends which connect the modern Pueblo peoples to the ruins which exist throughout the Southwest: the Santa Clara who claim their descent from the original inhabitants of Puye, all the Keres peoples of the Rio Grande valley who see the Rito de los Frijoles as their ancestral home, the recurrent visits by medicine men and other tribal members to sacred shrines among those ancestral ruins. The modern Pueblo ceremonial is thus best understood in relation to the history of its various rites and forms: "Religious form is always the last human habit to yield to change; and in the altars, sacred symbols, and customs of the modern Indian we can trace the history of his ancestors" (*DG*, 6).

Looking back to "history," the modern pueblo can be traced to the ancient Pueblo people, to the kiva or pre-pueblo people who dug into the ground and made a circular room, "roofed with mud-daubed logs and entered from above by means of a ladder," and to the prototypic wandering *kisi* who made no permanent homes, only brush shelters. The causality is more complicated, but Fergusson's explanation is simplified and readable, with enough suggestion of the greater complexity behind her narrative to make it convincing as a mere outline.

Fergusson's intended reader was a general reader receptive to both history and legend, recounted in comprehensible terms and made palatable by the author's attention to "style." It is the kind of readability which Lawrence Stone cites as a reason why certain latter-day twentieth-century "new historians" find themselves turning from strictly analytical, quantifiable, social science history back to narrative history and its open artistry: "One further reason why a number of 'new historians' are turning back to narrative seems to be a desire to make their findings accessible once more to an intelligent but not expert reading public, which is eager to learn what these innovative new questions, methods and data have revealed, but cannot stomach indigestible statistical tables, dry analytical argument, and jargon-ridden prose. Increasingly the structural, analytical, quantitative historians have found themselves talking to each other and no one else."[7] In her writing of history, Fergusson—in Stone's context—enjoys the paradoxical status of an innovator, an "old" narrative historian whose methods are being revived for reasons which include, but not exclusively, readability.

In Fergusson's account, although the pre-pueblo people left little other than their kivas, some crude pottery, and a bit of weaving, their descendants of the cliff dwellings and communal villages are relatively easy to study and their lives possible to recreate. The Puye, Rito de los Frijoles, Chaco Canyon, Pecos, Mesa Verde, and Gran Quivira dwellings are cited as instances of prehistoric Native American life. Although she remains relatively scientific in her accountings of Puye and Frijoles dwellings, Mesa Verde provides the occasion for sustained poetic description: "Just under the canyon's brim stand those marvelous dwellings, still in the sunlight, just as they have stood for more than a thousand years. The walls of stone, finely worked and fitted, are solid, rising as high as five stories and giving the general effect of an enchanted castle held under a spell of silence and distance" (*DG*, 8). Fergusson, on the spot (somewhat like Willa Cather in *The Professor's House*) intrudes as a modern, viewing the past as it extends into the present. It is precisely because of such outbursts of eloquent description that an otherwise dry sequence of archaeological phases takes on a special gusto.

Fergusson cites authorities of the time, such as A. E. Douglas, of the University of Arizona, who made prehistoric dating more verifiable by the use of analyzing tree rings. She cites statistics and draws analogies between the events of Southwestern Native American history and the history of Europe. But it is in her imaginative projections of what life was like— based on the extrapolations of what may be seen and experienced now by a knowing individual such as herself, such, perhaps as her ideal reader as well—that her history takes on the excitement of story.

In her condensed account of the coming of the Spanish conquerors, Fergusson is in greater sympathy with the Great Age of the Pueblos than with the conquistadors—intruders she sees as a blight which "checked the growth of a truly democratic state" (*DG*, 13). In Fergusson's version of the various sixteenth- and seventeenth-century Spanish explorers and settlers, the Pueblo Indians were friendly enough but mistreated because—among other reasons—they did not possess the gold and jewels, the great wealth which the Spanish believed were cached in the cellars and kivas of the pueblos.

She summarizes the individuals and their misdeeds: Fray Marcos de Niza, the Franciscan monk who headed the first expedition which came up from Mexico into the Southwest in 1539 and reported the wealth of the legendary Seven Cities of Cíbola; Esteban, Fray Marcos's black companion who allegedly seduced the Indian women; Francisco Vásquez de Coronado, who followed Fray Marcos's route in 1540, visited all the Zuni villages, saw Ácoma, reached the Rio Grande south of where Albuquerque now stands, and followed the river north to Taos; Tovar and Alvarado who fired on, flogged, and imprisoned peaceful inhabitants of the pueblos; the martyred monks, Juan de Padilla and Luis de Escalona, left behind by Coronado and killed by the Indians they sought to convert. In these accounts Fergusson concedes that the Church and its emissaries were much more benevolent than the Spanish soldiers who were presumably motivated largely by greed, saying, ". . . much of the history of the province of New Mexico deals with the conflict between the Church, which sought the souls of the Indians, and the civil government, which sought their wealth and their bodies in slavery" (DG, 15–16). Fergusson credits Antonio de Espejo's 1581 tour of the region as being the most kindly and the fairest in dealings with the indigenous peoples he found. But Espejo was the exception and Fergusson is harsh in her indictment of Spain's imperialism: "Later leaders were not always like Espejo, and the Spaniard soon forgot the original kindly welcome of a people who might easily have exterminated the first expeditions. So began the long course of the white man's encroachment on the Indian's land, breaking treaties and agreements until finally it came about that any Indian, claiming his own, was looked upon as a treacherous savage" (DG, 16).

In her description of Juan de Oñate's settlement of Nueva Granada in 1598, Fergusson depends again on her special kind of "New Mexico baroque" style while portraying again the spectacle of Oñate's train of colonizers: "He brought cattle and sheep, wagon-loads of household goods, artisans and priests, women and children. His wagons were of the type we know as *carretas*—inadequate-looking baskets of saplings mounted on groaning, screeching wheels of solid wood, and loaded, no doubt, with furniture, tools, food, and seeds, and surmounted with frightened women holding babies" (DG, 17). The "no doubt" is a revealing qualifier. Characteristically, she tended to stage a scene whenever possible, and get at the subjective as well as the objective truths.

In her account of the Pueblo Revolt of 1680 and of the role played by the San Juan leader Popé, Fergusson again comes down on the side of the Pueblos. In their uprising against Governor Otermin, Popé is viewed as the pueblos' liberator, at least in principle—until he becomes "swollen with pride and full of Spanish ideas" and tries to make himself a kind of king, thus bringing about the "downfall of his people" (*DG*, 20). His culpability, such as it is, is attributed to Spanish ideas, his tyrannical behavior associated, in Fergusson's account, with the Spanish.

Thus Fergusson anticipated the revisionist histories of today and the 1970s and 1980s which seek to tell the American Indian side of Anglo-European and Anglo-American "imperialistic" and "hegemonic" conquests of the dark-skinned races of Mexico, the Southwest, and the other regions of the United States. In her accounts of the reconquest of New Mexico by Don Diego de Vargas in 1692—his winning back control over the Keres people, the Tewas who held Santa Fe, the Jemez Indians allied with the Navajos, the Taos Indians allied with the Utes of southern Colorado, the Ácomas, the Zunis, and the Hopis to the west—Fergusson's sympathies are clearly with the conquered peoples: "The Indians, very naturally, drew into a hard impenetrable shell of silence and concealment. The old forms of worship were not abandoned; they were performed secretly in the kivas or in hidden places, thus establishing the custom of concealing all important ceremonies from the whites. The priests, in their efforts to suppress these rites, adopted the custom of considering them witchcraft and of treating the Indian *caciques* as wizards and sorcerers. Many of them were whipped, branded, enslaved, even killed for practicing the old religions" (*DG*, 22).

Fergusson's survey of the "Pueblo Indian and the American" is even briefer—but still empathic with American Indians. A few brief pages span the time from Mexico's independence from Spain in 1822 to the twentieth century: Fergusson zeroes in on General Stephen Watts Kearny's taking of New Mexico for the United States in 1846, Abraham Lincoln's presentation of all Pueblo leaders with silver-headed canes of symbolic governance in 1863, and the establishment of Indian agents to look after the Pueblo peoples. Here too she cites the injustices and abuses, "especially in the matter of encroachment on Indian lands and the violation of Indian water rights," for which legislation of her era, the 1930s, was then attempting to make restitution.

Fergusson's narrative telling of history, her "explanations," her tendency toward argumentation cannot be separated from her stance as an advocate of American Indian rights and reparations. Fergusson was not just swept up in the new sensitivity toward American Indian culture espoused by the increasing numbers of artists in New Mexico. In many ways, she was in the vanguard of the wider acknowledgment of those sentiments. Witness this climactic peroration in *Dancing Gods*, her "history" of intercultural relations in New Mexico and the Southwest:

All of this means that the Pueblo Indian is a person of dual nature. The white man's Indian is trained in a government school and turned out as a fairly good carpenter, farmer, and Christian. In so far as the education has been a success, he apes the ways of the white man even to the extent of living in the white man's town rather than in his own. The other face of him, however, is turned away from the white man and everything he typifies. Turning his back on the government school, the Catholic mission, and the Protestant church, he is dominated by his ancient beliefs, guided by his ancestral leaders. His real life centers in the kiva, his real hope is in the gods of the ancients, those potent beings who still bring him water and corn, prowess in the hunt, happiness in his life, and a deep spiritual understanding such as the white man does not know. (*DG*, 27)

By later standards and sensibilities, Fergusson's ethnocentrism might be construed as patronizing, even offensive if unintentional. But for her time, the regret she communicates concerning the creation of the "white man's Indian" went far to lay the groundwork for a fairer, less patronizing view and for the writing of a new history—not just of the white man's Indian, but of American Indians and Native Americans more broadly as they presumably might see themselves. Today, American Indians speak forcefully against cultural appropriation, and rightly talk much for themselves, and eschew—indeed, protest—"outside" interpreters, whatever their motive. The "new" history, the "new" ethnicity pleads for perspectives of greater thickness, greater allowance for inside/outside, dominant/downtrodden points of view and versions of "truth," be it "factual" or impressionistic and subjective.

OUR SOUTHWEST

Our Southwest (1940), Fergusson's next book about New Mexico, Texas, Arizona, and Colorado, has also achieved something of a classic status. Lawrence Clark Powell categorically views it as "the best general work on the region."[8] Another Fergusson friend and partisan, Dudley Wynn, although he (like David Remley) struggles with classifying Fergusson's writings and her role as author, eventually reached an apt enough conclusion, finding her a "historian" of a special mold: "*Our Southwest* is the kind of book that no mere historian, on the one hand, and no mere reporter, on the other, could write. It has clarity, well-directed scorn, the occasional warmth of a justifiable infatuation."[9] Also calling attention to the special persona of the author, which is so prominent throughout the book, Katherine Woods, reviewer for the *New York Times,* made this judgment: "Through contrasted scenes that are like scenes of enchantment, through man's passage in ambition and enterprise across changing time, into today's new problems and responsibilities, Erna Fergusson guides her readers with a gifted pen. She has a warm, human social sense and a keen sense of humor, and neither forsakes her; and her clear visualization, with its assimilation of honest study, stamps her work with a rare literary excellence. Her book is as comprehensive as her mind is many-sided and her sensibility broadly acute.[10] What Woods notes is the presence of Fergusson as historian/artist, the presence of a traveler and a humanitarian capable of caring for the people and the places about which she writes and of writing about them with "rare literary excellence." Although somewhat less enthralled in his assessment of Fergusson as a writer of history and uncomfortable with what he calls "a touch of the chamber of commerce complex" which he finds in portions of the book, Edgar C. McMechen judged *Our Southwest* "well-written in an easy, flowing style" and "truly admirable and authoritative in its descriptions of Pueblo life and customs."[11]

What most reviewers at the time of *Our Southwest*'s publication seemed to sense but never said outright is that Fergusson combined history, travel, journalism, and advocacy in a bold and successful amalgamation. Fergusson's ubiquitous and persistent reviewer and all-around Southwestern culture commentator, Stanley Walker, touched on this in his review for the *New York Herald Tribune*'s Sunday edition books supplement. In *Our Southwest* Walker sees "Miss Fergusson" (an obvious projection of her assumed "female" persona) balancing many forms and impulses, including romance and skepticism:

> Miss Fergusson, who has a shrewd talent for sizing up a country and a people, a good reporter's instinct for detail, and a sensitive appreciation of the currents of history, has set down . . . a full bodied picture of the American Southwest as it is today, and has placed it accurately and with a fine sureness of touch against the backdrop of four centuries. . . .
>
> Here we have not merely a portrait but a history. The subject is vast—so vast that even this long book seems extraordinarily compact when one considers the mass and diversity of the subject matter. . . . There is no question of the research and scholarship that went into the making of this volume; they are implicit in the text. Likewise, there can be no doubt of the integrity of the calm, level-headed judg-

ments of the author. She knows when high romance is justified and when to be skeptical.[12]

This same vastness of scope bothers David Remley who views *Our Southwest* as one of Fergusson's "least satisfying books" because she attempts to cover too much geography and subject matter; however, he concedes that "her observations and her pattern for touring the Southwest are interesting in themselves."[13] The narrative pattern Fergusson uses, which Walker praises for its diversity and scope and which Remley finds interesting in and of itself, is nothing less than a travel framework for the history of the lives and landscapes of the region. The travel pattern in which the narrator portrays herself as automobile tourist is not that much at odds with the history of the Southwest. Much of the history of the region is the history of travel, of journeys, of migrations, of quests and escapes; also, the literature is often travel literature and an accounting of discovery, exploration, and pioneering. The "narrator"/historian in *Our Southwest* stresses "tourism" for the serious purpose of seeing and experiencing the past in the present, of giving life to living history.

The narrative framework of *Our Southwest* is a purer form of travel narrative than *Dancing Gods,* and therefore contains even more anecdote and description and comparatively less cultural and social history and ethnology than Fergusson's examination of Indian ceremonies. Although Fergusson had distanced herself very slightly from her subject in *Dancing Gods* and although it was there that the personal cast of narration was set, she is even less distanced in *Our Southwest.* She writes more intimately and in a less philosophical vein than in her first book. Use of first person continues its prevalence, and when American Indians are interviewed or quoted (either casually as a result of a ride given in her car or as a result of a walk through a pueblo), personal names are given, suggesting how much she is held in friendship and confidence.

Fergusson's "touring" point of view in *Our Southwest* renders it a "period piece" which portrays travel—at least Anglo-American travel—as the travel of automobile or train. In a very special sense *Our Southwest* can be read as a "history" of automobile Southwestering in the 1930s. Like the accounts of other literary travelers during the evolution of transcontinental railroad and automobile tours, here too the automobile is at the center of Fergusson's perception and definition of the Southwest as travel. She dramatizes herself quite explicitly as the driver/"historian" who sees beyond the places and people she encounters and grasps the historical and cultural forces which shaped them.

Lawrence Clark Powell's autobiographical essay, "The Southwest of the Traveling Reader," accounts for the auto trips on which he based his books and his column for *Westways* magazine and underscores again just how important travel is in understanding the Southwest as place and as history. What shines through again is Fergusson's ability to render geography and culture into word. Likewise, Fergusson in *Our Southwest* takes herself and her traveler/reader, as she once did as a guide for the Koshare Tours and later as guide/historian in *Dancing Gods,* into New Mexico via the automobile.[14]

Our Southwest (1940) represents both an extension of *Dancing Gods* (1931) and a middle ground between *Erna Fergusson's Albuquerque* (1947), *Murder and Mystery in New Mexico* (1948), and *New Mexico* (1951). Coming nine years after *Dancing Gods* and more or less betwixt and between her Latin American and Caribbean books, *Fiesta in Mexico* (1934), *Guatemala* (1937), and *Venezuela* (1939), *Chile* (1943), *Cuba* (1946), and *Mexico Revisited* (1955), it shows her development as a seasoned journalist/traveler and a trained, experienced historian. Moreover, it demonstrates the polished result of Fergusson's anecdotal, personal-essay approach, first tried in her early newspaper pieces and later in *Dancing Gods.* Assuredly, the style (high romance and skepticism, "New Mexico baroque" and otherwise), the occasion (the tourist on the spot), and the historical framework of *Dancing Gods* are seminal, and Fergusson refined these techniques and affinities in other of her travel/history writings before turning to *Our Southwest.*

Our Southwest, however, represents a kind of homecoming for Fergusson and shows her at something close to the height of her form as a "popularizer" in the best sense of the word. It is, as Walker, Remley, and others have noted, a large and sprawling kind of a book, and—given the vastness of her subject—almost too ambitious. Knowing this full well, Fergusson first attempts to define her terms, to set the cultural and geographical boundaries of the Southwest. Fergusson is exuberant in her homecoming. She seeks to define the Southwest figuratively as a journey (implicitly a pilgrimage of reacquaintance with her homeland after sojourning in Latin America and Mexico) through her organization of materials—traveling west from Fort Worth and San Antonio to the border and towns such as El Paso, then on to Tucson, Phoenix, and Prescott, and back, heading east, to New Mexico and the northern towns of Gallup, Albuquerque, Santa Fe, the Rio Grande pueblos, and Taos. She also includes southern Colorado, primarily because of Mesa Verde. Finally, she discusses the high plains of the *llano estacado*—ending with summary chapters on festivals and other "interpreters" (literary and historical) of the region. The "mapping," inclusion of the states she discusses and exclusion of marginally southwestern states like Oklahoma and California, is determined in part by climate, season, and the seeking out of simpatico regions of Southwest as "winter and summer country."

At first glance, Fergusson, as the narrator of *Our Southwest,* seems much more rambling and disorganized, effecting much less unity and coherence than in either *Dancing Gods, Albuquerque, Murder and Mystery in New Mexico,* or *New Mexico.* She heads west and circles back to the east; she interchanges people and place, season and climate; and she almost serendipitously includes chance thoughts, including apparently tacked-on chapters by way of conclusion and rounding off. But there is a purposeful, albeit roaming, kind of design to the book which is altogether appropriate to the topic at hand—that is, identifying what constitutes the modern Southwest of 1940 and the changes which have taken place to make it that way—country and land related to city, subregion related to larger region. *Our Southwest* is much more mobile and kinesthetic, more given to touring than *New Mexico;* thus Fergusson here at once designs her book and defines the Southwest by means of travel, of actual highways on the map, by modern movements of a typical Everyman/Everywoman motorist, inquiring, seasonally touring, and relishing the Southwest and her moment in history.

And yet, such a practical, down-to-earth tour of the region is merely the basis of a more metaphorical mapping—the charting of a region's spirit and how it came to take the shape it does. In Fergusson's words of advice and counsel to one like her who is potentially of the place or soon wants to be, she says:

> The traveler who would explore our Southwest for the first time must know that it is divided very neatly into winter and summer country. The desert and near desert country from San Antonio, Texas, to Los Angeles, California, is delightful in winter; much of it is too hot for vacationing in summer. The northern half of New Mexico and Arizona and certain southward-reaching spurs of the Rockies are lofty enough to offer a fine summer climate; much of it is cold in winter. This book follows these lines, going westward along the routes best suited for winter travel and returning by the highways most comfortable in summer. And this being the erratic and contradictory Southwest, the plan will not be followed with any consistency.[15]

The design of the book, not just as road map but as the very vehicle for word travel, although it sounds too obviously contrived and something of a rationalization for disorder, by and large works as one of the more effective adaptations of form to material, of style to subject, that Fergusson ever hit upon. It is a natural enough design, given her personality, and that is why her persona and point of view seem so appropriate, if not totally captivating amidst the current culture wars here on the cusp of the twenty-first century, and should strike today's "politically correct" reader as humanely personable.

Much of the narrative conception of *New Mexico* is present, at least in outline, in *Our Southwest*. Here is Fergusson's early attempt at rendering the timeless, imagined vision of Sandia Man and Folsom Man, of a "pageant of three peoples" passing panoramically, as if in a prose mural, across the everlasting landscape of the Southwest as viewed from a breathtaking, sublime prominence. Here, though, it is done in less grandiose terms than in *New Mexico*. By this time she had clearly reread and registered her brother's panoramic history, *Rio Grande* (1933). At one point, Fergusson introduces the same image she would later expand when, in relation to the ruins of Montezuma Castle in Arizona, she says, "Such monuments . . . impress even the most thoughtless with the length of the Southwestern pageant in which we, with all our noise and trumperies, are just one episode" (*OS*, 112). It is a metaphor which Fergusson fondly reuses frequently, and it bespeaks her own and her brother's perspective of the Southwest as spectacle, as history dramatically staged against the laminations of three cultures, against the picturesque and sublime, the enchanted landscapes of New Mexico.

In *Our Southwest* Fergusson's larger design is to get at the entire region, "from the inside out" (*OS*, 6). For her this means the historical and cultural essence of "the Indian, the Spanish, and the Gringo"—as she says again in the organizational scheme of *New Mexico* and in the introduction to *Dancing Gods*. The Southwest also means other essences, most notably aridity, the need for water. In this regard she openly borrows from Walter Prescott Webb's ninety-eighth—meridian demarcation in defining the Southwest as a uniformly and characteristically arid region (*OS*, 9). Thus, the relationships which exist between climate and cultural mix, between geography and social and racial history, go far in identifying the Southwest "from the inside out," and from this premise she offers details, amplifies by means of interview, anecdote, and statistic—and editorializes humorously, at times satirically, along the way.

Her universal motorist/historian persona, together with her implied reader/traveler, experiences both the facts and the implications, the seen and the unseen, of the elements, the climate, the flora and fauna, and the geography, as well as of the human contributions to the landscape and all that is entailed in mankind's presence (going and coming) in a place. The Southwest is thus pictured historically as a composite of weather, society, and overall regional ambiance, pictured as a nodality where various kinds of people travel to and through and as a place where all are influenced by what they find, reciprocally attempting to influence what they find. In her characteristic lyricism, Fergusson's prose attempts to match and confirm the spirit of change amidst changelessness, of renewal out of the past, which she senses in the totality of the place:

> The arid Southwest has always been too strong, too indomitable for most people. Those who can stand it have had to learn that man does not modify this country; it transforms him, deeply. Perhaps our generation will come to appreciate it as the country God remembered and saved for man's delight when he could mature enough to understand it. God armored it, as the migrating Easterner learned in his anguish, with thorns and trees, stings and horns on bugs and beasts. He fortified it with mountain ranges and trackless deserts. He filled it with such hazards as no legendary hero ever had to surmount. The Southwest can never be remade into a landscape that produces bread and butter. But it is infinitely productive of the imponderables so much needed by a world weary of getting and spending. It is a wilderness where a man may get back the essentials of being a man. It is magnificence forever rewarding to a man couraged enough to renew his soul. (OS, 18–19)

This is, in a sense, strange history, at least stylistically, and is more lyrical and imaginative than strictly factual. And yet it possesses a certain truth which, in the motive and the manner of telling, transcends quantifiable matters, a truth which, although phrased lyrically, penetrates the spiritual essentials so crucial to the motivation of any human history place—call it Rudolfo Anaya's "epiphany in landscape" or the inspirational effect of place and its spirit on the soul of humanity. Although some readers, like Walker, might well consider such prose—in form and content— "New Mexico baroque," such language, phrasing, and rhythm go beyond the cataloging and translations of the common traveler/historian into the larger issues of human capacity for wonder and how that capacity works itself out in human history. It is Fergusson's attempt in *Our Southwest*, as in other of her Southwestern writings, to express such a feeling about the interrelations between human spirit and the spirit of place that allows her to capture (within the artistry and design of her "inside-out" pincer design) the multitudinousness of the Southwest, to enter it and pass across it involved in a manner similar to the likes of Cabeza de Vaca, as Wayne Franklin accounts for him.

Not only does Fergusson communicate her own kinship with the region itself, the enchantments it works upon her, she also tells of a shared sense of awe at the perception of its very existence, a sense of wonder and appreciation and reverence for humanity in the landscape such as that known initially by Native Americans, and later by some of the Spanish and Anglo-American discoverers.

Of the twenty-two chapters in *Our Southwest*, only three focus on Southwestern Native Americans: "Broken Pots and Prehistoric People," "Gallup and the Navajos," and "The People of the Pueblos." A fourth chapter, "Uncle Sam's Southwest," touches on government Indian policies. It is clear that Fergusson is amplifying on her *Dancing Gods* survey of New Mexico history as it touched on American Indians, which she would develop further in *New Mexico*. In her correspondence with her publisher, Alfred A. Knopf, Fergusson remained always leery, though, of repeating what she had already said in both *Dancing Gods* and *Our Southwest*.

The "Broken Pots" chapter reflects Fergusson's interest in archaeology and, more directly, archaeologists themselves and their personal histories, and the history of their discipline in the Southwest and how it has contributed to the way Southwestern history is known. She discusses in detail the projects of discovery and restoration at Casa Grande, on the Gila River, and the Hohokam peoples whose culture it represents, as well as the institutions and groups responsible for studying them. Mesa Verde National Park in Colorado and the spectrum of American Indians which it represents—from Basket Makers to those who immediately preceded the Pueblos—occupy much of her attention as it did first in *Dancing Gods* and does again in *New Mexico*. The role played by Edgar L. Hewitt and the School of American Research, which he helped found at Santa Fe, in Southwestern archaeology is similarly explained, allowing some entrance for her own authorial role as American Indian advocate.

New Mexico's Pueblo people occupy much of her interest—Chaco Canyon and its migration mysteries; Adolph Bandelier and his explorations of Frijoles Canyon; the Puye ruins above Santa Clara Pueblo; the disappearance of certain murals at Kuana, near Bernalillo, once seen and described by Oñate's historian, Gaspar Pérez de Villagrá. All these aspects of New Mexico history, which Fergusson chronicles even more fully in *New Mexico*, are here dealt with in early form.

In her chapter on "Gallup and the Navajos" Fergusson combines forcefully a narrative history of people and place with social commentary about them. The remote canyon sanctuaries of the Navajos are described and presented as vulnerable to the encroachments of Anglo history and influence. Gallup is described as the lodestar for Navajo and Anglo intersection, a cultural, interracial crossroads, as witnessed in this imagistic evocation of people and place:

From a few miles west of Gallup to thirty miles east of it the road runs along tall sandstone cliffs like battlements. Streaked with purple, varied with ochres and toneless buff, their canyons are so concealed that they seem to have no opening. One might believe the Navajos were forever safe behind them, protected from the noisy life of the white man, speeding along the tracks with jettying white steam or rolling black smoke, honking in motors, or building towns loud with whistles and bells.

But the Navajo is not apart. All along the road one sees him, riding a pony, driving a wagon or a creaking jalopy with his mothers, sisters, cousins, and aunts. (Only never his mother-in-law.) In every town they trade wool for canned goods, blankets for clothes, jewelry for the luxuries they are learning to like. Gallup, especially, is the Navajo's town. (*OS,* 207)

With such a process of convergence of two cultures—one pastoral, one industrial—to serve as a prefatory narrative frame (a compositional technique of Fergusson's which is often used for considerable effect), she begins her "history" of the town by stressing the significance to Gallup—to the Navajos and to the Anglos—of the intertribal Indian ceremonial. Gallup itself is described as a historical hub of travel activity, a place visited by trappers in years past, by the Army in their nineteenth-century expeditions into Navajo country and then on their way to Fort Wingate and Fort Defiance, and by the Santa Fe Railroad which led to Gallup becoming an "Indian show town" (*OS,* 208). Many subsequent students of Southwestern history have chosen to focus on town histories as microcosms of greater dynamics of regional identity and change; in this respect, as an "urban" historian—in addition to her accounts of American Indian ceremonialism—Fergusson is an early twentieth-century prototype.[16]

In her town portrait, Fergusson (ever familiar with and, to an extent, admiring of them as colleagues) mentions the Anglo-American automobile tourist guides who "wrangle" the influx of dudes in Gallup. One such individual is representative: "Dick Maddox, dean of them all, whose Ford and his driving of it have grown into a legend of mechanical sturdiness and the tenacity of human life, still twirls his mustache and rolls out his resounding remarks around El Navajo" (*OS,* 209). It is a touch of the past made modern, the historic wagon guide brought into step with the automobile age. Traders, the bustle of activity surrounding trading posts, and their flow of goods, of Navajos, and of tourists—these too are described with the detail of one who knows, who is part of the past renewed in the present.

Fergusson's wilder enthusiasms for Southwestern history made modern are also softened. Such a meeting ground as Gallup for Native American and Anglo-American cultures also has its disadvantages: "Navajos and Zunis trade in Gallup, too, picking up the worst of the white man's liquor, diseases, and habits in exchange, often for the worst of their own handiwork. To its inhabitants, Gallup is much else. To the traveling public, it is the taking-off place for the Navajo country" (*OS*, 209). Again, her empathy for Native American culture, seeking to fight off the material and spiritual corruptions—such as they are—of Anglo culture, is made apparent.

To illustrate her own involvement as an Anglo in the hustle and bustle of Native American–Anglo-American mixings at Gallup, she resorts to a characteristic anecdote. Fergusson, traveling with an unidentified companion, stops to eat while en route to the Gallup Indian ceremonial. A family of Navajos in another car also stops to eat at the same time and place. Fergusson seizes upon the occasion to speculate about the Navajo mind and imagination and does so with a proportionate blend of realism, good humor, and social conscience. Fergusson's presumably Anglo traveling companion queries, "I wonder . . . what those Indians think about when they sit so quietly?" The response as author/historian/traveler and friend to her naive companion's bemused questioning does not so much idealize the American Indian mind and individual presence in time and place as it does the landscape, particularly nearby Mount Taylor, a sacred place for the area Indians, and the enchanting New Mexico sunset. Always the respectful historian/traveler, Fergusson offers this reply—in ways skeptical, in ways believing—in her speculations about American Indian consciousness, speculations and projections which place her in at least a kind of kinship with the "others" who have "passed by here" in their travels for much the same reason as hers:

> Thoughts no more memorable, probably, than mine, as I watched the shadow slide up Mount Taylor's flank, while the sun lowered itself through horizontal clouds of rose and silver in the west. But they could call up many images out of their racial consciousness—if there is a racial consciousness, and if the schools did not catch them too young. For Mount Taylor, whose shapely crest would be the last to let the sunlight go, is the southern outpost of the Navajo legendary world. There the sacred twins were born, from there they journeyed in the four directions, defying the unconquered monsters and preparing the world for the coming of the People [i.e., the Diné]. Yet, gods inhabit its slopes as they do those of the other mountains which guard the Navajo's land: the San Francisco Peaks on the west in Arizona, *El*

Pelado [Baldy] in the Jemez Mountains to the north, and the San Juan
Mountains in the east. (*OS,* 209–210)

Such, on the one hand, clearheaded reluctance to second-guess a car-
load of Navajo travelers, her skepticism about theories of "racial consciousness," balanced, on the other hand, with her display of knowledge about
the richness of the legends and folk history of the Diné and her outright
captivation by the ways of their enchanted world, tell much about Fergusson's person and persona as a historian/traveler. In seeing points of unity
and of diversity she, as an Anglo-American, is able to empathize with
American Indian culture and talk about Navajo origin, myth, and landmarks, but she never loses consciousness that she is indeed attempting to
enter another culture's worldview, that she is empathizing. Nevertheless,
she momentarily enters, travels into the world of the Navajo as a person,
as a historian, and, above all, as a writer and artist. In this latter context,
she builds upon her anecdotal musings.

From such thoughts about the incongruities of a car of traveling Navajos and whether what they are thinking is different from what she and her
friend are thinking, Fergusson extends her "survey" of Navajo history and
origins to their relationship with the Pueblos and speculates about Anglo-
American influences on the Navajos and the changing, modern world
which they face—always a concern of hers in her Southwestern writings.
She discusses the Navajo life-style as "wanderers of Athabascan stock";
their conjectured descent from Hopi, Zuni, and Jemez peoples; their adoption of Pueblo, Spanish, and (later) Mexican crafts—especially their learning to "weave better blankets than their Pueblo teachers" (*OS,* 211).

She mentions the travels of James Pattie who crossed the Southwest
in 1826 and his own praise of Navajo weaving. The etymology of the word
"Navajo" is traced to the 1620 translation of early Spanish travelers as "great
planted fields" and then as a word associated with the Spanish word for
knife, *navaja.* Peaceful and violent connotations of the word are acknowledged, with, some readers might insist, the violent association getting more
emphasis, presumably because Fergusson accepted such behavior as historical fact: "Certainly the Spaniard had reason to use the more bellicose word
[*navaja*]; the history of every village in New Mexico is marked by gory
tales of rape and slaughter. The Spaniard fought back, of course, but until
the Unites States Army faced him along a gun-barrel, the Navajo roamed
unconquered and ravaged where he would" (*OS,* 212). One can presume,
too, that Fergusson felt a deeper fondness for the Pueblos, especially the
Zuni, than she did for either the Navajo or the Apache. And this is confirmed in her treatment of the Apaches in *New Mexico.* As ethnocentric

such a portrayal of the Navajos is, Fergusson's conscious intentions are to show the hard times they faced at the hands of U.S. government and military policy—again tending toward her role as outspoken advocate for rethinking the history of the U.S. government's "white" policy concerning the "Indian problem." The infamous exile of the Navajos to the Bosque Redondo is pictured as an outrageous Anglo-American injustice on American Indians.

There is nevertheless an ingrained ethnocentrism—at least by today's standards—in her accounting of the result of Anglo injustices perpetrated against the Navajo: "Those bitter years left a mark not yet eradicated. The Navajo is still a man of spirit, but it is now a smoldering, under-cover temper which breaks out only in bitter mirth, in sullen distrust of the government, or in enjoyable outsmarting of the white man. Navajos, as a people, are never pitiful. Tragic, yes, but their strength and cleverness preclude so soft an emotion as pity" (OS, 214). There is something of the stereotype lurking here, and one must admit to a certain disappointment in such a portrait, mitigated though it is by Fergusson's sincerity.

Touching on the more distanced role of the historian as social scientist rather than as artist, Fergusson traces key dates in the Anglo scheme of events, such as the 1868 treaty in which the Navajos agreed to cease fighting the United States, the establishment of government Indian schools in 1887, the appointment of John Collier to head federal Indian affairs in 1933, and the discovery of oil on Navajo land in 1923. Throughout her chronological survey she attempts to give the reader a sense of why in 1940 the whole involvement of governmental agencies, missionary and welfare efforts, and the overall politics of the "white man's Indian" and the "Indian problem" seemed so appalling. The history of Fergusson's Southwest, then, inevitably merges with tract.

Returning to the anecdote which began her chapter on "Gallup and the Navajos," Fergusson concludes that the crux of the "problem"—offered as another answer to her naive traveling companion's speculation about Navajo thinking—is that "Indians do not think as white men do" (OS, 224). It is a view similarly held by her brother Harvey in McGarnigal and Rio Grande and common enough to the Anglo interpretations of the Indians of the time. This difference she attributes, in part, to the inability to communicate through language, the failure to catch the meanings of words, and to differing sets of assumptions by the federal government and by the Navajos. She in no sense sets out to be condescending. To the extent that she is, it is a condescension levelled at the whites as much as at the Navajos: "When a Navajo interprets what an expert from Washington says, not all the gods of medicine men and missionaries could guess what the Navajo thinks. . . . The Navajo's mind is quite the equal of the white man's, and different only in content, in habit, and way of thought. If he often does not understand, neither do we" (*OS*, 224). Laced with the historical conjecture and speculation is the familiar editorializing about what is needed politically. She ends her chapter about the Navajos in favor of continued government assistance and involvement by Anglos on behalf of American Indians.

She is strongly against termination policies of the era which would leave American Indians alone. And although her own accounts about the Navajo in his land stylistically tend toward the sentimental, the romantic, the transcendental, if not the mystic, Fergusson comes down hard against the brand of sentimentality which would in the end serve to dehumanize all Indians. She targets insensitive tourists as the worst offenders in such attitudes: "Many tourists want all Indians kept primitive and picturesque, though dirty, diseased, and underfed. These sentimentalists, bounding over the reservation in a motor car, shudder away from the sight of a cement dam, a Navajo wielding a hoe or driving a truck. The shrillest of them advocate 'letting the Indian alone,' but they submit no detailed plan for letting alone forty-five thousand people in the midst of the United States" (*OS*, 224–25).[17] The Navajos remained of interest to Fergusson throughout her New Mexico writings; however, as chapter 16 of *Our Southwest* illustrates, the Pueblos were her chosen Native Americans. In that chapter she returns to a discussion of "The People of the Pueblos." They provided the focal point for *Dancing Gods* and continued to dominate *Our Southwest* and *New Mexico*. In *Our Southwest*, however, Fergusson devotes most of her attention on the Pueblos to a discussion of the issues surrounding the Bursum Bill, introduced in Congress in 1922, and to the efforts of John Collier and lobbying groups to preserve American Indian lands. Had it not been for the establishment, instead, of the Federal Land Board to deal with each claimant to land on an individual basis, the passage of the legislation outlined in the Bursum Bill and supported by Collier would have turned all settlement to the state courts. Much of what Fergusson says in *Our Southwest* she repeats again in *New Mexico*. The whole spectrum of pros and cons which surround the Bursum Bill is one of Fergusson's most fascinating roles as a propagandist.

Beyond her treatment of the history of Gallup and of the Navajos and the Pueblos of the Rio Grande valley, Fergusson includes enlightening "historical" chapters on Fort Worth and El Paso; on Tucson, Phoenix, and Prescott; on Albuquerque, Santa Fe, and Taos; in addition to one of the most authoritative chapters yet written on the life and times of Fred Harvey, Southwestern "Civilizer," as Fergusson calls him. Taken all in all, *Our Southwest* must be seen as an early attempt to arrive at an assessment of the interrelationships of Native American, Spanish/Mexican, and Anglo-American cultures in the cities and towns of the growing and changing Southwest. Besides her accounts of ethnic and racial minorities of the region and the forces they exert against and with the ambitions of the Anglo culture, Fergusson's documenting of how Albuquerque came to be a haven for pulmonary patients of all kinds, but especially of tuberculosis patients, begins the accumulation of description and data and general information which makes *Our Southwest* one of the earliest and most informative, albeit "popularized," compendiums of Southwest studies yet published. Here too are accounts of how Santa Fe and Taos became settlements for painters and writers, of the long and illustrious list of authors who found the modern Southwest an inspiration.

Our Southwest sold better than Fergusson's other Southwestern writings. By 1946 it was in its third printing. In the late 1930s Knopf had suggested to her that she write a generally informative book on the Southwest for the general reader. By the spring of 1939 Fergusson was hard at work planning the book and the trip which she would take to "make it"—both literally and figuratively. She told J. Frank Dobie about her projected route and wondered if he might make some suggested refinements on her itinerary: "My plan is to hit from here [San Antonio, Texas] to the best example of a border town. Then the Big Bend. And later, Amarillo. El Paso on my way to Arizona."[18] She also told Dobie that her plan was to give the general reader a once-and-for-all answer to the Southwest and the information about it: "You know, we always have to give him a list of books now. Mine is to put an end to all that. He will just read mine and it will refer so alluringly to others on more specialized subjects that he will be inevitably and painlessly led along."[19]

Dobie responded with both encouragement and information, although their schedules made a rendezvous in El Paso inconvenient. But in subsequent letters Fergusson continued to think out loud, telling Dobie of her purpose and how the traveling and the writing were affecting her personally, while continuing to make queries about his notion of the Southwest:

> What does the intelligent, but unknowing new-comer to the Southwest want to know? Clearly, what is the Southwest now and how did it get that way? This has been my criterion in writing about foreign places and I'm trying to apply the same scheme to my own bailiwick: quite an experience in itself. My book, if it is any good, will be a fair and decent and dependable introduction to the immense literature of the Southwest as well as to the country itself and what may be done there. My emphasis, I think, will be on the country as a

vacation country, the country God forgot, thank God, so it would still
be good after they had used up the rest of the United States. . . . My
notion of the Southwest is something that begins really west of the
moss-hung live oaks, cotton, . . . to say nothing of ladies of the southern tradition. It includes Mexicans and Spanish influence, Indians
still extant, cowboys and oil. As I must stop somewhere, I almost limit
myself to land that includes all of these, making a territory that runs
pretty close to Webb's Great Plains, as an east and west delineation,
and that stops where the Penitentes end in Colorado. . . . Many objections can be made to that, but I can make out a good case too for
leaving out citrus fruit and a purely gringo cow country. . . .[20]

Fergusson followed her original plan almost to the letter, except for
incorporating the recommendation of Harold Strauss, who read the manuscript for Knopf and suggested that since the transitions were inadequate—
in his opinion—the various chapters tended to "fly apart" as she jumped
"arbitrarily from town to town, and within each town, from topic to topic,
without so much as a line space."[21] The "dozen or so transitional passages"
which Strauss recommended were incorporated between chapters and
stressed Fergusson's own motorized route as traveler/historian.

The final result was a success with the general book buyer and with
most reviewers. Fergusson was so pleased that she had great fun with the
reviews as they came in and was able to joke to Dobie, "Happily for my
self-conceit I got well panned by Dallas and Phoenix."[22]

Twenty years later, June 17, 1959, Knopf contacted Fergusson about the
possibility of rewriting and resetting *Our Southwest* for a new edition. The
book had endured. But Fergusson, by that time, after two operations on
her hip for arthritis, was able to walk only with difficulty and unable to
drive. She had changed and so had the Southwest—so much so that she
wondered whether she could adequately incorporate those changes, especially given her immobile condition. In responding to Knopf's suggestion,
Fergusson thought she could bring off an adequate rewrite but only under
certain conditions: that she had an editor "who knows the Southwest and
can understand my point of view, and who likes my style well enough not
to feel obliged to change it"; that she be allowed to include new chapters—
"needed in view of the enormous changes, especially in New Mexico, due
to the atomic bomb and subsequent developments, and to the discovery of
uranium"; and, quite significantly, that somehow (given her handicaps and
the resultant difficulties and expenses of travel) she be able to "visit some
places and talk with some people to get my own impressions and make my
own evaluation of the present situation."[23]

Throughout such correspondence runs the unspoken realization that Fergusson, although she would nobly attempt to gather material, would never gather the strength to do the job needed for a first-rate revision of *Our Southwest.* Perhaps Alfred Knopf realized this and merely attempted to cheer an old friend. Clearly history had outstripped the historian. While change as growth and "progress" continued to accelerate, change as old age and illness worked its way on her. She had the Tingley book to finish, another book which was beyond her physical resources at the time. And the full scope of the "history" which the intervening years had brought to the Southwest, to New Mexico, and especially to Albuquerque was startling and intimidating. As Fergusson told Knopf, "I am not the woman who wrote *Our Southwest,* not only because of the added twenty years, but because drastic surgery has reduced my strength far below par."[24] Her spirit, however, was game enough:

> I am trying to be as realistic as I can in considering this revision of *Our Southwest,* but it is hard for me to be sure how much time the job will take until I know how much rewriting will be required. And this I really do not know. I have not seen the Texas and Arizona centers I featured for twenty years. Naturally I know New Mexico better and Albuquerque best of all. But Albuquerque's population, 35,400 in 1940, is now estimated as 256,000 and its character has changed completely. . . . This boom, the most striking is probably typical, but I greatly need to talk over the other situations with an editor who can advise me. It would be wonderful if you could give me some time, at least to get me started right and perhaps to keep an eye on my progress.[25]

By April 14, 1960, it was clear to Fergusson that she could not finish the Tingley biography and begin the rewrite of *Our Southwest* by a certain deadline, explaining to Knopf, "Try as I may to work more and faster, it only becomes clearer that I cannot push myself into any more speed than the very slow rate at which I am going."[26] She knew and reluctantly accepted her own history, her own biography, and could only be thankful she had known her Southwest, had traveled it, seen it, and talked to its people when she did. The book, though dated, exists and endures (as do her other Southwestern writings) as a piece of history of its own.

CLIO AS COLUMBO:
MURDER AND MYSTERY IN NEW MEXICO

The best showcase for Fergusson's abilities as a narrative historian is *Murder and Mystery in New Mexico,* published in 1948 through the efforts of private backing, in collaboration with local Albuquerque bookseller, Jim Threlkeld, and the designer of *Erna Fergusson's Albuquerque*, Merle Armitage, an editor and advertising executive who specialized in custom-made books. In a sense *Murder and Mystery in New Mexico* is a companion book to *Albuquerque*, looking very similar in appearance and following it into print by only one year. *Murder and Mystery* is clearly a work of regional literature which focuses on several communities and subregions within New Mexico, and this explains, in part, why Knopf—when first presented in the early forties with the idea for a book of several spine-chilling and bizarre New Mexico murders and thinking it too quaintly local—turned it down. But unlike *Albuquerque* it ranges far and wide across New Mexico and reads more like a series of detective or mystery tales than it does as a travel book, notwithstanding the amount of travel and interviewing Fergusson had to do in compiling her information.

She kept the idea for a book of murders in mind for some years before she followed through with her design and found a publisher. The entire project was closely linked to her respect for her father, H. B. Fergusson, and his livelihood as a frontier attorney and territorial politician. In an August 21, 1948, letter to Judge J. J. Willett in which she queried the Alabama heritage and ancestry of her grandfather, Sampson Noland Ferguson, Fergusson volunteered this summary of her motive and method in writing *Murder and Mystery:*

> I have just done nine murders; and I am sure that you, as an attorney, will admit without argument that such a chore might well absorb one's time. As a lawyer too you may be interested in what I have done. The book is promised for November 1, and I shall then take pleasure in sending you a copy. It is a collection of nine true tales out of New Mexico's history. I began gathering material twelve years ago and so got several interesting people who have since died. I interviewed all extant, except one or two of the plaintiffs who declined to see me. When there was a transcript of testimony I read that, as well as charges to the jury, and newspaper accounts. I had the whole checked by a lawyer with a fine sense of humor, and he tells me that he believes I can be kept out of jail.[27]

Fergusson explains further to Judge Willett that her father figures directly in the case of Colonel Albert J. Fountain in Lincoln County in the 1890s and indirectly in the instance of Colonel Ethan W. Eaton, who headed the vigilantes in the town of Socorro in the 1880s. The attorney who advised Fergusson on keeping out of jail herself was no doubt her personal attorney and family friend, William A. Keleher, who, in his review of the book, comments with tongue in cheek:

> To this date [Dec. 23, 1948], so far as reporters know, Erna Fergusson is still enjoying life, liberty and the pursuit of happiness guaranteed under the American form of government. But there is no telling when she may be sued for damages for alleged defamation of character; when a judge of a court of competent jurisdiction may cite her in on a bench warrant to show cause why she should not be placed in jail or when a deputy sheriff decorated with a big sombrero, a shiny badge, and a pearl-handled six-shooter, may not serve a warrant on her charging criminal libel.[28]

Keleher spends less time reviewing the book than he does relating anecdotes about H. B. Fergusson and some of the cases he prosecuted as district attorney, most notably the time he unsuccessfully prosecuted the celebrated Elfego Baca on first-degree murder charges. In any event, the book's and the author's ancestral link with H. B. Fergusson and the history of the Southwestern legal system is implicit.

Reviewers, although uniformly favorable, had some difficulty in actually labeling just what kind of book Fergusson had written—and called it reporting, history, and even, as in the instance of the *Saturday Review*'s "Guide to Detective Fiction," unadulterated "detective fiction."[29]

When soliciting responses from readers before she decided just where to try and place it—or whether to publish it privately as she had done with *Albuquerque*—Fergusson consulted Horgan again. He advised that she speak throughout with the objectivity and authority of the muse of history and that she rewrite any portions—small in number though they might be (he counted six places in what turned out to be the fourth chapter, "The Mystery of the White Sands," on Colonel Albert J. Fountain)—where she intruded as narrator: "Since you do not orient us at the outset . . . to expect you as interlocutrix, directly, you would do better, I think, to keep all the telling objective and impersonally impressive with the authority of Clio."[30]

More than all of her other New Mexico writings, and certainly more than is given any real credit outside of early reviews, *Murder and Mystery* confirms just how good Fergusson's Southwestern narrative history can be. In the 1990s her writing might also be called "new history" or "new journalism" or even "faction," and its narrative quality confirms just how authoritative and appealing a storyteller Fergusson's muse, Fergusson as Clio, really is. It is the kind of historical digging, reporting, and telling that recent commentators like James West Davidson and Mark Hamilton Lytle extol as both a scholarly and a "popular" ideal when they make this observation:

Undeniably, history would lose much of its claim to contemporary relevance without the methods and theories it has borrowed from anthropology, psychology, political science, economics, sociology, and other fields. Indeed, such theories make an important contribution. . . . Yet history is rooted in the narrative tradition. As much as it seeks to generalize from past events, as do the sciences, it also remains dedicated to capturing the uniqueness of a situation. When historians neglect the literary aspect of their discipline—when they forget that good history begins with a good story—they risk losing the wider audience that all great historians have addressed. They end up, sadly, talking to themselves.[31]

In *Murder and Mystery* Fergusson succeeded in combining fact with imaginative telling in a way that entertained and informed general readers and more analytical reviewers as well. She even succeeded in winning over Stanley Walker, who had nothing but praise for the book, controversial subject matter and Fergusson's at times "baroque" style notwithstanding. Writing again in the *New York Herald Tribune*'s books supplement, Walker calls Fergusson's book, "Good entertainment, absorbing mystery, and sound history, . . . [a] book [which] serves to bridge the gap between the wild old days of the vigilantes and modern times, when law and order are pretty much in the saddle in New Mexico."[32] Walker chose the story of Colonel Fountain and his son (chapter 4) and the story of Manuel B. Otero and his conflict with Joel P. Whitney over Estancia Valley land rights (chapter 2) as his favorite chapters, saying most of the other "tales" were "already pretty well known," but he gives the entire book high marks: "Here are nine neat tales, told with charm and simplicity by a lady who knows her New Mexico from way back. This is, moreover a handsome little volume, a distinctive contribution to regional literature."[33] Walker rightfully implies no real distinction among Fergusson's "tales," true stories," and "history"— for, indeed, this merging and alternating of story and history in the most readable of ways is the book's real accomplishment. And Horgan was effusive in his reaction to the manuscript when he first read it and told his friend of his enthusiasm:

I read them all, right straight through, thinking at first that I must do this in all fairness to my agreement. But after a few pages, I found myself reading for the sheer interest, readability and fascination of the pieces themselves. I devoured them. I learned infinitely more than I ever knew about the episodes in point. All the information is most interesting, and the telling fluent, skillful and persuasive—and that last point is important in any such highly controversial subject matter. As usual, you make the reader yours all the way.[34]

One of the few academically affiliated individuals who reviewed the book, Levette J. Davidson, of the University of Denver, also had high praise for Fergusson's ability to involve her reader in both "facts," and their "suspense," in matters of plot and story and arrangement as much as of data: "All of the stories hold the reader's interest, even better than do the ever-popular fictional 'who-done-its.' Here fact itself falls into patterns of suspense, and the assembled clues have a concreteness difficult to rival by invented circumstance. The characters, also, are more varied, colorful, and convincing than are the creations of even top level purveyors of today's crime and mystery best sellers."[35] Davidson also touted the book for its "regional quality": "Racial and physical backgrounds, common occupations, local customs, ethical and cultural standards, and characteristic ways of thinking and speaking permeate the stories."[36] In addition to praising readability and regionalism, Davidson also found an important aspect of the book to be "the artistry of the narrator." By narrator, of course, she meant Fergusson the author, who apparently had succeeded in distancing herself somehow from her teller.

In actuality, there is more of Fergusson—author and person—in her telling than either Horgan or a reviewer like Davidson would seem to allow. Among other reasons, this presence is due to Fergusson's subtle intrusion of some of her own family history into her stories/histories, as family biography coincided with the history of New Mexico.

Although he finds *Murder and Mystery* a more interesting book than its immediate predecessor and other Merle Armitage-illustrated book, *Albuquerque,* David Remley believes that Fergusson does not live up to the potential of the book, that although she raises some interesting questions about violence in New Mexico and the Southwest, "she misses an excellent opportunity to analyze 'violence' in the Southwest."[37] Remley is correct insofar as Fergusson does not offer any real answers to the "mysteries" she presents. In one sense, this is consistent with the dimension of mystery she is trying to establish.

Readers might also criticize her objectivity and tolerance: she argues for the relativity of right and wrong too strongly. Murder is not presented as an absolute evil, as an absolute wrong or crime. Her assumption is that not only do smaller circumstances color the right and wrong of an act of violence, the larger changing conditions of society and history affect such judgments also. Thus it can be asserted with counterforce that *Murder and Mystery* is a historian's look at not only the cruel and mysterious turns of human history but also at the ironies involved in the working out of history and the motivations and actions of mankind. If Fergusson's voice has in any way the authority of Clio's in this book, it is, tale after tale, narrative after narrative, with both a certain wisdom and resignation about the doings of the Southwest and "people" as "killers":

> Probably people are never so much themselves as when they are killing or being killed. Perhaps there is no better way to know a people than to understand why they kill. Not only the moment's hot compulsion but all the deep currents of thought and habit that made that killing at that time seem both right and necessary to the killer.
>
> This is most true in New Mexico where within the memory of living men and women killing has come all the way from a manly and needful act to an intolerable offense. Good men, in all eras, have regard for the general good; bad men consider only their own selfish ends. But what seems good in one period may seem evil in another. Standards change as surely as times change.[38]

Fergusson thus acknowledges civilization's need to abolish murder and violence, while at the same time conceding that the settlement of the frontier was also a necessarily violent era. What will the final judgment be of such ambivalence, and who will make it? If Clio does not make the final pronouncement, then perhaps a pronouncement will be made on Clio. Or so Fergusson suggests, for she does not presume to pass final judgment on the strivings, blind or directed, of the past.

She, however, did not intend to write a book, at least explicitly, about the mysteries of history and historiography. She sought to entertain her reader and to make a living as a popular writer. Her correspondence with Merle Armitage in particular reveals this. *Albuquerque* was intended as a book essentially for tourists. Travel, history, autobiography—all of these elements combined to make for successful sales. As she thought of ways to "pep up" her market when the "tourists start to run," she wrote to Armitage proposing a book which she initially called *New Mexico Murders* or, later, *New Mexico Killings:* ". . . I'd love to see another MAE [Merle Armitage Editions] book. It's too good a proposition to let die. A new book would help my lecture prospects. And I'm beginning to itch to do those *Killings.*"[39] One of Fergusson's lecture prospects had included, fittingly enough, a series of nine lectures on "how to write non-fiction," which she and Horgan discussed in specific, outlined detail as early as 1940.[40] In letter after letter to Armitage, she demonstrates that there is indeed much method behind both *Albuquerque* and *Murder and Mystery;* they are products of her interest not only in how to write nonfiction, but also in how to get it published and how to market it.

In April, 1948, Fergusson had six "tales," as she herself called them, ready to go (i.e., "The Killing of Manuel B.," "The Vigilantes of Socorro," "The Fountain Case," "A Navajo Killing," "The Manby Mystery in Taos," and "Gallup and the Communists"). In December of 1947 Horgan had encouraged her to add more chapters to her manuscript. She made the additions primarily on the basis of reaching the right number of words, the right length for reasons of cost, and added three more tales: "Billy the Scapegoat," a sympathetic account of Billy the Kid's role in the Lincoln County war; "How Black Jack Lost His Head," an account of the ghastly hanging of the train robber and bandit, Tom (Black Jack) Ketchum; and "Woo Dak San and the Bird," a blackly comic tale of the murder, in Silver City, of Chinese merchant Yee Fong and of the arrest, prosecution, and eventual pardon of Woo Dak San. Moreover, she revised the chapters, changed the titles, and decided to arrange them in chronological order, from the earliest in 1880 to the most contemporary in 1935. "The Vigilantes of Socorro," dealing with the murder of A. M. Conklin, editor of the *Socorro Sun*, by Antonio Baca and his two nephews, Onofre and Abrán, turned out to be chapter 1. "New Mexico Tries Its Own," dealing with the dispossession of Victor Campos and the murder of Sheriff M. R. Carmichael in Gallup, originally "Gallup and the Communists," concluded the book.

In all, Fergusson—with Clio at the wheel—takes the reader on a tour of more than a dozen New Mexico towns and villages in all quadrants of the state and cites countless historical records, including newspapers, memoirs, diaries, and interviews with participants. In addition, she generally shares with the reader her own family heritage, alluding to various pioneer families. Central to the overreaching motive of the book is her dedication of the volume to her father, one-time frontier attorney in White Oaks, New Mexico, and then lawyer in Albuquerque, as well as district attorney, Harvey Butler Fergusson, a man who "believed in law and order."

Her artistry as a storyteller and "detective" of historical fact is supplemented by photographs in the book of many of the parties involved in the murders, by silhouettes by Al Ewers at each chapter heading, and by a frontispiece by famous Southwestern artist and personal friend Peter Hurd. The amount of planning that went into the minutest detail, such as the frontispiece, is evidenced in Hurd's description, quoted by Fergusson, of his "gun in hand picture"—a Colt, long-barreled "Peacemaker" revolver, cocked and ready to fire: "Colt six shooter at full cock, carefully and yet boldly drawn. . . . I picture the hand holding the gun as emerging from a star-studded leather cuff of the type we remember as children. . . . Design as I picture it calls for a pale shell pink paper stock, a black master plate, then one additional painting of ultramarine blue ink."[41] The colors did not work out as Hurd had hoped, but the black-ink drawing on white stock, accented by the red lettering of Hurd's name, is essentially the same.

Fergusson estimated 240 typed pages of manuscript at 250 words per page, resulting in less than 100 printed pages. The manuscript ran to about 60,000 words and slightly under 200 typed pages, and in Armitage's design, the total number of printed pages ran to 192, plus 3 pages of photographs. *Albuquerque* sold about 2,500 copies in its first 9 months, and she requested that the first run of *Murder and Mystery* be that same number.[42] *Murder and Mystery* was ready for publication in the fall, November 5, of 1948. In October she was able to send an advance copy to Herbert Weinstock at Knopf's and began discussions for her next project, *New Mexico,* which she was able to finish and see published only three years later.[43]

Any of the nine narratives in *Murder and Mystery* show Fergusson at the height of her form as a popular historian. All of the tales reveal her knowledge about and fondness for New Mexico—its landscape, its cultures, its towns, its people, and its past, especially the past of her father, H. B. Fergusson, and the heritage he left her. Each tale can be read for any one of several ideas as well: for the mind and sensibility at work in retelling the notorious murder in question and its attendant mysteries, whether about human behavior or the vagaries of time and place; for the biographies of killer and killed; for the descriptions of setting and ambiance; for insight into the interrelationships, both cultural and racial, of Mexican American, Native American, Anglo-American, and, in one instance, Asian American; for the various profiles of Southwestern women as they confronted the issues and roles of gender during the late nineteenth and early twentieth centuries; for the horrors and imponderables about not only human violence and revenge, anger and fear, but about more noble emotions and traits, such as loyalty and courage, love and rescue; for a greater understanding of the workings of frontier and modern justice; for the ways in human nature and geography which both change and never change. And the list could continue, for the book is a treasure of fascinating subject matter and narrative technique, history and story, combined in the most satisfying of ways. Fergusson supplements her own inventions and arrangements with accounts from territorial newspapers such as the *Albuquerque Morning Journal* and the *Las Vegas Optic;* with the memoir of Sister Blandina Segale, *At the End of the Santa Fe Trail;* with reports and court records; and with verses from the ballads which were sung after Manuel B.'s death.

All of her (Fergusson's and Clio's) tellings, her "retellings" more accurately, bespeak her soul-felt feeling for New Mexico as a special phenomenon, a true land of mystery in and of itself. Two of the narratives touch more closely on her own life—her genealogy and family heritage. Those narratives are "The Ballad of Manuel B." and "The Mystery of the White Sands," chapters 2 and 4, respectively. The former tale takes place in the 1880s in the Estancia Valley east of Los Lunas, a small farming community about twenty miles south of Albuquerque, and the latter takes place in and around Las Cruces, New Mexico, some two hundred miles south of Albuquerque and near the Mexican border. Both locales were known to her family during territorial days since Louis and Carl, the two brothers of her maternal grandfather, Franz Huning, had settled in Los Lunas and had built up a mercantile business and sheep-ranching "empire" there at the turn of the century; and her father, H. B., had practiced law throughout the state. He enters the events in "The Mystery of the White Sands" as one of the defense attorneys, along with his colleague and friend, Albert B. Fall, later of the Teapot Dome scandal.

Other narratives, notably "Billy the Scapegoat" and its account of the Lincoln County war, also touch on her father's familiarity with the town and county of Lincoln, while one of the most horrifying and bizarre murder accounts, "The Manby Mystery," deals more directly with her own first-hand knowledge of Taos and northern New Mexico in the late 1920s and early 1930s. Although she understates her own links with the history she is retelling and, in the process of codifying, making it herself, or at least putting her stamp on it, her involvement with the living history of the past in the living present is implicit on every page.

In many ways "The Ballad of Manuel B." represents Fergusson's feel for folklore as history, for the historian as folklorist and oral historian. It is part of a larger tradition of the Mexican *corrido* so expertly expounded by Américo Paredes in *"With His Pistol in His Hand,"* the "ballad" of Gregorio Cortez.[44] As well as any of the other narratives in *Murder and Mystery*, this tale also demonstrates her assumptions about and knowledge of interracial and intercultural relationships between Anglo-Americans and Mexican Americans as they struggled for dominance, fought with each other, and made friendships in the days before statehood. Aside from what the narrative reveals about interracial hostility and violence, there is much background here concerning the knots and tangles of Spanish land grants and claims of ownership which extend well into the present-day conflicts and "history" of the state.

The Manuel B. of the title is Manuel B. Otero, son of Manuel Antonio Otero, one of Valencia County's earliest Hispanic settlers and *patróns*. The murder in the story involves the shooting of Manuel B. Otero by James Whitney, the brother of Boston millionaire Joel P. Whitney, in a dispute over the rightful ownership of the Otero ranch near Antelope Springs on the Estancia plains. But in the midst of telling of Otero's killing and the ballads which his people composed and sang about it, Fergusson works in much family and state history, shifting from drama and dialogue to description of people and place, to exposition and editorializing. As in all the narratives, she bends the boundaries of pure history and pure fiction, adapting techniques of each for something of an even more enlightening "truth."

In these narratives, as in her other writings, she begins dramatically by staging a scene. And the scene involves one of her own family, her aunt, Mrs. Louis Huning, of Los Lunas. Significantly, Fergusson does not identify Mrs. Huning explicitly as a relation; however, she does say that she learned much of this incident from hearing Mrs. Huning talk about the notorious murder of pioneer times. The interview provides an especially useful tool for Clio's tellings. Whatever the means which allowed her to do it, Fergusson, as narrator, places the reader in the middle of history, shows what it was like—what was said, what was sensed, felt, seen, smelled, heard—on the spot, *there*. Much Los Lunas history is revealed in the process.

As it happened, Mrs. Huning was on the fringe of events as they began to unfold in the summer of 1883. As Manuel B. was on his way to his ranch at Antelope Springs and to what would be his fateful shoot-out with Whitney, he stopped for a chat with Mrs. Huning. She was in front of a cabin in the Manzano Mountains east of Los Lunas with her children, whom she had taken there for a brief vacation. The scene is the stuff of fiction and drama: "Early on a hot August morning in 1883, Manuel B. Otero drew rein in front of a little cabin in the Manzano Mountains" (*MMNM*, 33). Through the eyes and memory of Mrs. Huning, the character of Otero is established, as is his civility and his claim to aristocracy. And from such refinement comes the mystery of a murder which, ironically, at least partially results from high principles of chivalry and honor, not to mention the obligations of ownership. In Mrs. Huning's memory—naive as to what catastrophic events would transpire, but keenly attuned to each detail in retrospect—Manuel B. was something of a knight of the plains. In effect, what Fergusson relates amounts to Mrs. Huning's own "ballad," in Anglo-European terms (she, like her husband, was an immigrant from Germany) rather than Mexican or Mexican American terms.

Here is some of that opening scene, that opening "balladry" which allows Fergusson to link implicitly and artfully the personages involved to the courtly and feudalistic traditions out of which so much Southwestern violence—gunfights and shoot-outs—evolved:

> She was fond of Manuel B., a handsome and charming young man; she loved to talk with him because he had studied at Heidelberg and could converse with her in her native tongue. The two families were closely linked because her three children were the age of Don Manuel's two; and his wife, the lovely Eloisa Luna, was a close friend. . . . Altogether, the joining of two of New Mexico's most prominent families had been like a picture of old Spanish court life.
>
> Don Manuel, standing now with hat in hand—for no gentleman would address a lady from his horse—gave Mrs. Huning news of Doña Eloisa, expecting her third child, and asked about her family. He did not mention the business which was taking him down to Antelope Springs. (*MMNM*, 34)

From such a courtly scene, Fergusson shifts to Manuel's journey, describing in vivid detail the Estancia plains which he crosses and filling in as he travels pertinent information about the history of the land in question—the Baca Grant—and the convolutions of ownership involving Spain, Mexico, the United States, and New Mexico. Showing turns to telling and then soon back to showing the murder, the players, and the protagonist/antagonist parts they played.

What Manuel sees (or what he must have seen in Fergusson's and Clio's conjecture) is narrative history at its best, fact blending with the imagination and mind's eye of the historian/narrator: "As he rode he could see the early mists lifting from the Manzano Range to the west. Eastward the mountains sloped steeply down to the long stretches of the Estancia plains where myriads of antelope fed. It was rich grazing, thick with nourishing grama grass and showing an occasional spring, marked by cottonwoods, like La Estancia and Antelope Springs five miles to the north" (*MMNM*, 34–35).

All is not, however, merely an imagistic projection or recreation of what a historical figure "saw." Fergusson also quotes from historical documents, not the least of which is the report of the alcalde, acting for the governor of New Mexico, in 1819, making the grant to Bartolomé Baca, while oblivious of the fact that the Republic of Mexico had been established eight years earlier in 1811. Building on this document, Fergusson, in patient detail, explains that Manuel A. Otero, father of Manuel B., purchased half of the Baca Grant before the U.S. occupied New Mexico in 1846 at the time of the Mexican War. His brother bought the other half for a combined holding of 1,232,000 acres. What the Oteros—father, uncle, son—did not realize is that Baca never perfected his claim and that the alcalde had made the grant in the name of the king of Spain after Mexico was a republic. This "fact" was complicated by another one: the Whitneys of Boston had a conflicting claim based on the Estancia Grant, 300,000 acres of land right out of the middle of the Baca Grant, this one made by the governor of New Mexico in 1845 to Antonio Sandoval. Governor Armijo was acting for the government of Mexico which then governed New Mexico as a province. Sandoval later deeded his land to his nephew, Gervacio Nolan, and Nolan's heirs sold to Joel P. Whitney. It was a legal question for three countries—and two cultures.

The confusion of the situation was compounded by a supreme irony. After the personal tragedies involved in the shoot-out, and subsequent charges and countercharges between the Oteros and the Whitneys, when the final disposition of the land grant case went before the Supreme Court of the United States in 1898, the decision was to find "both parties right as to the faultiness of the other's claim" (*MMNM*, 48). The land was declared public domain, and the whole valley opened to settlement—of bean farmers. Fergusson's final comment underscores her sense of the mysteries of history itself: "The irony of the tragedy was that though each man believed he was right, both were in fact wrong. It was all for nothing that two high-spirited and impetuous young men had shot each other in that blood-spattered room by the big Estancia Spring" (*MMNM*, 48).

Fergusson's description of the room and the blood-splattering is presented as the climactic point of the narrative—complete with dialogue before, during, and after the shooting. That confrontation is almost as chaotic as the legal issues involving the grant itself. All of the disputes surrounding the claim were in litigation in August of 1883 when Manuel B. met Mrs. Huning on his way to throw Whitney off what he considered his land. James Whitney had precipitated matters by attempting to secure judgment against one of the squatters on the grant, a man named McAffee, who decided to settle out of court and leave the valley. When Whitney tried the same tactics against Otero, the showdown resulted. In Fergusson's account: "Manuel B. was no small squatter to be removed with a word and a few dollars. To him, Whitney was the squatter who had moved in on land to which he had no right or title. Of a proud governing group, young Otero was fiery by nature, a fearless fighter, a good shot, and a man not at all averse to meeting his enemy face to face. So here he was, riding down the slope toward Estancia Springs" (*MMNM*, 37).

When Otero rode up to his ranch house at Estancia Springs, where Whitney, after leaving Antelope Springs, awaited him, and ordered him off the premises, Whitney pulled a gun and shot Otero in the neck—but not before Otero shot him, wounding him in the jaw and one hand. Whitney's brother-in-law, Alexander Fernández, was killed in the melee. And Dr. Henríquez, who was backing Otero, was wounded in one hand. Ten shots were fired all together, resulting in Whitney's surrender. Fergusson quotes one of the men who reached the ranch to attend the wounded and take Fernández's body back to town—all of which adds to the credibility of the description, though it too is clearly recreated in the author's dramatization. Manuel B. died on the way back to his home in Los Lunas.

Some of the ballads sung in tribute to Otero stress the sorrow of Doña Eloisa, and Fergusson reports that Casimiro Lujan, a famous minstrel of Torreón, was invited to Los Lunas to sing while the widow was still dressed in mourning. Lujan's ballad ran to eleven verses, with a long chorus repeated between each verse. Fergusson quotes some of the verses in both Spanish and English. Other ballads stress the hatred felt by many of the Mexican American friends of Otero for intruding foreigners, such as Whitney. The composition of *Plácido Romero of Peralta* is one such song. And she explains both the subject and motive behind some of the alterations in "fact" this way: "[Peralta's ballad] describes the killer as a coward, a Texas robber, and a murderer whom devils await in hell which is the place (*la estancia*) for him. The killer was well known to be a Bostonian; the poet used the word *Texan* epithetically, not geographically—for the worst you could call a man was a Texan" (*MMNM*, 43). But Fergusson balances the sense of hatred and hurt reflected in such ballads by quoting from Sister Blandina Segale's account of the killings and their aftermath. Sister Blandina was the director of Saint Vincent's Hospital in Santa Fe where Whitney was taken after the shooting. Sister Blandina resolved to visit Whitney, not as the gringo murderer her *familia* thought him to be but as a patient, saying, "I forgive you as I hope to be forgiven, I am Manuel Otero's sister" (*MMNM*, 44).

Fergusson is particularly adept at recording the tensions and intrigues of litigation. And most of the narratives in *Murder and Mystery* deal at one point or another with a trial and the drama of the courtroom. In the instance of Whitney, he was charged with the murder of Otero even while in his hospital bed. Because of their money and their shrewdness—"acumen" she calls it—the Whitneys were able to retain Colonel José Francisco Cháves of Peralta as their attorney. Since Cháves reputedly had the ear of Judge Axtell, who was to hear the case, a verdict of not guilty was more or less assured. Through the use of territorial news accounts, plus interviews—including one with John Taylor of Springer, in 1935, the only surviving juror—Fergusson recreates Whitney's trial, which was held on April 29, 1884, in Colfax County. When the verdict for not guilty came, as anticipated by most, the editor of the *Las Vegas Optic* wrote, "A man who kills another in New Mexico has a much better show than if he stole a cow" (*MMNM*, 48).

The "verdict" for the author of such narrative retellings does not really depend on whether Fergusson is better at showing or at telling, more adept at the techniques of fiction or history, drama or description. Rather, it depends on recognizing her ability to blend these techniques into a meaningful replication of what happened, what led to it, and what resulted. With the talents of an accomplished historian/detective (Clio as Columbo), Fergusson adeptly unfolds the many layers of mysteries, multifold as they are, which surround an era of transition from frontier justice to modern justice, the mysteries of this or that series of events in a place such as New Mexico, in the Southwest. Although Otero is something of her favorite, her "protagonist" (Fergusson relates the story from his vantage point), Whitney is also given fair treatment, reinforcing Fergusson's presence as a sort of Clio-like observer of and driver in the parade of history. If from time to time she sought to join the parade or even to lead it, Fergusson was always loyal to her own New Mexico muse, and the reader is all the more respectful of Clio's claim to authority because of it.

The disappearance of Colonel Albert J. Fountain and his nine-year-old son, Henry, in January, 1896, provides Fergusson with the subject matter for perhaps her best narrative history in *Murder and Mystery*—and the one most directly related to her father. Here she is able to combine her flair for travel narrative with historical research (and its various forms of "digging") and to top it off with consideration of a chapter from her own father's biography—and, by extension, a portion of her own Southwest as well. In Fountain's story—the mysterious disappearance of both Fountain and his son, the resultant accusations of foul play, the trial of rancher Oliver Lee and his defense by none other than Albert B. Fall, Harry Dougherty, and H. B. Fergusson—is found all the makings for prototypic Southwestern frontier history (legal, political, and social) and for "classic" Western melodrama as well. (For example, Pat Garrett makes a dramatic appearance as a detective). In "The Mystery of the White Sands," Fergusson's Clio and Calliope more than live up to the potential of both narrative forms.

She structures her recreation of persons, events, and places in basically three parts: Fountain's trip from his home in Las Cruces to court in Lincoln and his attempted return home, the search for Fountain and his son, and the investigation of the disappearance followed by the arraignments and trial. Each segment of the story/history matches the other in the laying out of careful detail and in the building of suspense. Certainly Fountain, his family and friends, Oliver Lee and his supporters, the prosecuting and defense attorneys, all of the individuals involved are made human and believable. Moreover, their relationships with each other and with their time and place—their society and their physical environment—are masterfully intermeshed.

In this narrative Fergusson again opens with domestic drama as Fountain prepares to leave on his business trip to Lincoln, over one hundred and fifty miles to the northeast. A description of his adobe home, its furnishings, and the mementos which adorn its walls establishes that Fountain is a prepossessing man with an illustrious past as a lawyer, a soldier, and an adventurer: "His legal diploma from Columbia University; the sword he carried as an officer in the California Column just after the Civil War; a hat from Panama, where he had shared in a revolution; fine blankets and beaten silver from Mexico; trophies from Apache fights; gifts from the Texas Rangers, and from the Masonic lodge he had founded in Las Cruces. In the parlour hung a painting of the Colonel in uniform, very military with keen blue eyes and flowing mustaches" (*MMNM*, 73–74). Mrs. Fountain, from Durango, Mexico, and married at the age of thirteen, is drawn as being apprehensive about the colonel's trip because of his many enemies and the nature of his business. His sons try to convince him not to go. And, as the chances and ironies of history will have it, little Henry persuades his father to take him along.

The immediacy of the moment of departure is recounted in the most convincing and credible detail and, not insignificantly, from the point of view of Mrs. Fountain as a frontier wife and woman: "The wife clung to her husband, weeping, and at the end she gave him a muffler of her own that he might at least be warm. She did not seem to have feared for her child. Maybe she hoped the boy would somehow be a protection to the man. She saw them drive away, and settled down in her big adobe house to wait, and to pray" (*MMNM*, 75). In this narrative and in such chapters as "Billy the Scapegoat," Fergusson uses such a female vantage point to great effect and seems capable of strong identification with pioneer women.

She identifies with Fountain's kind of man as well and no doubt saw her father in a similar light, strengthening the notion that this particular narrative, and for that matter the entire volume, is offered in tribute to him and those like him.

Even after Pat Garrett killed Billy the Kid, the struggle continued between men who preferred the old lawless ways and men who advocated the regular processes of the law. Cattlemen registered their brands and hired private detectives to pursue thieves and bring them to court. Rustling became a crime. The New Mexico Stock Association had become a power in politics, and Albert J. Fountain was its lawyer. He fought rustling in his paper as well as in the courts, demanding exposure of men in high office who connived at it. He named names and made himself a formidable collection of enemies. (*MMNM*, 75–76)

As the trial surrounding Fountain's and Henry's mysterious disappearance took shape, the adversarial lines took on the definitions of not just prosecution versus defense but Republican versus Democrat, respectively. And among the "fighting Democrats" were Albert B. Fall and his friend, H. B. Fergusson. Fall and Fergusson had first become friends in the mining town of White Oaks and shared a cabin together for a time—along with Western novelist Emerson Hough and William MacDonald, soon to be governor of New Mexico.[45] The successes of H. B. Fergusson were a continued source of pride for the entire Fergusson family and a part, naturally enough, of their identity as pioneer Southwesterners.

In her dedication and in "The Mystery of the White Sands," however, Fergusson makes no explicit mention of H. B. Fergusson being her father. She does quote what the *El Paso Herald* had to say about his courtroom style and eloquence in making his points of argument: "Mr. Fergusson's style commands attention. He talked straight to the jury as individuals, sometimes calling the men by name. He said that no evidence had been presented to prove that anybody had been killed or was dead. . . . He hinted at the use of bribery and ended that 'Colonel Fountain, who was the soul of honor, would not have lent himself to such methods as have been used to make a case against these two young men' [i.e., Oliver Lee and cowhand James Gilliland]" (*MMNM*, 92). Because of the blunders of the prosecution in losing key evidence and because of the abilities of the defense, Lee and Gilliland were found not guilty. The mysteries surrounding the case—including whether or not Fountain and his son were murdered— never were solved. Fergusson concludes her account of the case by reintroducing a continuing metaphor whereby she compares the shifting sands of time with the mysteries of the natural driftings of the inscrutable white sands of southeastern New Mexico (still mysterious, White Sands is now a national monument near Las Cruces and Alamogordo), and she makes a closing philosophical observation on behalf of herself as narrator and on behalf of Clio's "authority": "For years New Mexico was filled with rumors about Colonel Fountain and little Henry, with whisperings of people who knew just what had happened. But most of these eager wiseacres are now dead, as are all the principal actors in that stirring drama. Only the mountains and the great empty basin of the San Augustín Plains remain as they were. They and the shifting heavy waves of the White Sands keep their secret well" (*MMNM*, 93). It is prohibitive to analyze all of the histories in *Murder and Mystery* here. They are all so richly textured with their own intrigues of narrative form and historical process that their own mysteries are almost endless for general and more critically minded readers alike. For whatever reasons, whatever the combinations of forces and circumstances, Fergusson hit her stride as a writer in *Murder and Mystery*. Not only Clio's authority but Clio's blessing was with her.

The consensus of sales, if not critical opinion, might well see Fergusson's next book, *New Mexico: A Pageant of Three Peoples* as her best Southwestern writing. In actuality, however, that book, good as it is—as history, travel, and the advocacy of intercultural and interracial understanding—exists in the glow of the more tantalizing narrative talent of *Murder and Mystery in New Mexico* and of *Our Southwest* and their spellbinding records of Clio "at the wheel."

Chapter 4

· ·

Advocacy:
Pageantry and Prejudice

I think it is very important to show a lot of people
what we have done and are doing to helpless people
and how we might mend our ways and our manners.
—Erna Fergusson to Oliver La Farge, June 22, 1938

I find that one good way to work against prejudice is to show
how little reason there is for it.
—Erna Fergusson to Carey McWilliams, January 10, 1940

Although *Murder and Mystery in New Mexico* enjoyed some vigorous sales for a brief time, it was not a best-seller with the tourist crowd in New Mexico and soon receded into the relatively diminished popularity of a library book on the Southwest. As years passed, it was eclipsed in the Fergusson canon by *Dancing Gods, Our Southwest,* and *New Mexico: A Pageant of Three Peoples.* Ironically, the best-seller of all her books thus far was her *Mexican Cookbook* (1934)—a "little item," as Fergusson referred to it, which brought in five hundred dollars a year.

She still had more books left to write after *Murder and Mystery.* It remains, however, an undisputable, albeit neglected, major work. The books which followed it, namely, *New Mexico* (1951) and *Mexico Revisited* (1955) generally gained wider and, as it turned out, more lasting attention. Both books, as admirable as they are (especially when considering the trying physical and emotional conditions under which they were written), are essentially reworkings of previous books. Especially in *New Mexico*, Fergusson took yet another opportunity to speak out on behalf of American Indians. The Apaches of New Mexico thought Fergusson presumptuous to set herself up as their advocate and complained about her portrayal of them in *New Mexico*. Viewed against the values and assumptions of later less paternalistic attitudes and sensibilities, Fergusson did not do the Apaches as much justice as she intended. It is precisely this kind of controversy which lends added interest not only to *New Mexico* but also to Fergusson's earlier essays in which she takes up the cause as a proponent for fairness and equality in intercultural and interracial relations.

NEW MEXICO ADVOCACY

Fergusson was first contacted, as early as December, 1947, by Herbert Weinstock, an editor for Alfred A. Knopf, about the possibility of writing a "regional book covering all aspects of New Mexico."[1] Thus began one of the more troublesome times in Fergusson's long experience dealing with publishers, and especially with Weinstock. *New Mexico* would come into being, but it would cost her some personal agony—in the writing process, for her mother was aged and ailing, and in strained relations with Weinstock about just what kind of book he had in mind and what kind of book she wanted to write about the Southwest. Weinstock, an author in his own right of books on Frédéric Chopin and others, had in mind a book for Fergusson along the lines of *Pine, Stream, and Prairie* and *Call It North Country*, two books of the time which dealt, respectively, with Minnesota and Wisconsin, and with the northern peninsula of Michigan. In making his pitch to Fergusson for the comprehensive regional book he envisioned, Weinstock saw considerable sales potential. He wrote, "I believe that a book surveying the entire state, covering history, topography, Indians, Spanish background, industries, politics, the arts, prominent individuals, towns, and what you will, might have a very promising sale."[2] Weinstock was aware that much of this material was covered by Fergusson in *Our Southwest,* but not in quite the way he had in mind—not exclusively focused on New Mexico. In large measure, as Fergusson took hold of the idea, reworking some earlier pieces and introducing new ones, the difference became one of speaking out for American Indian rights, while still touching on the other areas Weinstock had in mind.

She realized from the first that it would be hard to write anything new about the Southwest, and her mother's ailing condition was not conducive to inspired writing. But she was interested and agreed to look at the model books Weinstock had in mind and think through her possible approach:

I am so involved in domestic affairs and in being ready to do what Mother needs when she needs it that it is difficult to see how I could sign a contract to deliver a book on a certain date. Still I am interested and would like to see the two volumes you mention. Just now we are planning a slow southern-route trip to California in February, and I certainly could not make any definite plans before that.

I do not really take fire from the idea you outline. Perhaps I shall see how the formula could be applied to New Mexico, but so much you mention was covered in *Our Southwest* that it does not strike me as anything fresh; at least a fresh way to handle it does not occur to me yet. I'd like to consider it after I see the other books.[3]

Rather than write so comprehensively about New Mexico in the format of other books about states, such as the ones Weinstock liked on the north-central U.S., Fergusson proposed to him that she write a book on Navajo trading posts instead. If not that topic, she expressed great interest in doing a book on Spanish contributions to American culture in the Southwest. Even in this early stage of query and rough prospectus, she took the opportunity to express her progressive position:

This appeals to me as a way to take the emphasis off my neighbors as inferior, put-upon, and discriminated against and to show that they have widely and deeply influenced the best Southwestern culture which has extended far beyond our borders.

Both these books are along my alley, I could find material for both without going too far afield, and they both strike me as offering a chance to write both informatively and with some humor and much personality.[4]

Clearly her desire, which would be transferred to *New Mexico* as it took shape, was to involve herself even further than she had done previously in the cause of intercultural relations in the Southwest just as she had in Latin America. Her father's progressivism and democratic allegiance had not only endured but also deepened in her later phase. Her method of operation had long been to write informatively and with humor and personality—whether as a traveler or a historian. Advocacy was no new motivation either. She had merely added a degree or two of stronger emphasis and urgency.

She was at work on *Murder and Mystery* at this time, and that was her priority—readying it for what she planned to be a November, 1948, publication. But all through the summer and early fall, in the back of her mind she was planning how to take on the giant task which Weinstock had suggested. Before she saw the project through to completion she would experience the anguish of her mother's death in the fall of 1950, her own painful problems with an arthritic hip, and a protracted disagreement with Weinstock over the issue of whether only map drawings and not photographs would be sufficient as illustrations.

By the time she saw *Murder and Mystery* through to publication she was ready, in January, 1949, to commit her energies to a new book on New Mexico. First, she and her mother would spend the month of February in Berkeley, visiting family—Lina and Harvey—and return to Albuquerque in mid-March, "ready for intensive work."[5] The trip to California would allow her some opportunities "to get in some interviews on the way," and she believed that an essay, "The New New Mexican," she was then working on for the winter, 1949, issue of *New Mexico Quarterly* could well be worked into a chapter for the projected New Mexico book. That essay, it is significant to mention, had already seen publication once in its earliest form in *Century Magazine* twenty years before as "New Mexico's Mexicans." Even then she represented a more indigenous perspective on New Mexico than would Carey McWilliams, and her role as advocate shines through in her account of what held her interest in the late 1940s: "This is a study of the new generation of Spanish heritage that is just now getting out of the University and into business, the professions, and social life without any of the old language and culture handicaps. I am sure again from Carey McWilliams' latest [*North to Mexico*] that most observers have missed the point in New Mexico and I am eager to get my theories into print."[6]

McWilliams's publisher, J. B. Lippincott, asked Fergusson to comment on *North to Mexico,* and she took issue with many of McWilliams's comments about Hispanics in the Southwest—particularly New Mexico. Moreover, she made her views in opposition to McWilliams the basis for many of her points of argument in *New Mexico.* On January 10, 1949, she wrote a heated four-page private letter to McWilliams in which she outlined in four major points, as well as in miscellaneous observations, her disagreements: (1) "The 'people who were here first' have suffered more in New Mexico from the language handicap and its manifold consequences than from any 'racial discrimination.'" (2) "As in all societies queerness is a bar—of language, custom, religion, looks. The great failure—and you seem to me not to perceive its importance—was that the United States did not teach English to the new citizens in 1846 and thereafter. Only recently do enough Hispanos speak colloquial English *without accent* to erase that stigma of queerness. . . . As fast as any Hispano family can it forgets its less lucky neighbors and family and rushes into the Anglo group." (3) "These are the peculiarities of New Mexico—especially in regard to 'those who got here first.' Naturally I am not talking about immigrant and migrant groups." (4) "The glory of New Mexico—as I see it—is in its young people of Spanish heritage who are now forging ahead and developing a new middle class on the approved US model."[7] These concerns and the assumptions behind them carry through in varying degrees in all her writing on Hispanics and Americanization.

Our Southwest had been structured around just the kind of travel she was undertaking again on her way across the Southwest to and from California. The new book would somehow take into account the tremendous changes history was working in the region—changes she had witnessed herself:

> There is, I think, much to be done in the changes brought by developing industries, by population changes due to incoming government scientists and other folk, and by radical changes in all sorts of Indians. As all these modern conditions are significant only against the background of old cultures and customs and against the climate and landscape I believe that it will be easy enough to get the whole picture drawn to scale. But this approach—it seems to me—will save my book from seeming to be a mere repetition of many former ones.[8]

Weinstock pressured Fergusson for a completion period of one year; she held out for "a year and three months," insisting that she had to protect herself—in time and money—against the chance of her mother's condition worsening: "Here again I have asked for insurance in case I get caught and have to employ nurses or pay hospital bills in order to keep working."[9] But even while negotiating a contract she indicated to Weinstock that her mind was "beginning to click" and that she had two more ideas for inclusion in the book: one idea was how modern business and industrial methods operated on an old Spanish grant, such as Tom Campbell's La Jolla Grant Ranch—"a big stretch of country including lots of New Mexico, lots of history, and a modern picture too"; the other idea was how the newly established Los Alamos atomic scientists and other companion Anglo civilians upset the political system of Sandoval County as run by the Montoya family. When the Montoya machine refused the vote to the Los Alamos residents, they in turn threatened to petition Texas for annexation.[10]

At the time she and Weinstock reached agreement on the contract, Fergusson was sixty-one and her mother was eighty-three. Stamina, time, and luck were all factors. The delivery date was first set for January 1, 1949, then changed to allow her the time she needed—until July 1, 1950, and then extended finally to March 1, 1951. The manuscript would be no longer than 125,000 words (a length that would cause her to do considerable cutting). The book would sell for between $3.00 and $7.50; royalties would be no less than 17 ½ percent and no more than 21 percent; and she would receive an advance of $2,000—$1,000 on signing and $1,000 on demand, with the condition that "any part of the second $1,000.00 unearned one year after publication . . . may be charged against E. F.'s general account."[11]

By the end of April, 1949, Weinstock and Knopf had read Fergusson's full outline for *New Mexico* in addition to her *New Mexico Quarterly* piece on "The New New Mexicans," and they liked what they read.[12] She explained to Weinstock that her idea, perhaps not as obvious in the outline as she intended, was "to make this a picture of the state as it is," admitting that she included "all this historical stuff" because she understood from Weinstock's letters that he "thought I must cover the entire field again"; however, all of the historical "stuff" was intended as incidental to an understanding of present-day New Mexico: ". . . as I think it out I find myself using Sandia Man and Folsom Man and the land they knew to explain certain geographical and climatic factors of today."[13] History, travel, and advocacy were indeed a part of her scheme, but her main concern was to explore present-day situations and issues.

Weinstock suggested that she rewrite her "New New Mexican" essay to avoid "fictionalizing." Their exchange over this matter, compounded by bickering over whether to use maps and photos or just maps, eventually led to Fergusson's requesting directly to Knopf that she never have to work with Weinstock again and that she be assigned another editor for *Mexico Revisited*, her last published book. What Weinstock meant by "fictionalizing" was not what she meant by it. And the whole matter underscores just how much of a "new journalist," she was for her time. Although not a pure fictionist, she was as much interested in personal anecdote and narration as in purely objective exposition. In her response to Weinstock's request, she replied, in part:

> I shall, of course, rewrite my chapter on the New New Mexican, but I believe that quoting individuals and citing individual experiences is not fictionalizing. Every person I mentioned is an actual person whom I interviewed; I have made up nothing. In fact, what I find out about people is so much more dramatic than anything I could invent that fiction has few charms for me. Now maybe I can make this somehow clear to the reader. But it seems to me to add force and validity if I say, "I knew a young man who did so and so and who said so and so" rather than to run on in general terms as though I could not document my statements.[14]

Weinstock replied that he did not mean to imply that she was "making things up," that when he complained of her "fictionalizing" he simply objected to her method of speaking about one of the families in the essay.[15] The whole squabble is indicative of what Fergusson came to understand as the differences in sensibility and background between her as a Southwesterner and Weinstock as an Easterner. It also demonstrates in explicit terms how she utilized various narrative techniques more common to fiction and the personal essay and shows how she was a proponent of new forms of creative nonfiction and of expanding stodgy boundaries of exposition and argumentation.

By June, 1950, she had finished her last long trip and series of interviews. She had all of her material and was ready to write, rewrite, and condense. She told Weinstock: "My material is practically all in hand, though new and fascinating data and new slants on old data are forever coming up. My big job now is rewriting and so condensing my manuscript that it will come within the number of words allowed."[16] Her plan was still to emphasize contemporary New Mexico and present the issues and data needed for a newcomer to understand what was happening: "My first idea—to present the various peoples of the modern state with enough background to explain them and to account for their effect on each other—seems to hold as I work along. My selection of material is based on what the intelligent visitor should know to understand what he sees and to explain the curious social conflicts he is sure to meet."[17] So tourism was still part of her way of seeing things, providing the same audience that it had in her life as a guide for her Koshare Tours and Fred Harvey's Detours, and for her books. Moreover, history was still essential to what New Mexico and the Southwest meant to her—as was landscape, geography, and geology. But the main idea, as she phrased it, was to stress the "curious social conflicts" at work in the state and, as is explicit in the book itself, argue her own point of view. And thereby she would sway an "intelligent visitor" toward acceptance of the diversity of cultures and peoples found, rather than to discriminate against them—to help "mend our ways and manners" toward "helpless people," as she had mentioned in correspondence with Oliver La Farge in 1938. Needless to say, most of those "intelligent" visitors were assumed to be Anglo-American. And this is perhaps as indicative of the history of tourism as well as of book buying at the time, as it is of Fergusson's ethnocentrism. Or, to state it differently, she was part of a larger, dominant, white ethnocentrism. Furthermore, she felt obliged to straighten out misinformed non-New Mexican authors like Carey McWilliams. In this regard, as in her dealings with Weinstock, there was, ironically, no small degree of nativism in Fergusson's motivation.

Although she dealt most directly with Weinstock on *New Mexico*, she did consult with Knopf too. At midsummer and well into the writing of *New Mexico*, she shared with him some of her reservations about the nature of the project she had undertaken as well as some of her resolve—if not enthusiasm—to bring it off: ". . . I am, at the moment, in a state of dismay at what I have undertaken. This state is so rich in everything human, scenic, and potential that at this moment it seems to me quite impossible to get it down in less than an encyclopedia. But maybe I can. Anyhow I am having fun seeking out the less-known places and trying to manage a book that will not be a rehash of what has been done."[18]

In general she found Weinstock to be too much of the "city man" who, in what she considered high-handed editorial decisions, demonstrated, ignorance," as she phrased it, "not only of my part of the country, but of frontier life in general, and of Indians."[19] Fergusson had worked with Weinstock on earlier projects, including *Our Southwest* and her aborted "novel," *Malinche*, which she was outlining in 1946 and had considered doing for quite some time. But after *New Mexico* she was adamant in her insistence to Knopf that she not work with Weinstock again. Their dispute climaxed over crucial maps which she could afford to have drawn by a local cartographer, Lee Truitt, who worked for the Soil Conservation Service. She intended to use only Truitt's maps, but Weinstock insisted that the maps be supplemented with color photographs. Throughout September and October of 1950 heated letters were exchanged between Weinstock and Fergusson, resulting in something of a feud. In fact, she felt all of her wishes about maps rather than photographs were disregarded, and she appealed to Knopf when he returned from a trip abroad. When Truitt submitted his drawings Weinstock found them commonplace, and the disagreement was agitated. Knopf later agreed to her wishes while still trying to be fair with Weinstock. He told Fergusson, "It is quite clear that you realize that I will naturally expect Herbert [Weinstock] to help in any way possible with anything we ever publish on Central or Latin America, but he will not be your editor and you will not have to be in communication with him at any time."[20] Knopf explained to her with some firmness that it was he who insisted on further work being done on *New Mexico* after Weinstock passed on it but never insisted on any changes in meaning or anything which would result in self-contradiction.

Fergusson's brother Harvey advised her not to overreact by trying to change publishers:

> I must say also I don't think your feud with Herbie is any adequate
> reason for making a change. You can't have to submit to his demands

and Alfred will doubtless let you work with . . . someone else if you ask. They are all eager to keep authors happy if possible.[21]

. . . If I were you I would do absolutely nothing about Herbie until you have finished a new book, which may be two or three years hence. By that time he may be dead or canned. If he is not, you can ask Knopf to let you work with someone else and I have no doubt he will agree. Author's bellyache is the worst endemic affliction of the publishing business and they are all eager to alleviate it.[22]

The exchange of letters between Knopf and Erna Fergusson which offered the accommodations Harvey Fergusson knew would be forthcoming took place in 1952, a year after the publication of *New Mexico* and after Weinstock had written an apology to her on August 9, 1951. In that most personal and gracious letter, Weinstock wrote: "I am extremely sorry that I was brusque and mandatory about the final map questions. I was harassed and driven. What I had been told firmly was a deadline was at hand. I lost my temper—not at you, but at the crowded shortness of time."[23] In her response four days later she accepted the apology, indicating to Weinstock that she still considered him her friend but that she would never work with him again as her editor and would tell Knopf of her decision.[24]

Five years later, in 1956, Fergusson and Weinstock were corresponding again about her writing—this time her projected biography, *The Tingleys of New Mexico*—and had reconciled past differences of the maps and other matters which so upset her in the preparation of *New Mexico*. She was struggling with the pain of her hip operations, and her convalescence was slow. By that time *Mexico Revisited* was in its second printing, and the photographs and a sketch for the disputed maps for *New Mexico* were found during the cleaning of the bins in Knopf's production office. Weinstock offered them to Fergusson. Whether she accepted them or not is not known. Weinstock's offer, however, marked the end of a particularly trying time for her in the publication history of her books.

Weinstock courteously expressed continued interest in seeing her book on Tingley even though he agreed from the time she first told him of her work on such a subject that university press publication might well be more appropriate. Throughout this sequence of letters is the theme that Fergusson was attracted to Tingley as a Southwestern politician for the general reason that he too was an advocate—for Albuquerque, as its mayor, and for New Mexico, as its governor. Linking the success of her recovery from hip surgery to her ability to get back to work on the Tingley book, she informed Weinstock that she had not yet mentioned the project to Knopf, convinced that to the Eastern publishing establishment "New Mexico rates as a literary field—folklore or nothing!" However, she was committed to finishing her manuscript on Tingley, already far along when interrupted by surgery: "The character is very interesting to me as a rough, almost illiterate but very bright man who became mayor of Albuquerque and governor of the state and such a good friend of FDR that he is said to have got more WPA money per capita for New Mexico than any other state got."[25]

Three years later, in 1958, she had yet to finish the Tingley book, but her letters to Knopf and Weinstock indicate that she hoped for their continued support and encouragement. They sensed that she needed hope and expectation of future writing prospects to hasten her recovery. A new printing of *New Mexico* in 1959 and yet another in 1964 (the year of her death) did more for her spirits than did work on the Tingley book, which never saw publication. During the early 1960s, while Weinstock was doing some of his own writing and not employed by Knopf, Angus Cameron, another editor at Knopf's, contacted Fergusson about reprinting *New Mexico*. With some help from Robert Feynn and Roland Dickey at the University of New Mexico, she completed the necessary revisions by December, 1962.

Thus, for roughly the last dozen years of her life, Fergusson was occupied by the rewards and the disappointments associated with the writing, editing, and marketing of *New Mexico*. As a final chapter in her own biography, and in the ensuing years which have determined Southwestern literary history, the tenacity and resolve associated with the book and its making contribute poignantly and triumphantly to the overall "pageantry" made explicit in the subtitle and structure of her last published Southwestern writing. *New Mexico* subsumed, in ways too involved to trace completely here, the pageant of her own life and times as Beautiful Swift Fox, the motoring Clio of early twentieth-century Southwestern letters.

NEW MEXICO PAGEANT

In addition to presenting herself as an artist/discoverer whose conception of Southwestern history owed much to her pioneer heritage, Fergusson felt an obligation, deriving from her Anglo pioneer genealogy, to accept and promote American Indian and Hispanic cultures. These cultures which had historically preceded her own roots now in her own time were not given their due credit and respect. It is no surprise then that she dedicates *Our Southwest* to her mother, Clara Huning Fergusson, "daughter of pioneers and a real Southwesterner," and that she dedicates *Murder and Mystery in New Mexico* to the memory of her father, "Harvey Butler Fergusson who believed in law and order." The various phases of conquest and settlement of Native American, Spanish, Mexican, and finally Anglo-American provide the historical basis for the "pageant of the three peoples"—in her terms, "Indian, Spanish, and Gringo"—which gives structure to *New Mexico*. But her controlling assumption is that all three peoples can and must live in harmony with each other. It is this controlling assumption which gives the book its dialectical edge, creates the tension of ideas, and informs her conception of the Southwest.

In terms of the considerations of travel literature as genre, discussed earlier, *New Mexico* is Fergusson's least traditional account of a trip (or trips), although she did travel once again many of the same routes she did in *Our Southwest* and, to a lesser extent, in *Dancing Gods, Albuquerque,* and *Murder and Mystery in New Mexico*. Certainly the reader of *New Mexico* is taken on a panoramic tour of three centuries of the state's history—and, by extension, of the history of the Southwest as it converges with the history of New Mexico. But as Fergusson indicated in her correspondence with Herbert Weinstock and Alfred Knopf, her intention was to present history as a means of understanding New Mexico "now" and to present also the complex cultural and social issues which faced her contemporary Southwest in the twentieth century—a century complicated by nuclear energy and all kinds of new, awesome technologies. In New Mexico, as perhaps nowhere else in the world, prehistoric Indian dwellings in Frijoles Canyon existed virtually side by side with Los Alamos, where the atomic bomb was developed, and just a hundred or so miles from another "atomic" city, Albuquerque, where assemblies and shipments of nuclear armaments were carried out. Trinity Site, near Alamogordo, and White Sands, where atomic testing took place, added to the strangeness of such a spectacular triad.

The bafflement and wonderment Fergusson always felt when contemplating the Southwest were influenced by such unsettling social, political, and technological changes, both in the rate of changes and in the very nature of the changes brought about by World War II. She still attempts to intrude on her subject, to present herself as a part of it, and yet there is the distinct sense in *New Mexico* that time is passing her by, passing by her generation of Southwestern pioneers and nodding to another. She still has recourse to her characteristic narrative and structural devices—that is, the firsthand, on-the-spot interview with American Indians, Hispanic, and Anglo sources (either dramatically told in the present or remembered); the abstracting of this or that assertion or thesis from secondary expert or otherwise scholarly, historical, and authoritative sources; the journey by automobile on highways and back roads across sublime and exotic distances into the strangeness of "Indian" and "Mexican" locales, and away from them, back to the comfortable, dominantly Anglo urban areas from which such journeys into exoticism began; and the posing of tourist versus indigenous and, at times, ethnocentric and nativistic attitudes.

All of these narrative "techniques" and interests, developed over thirty years of traveling and writing, are still present in *New Mexico*. However, what takes precedence, in both political and human terms, is her foregrounding of the "problems" of intercultural and interracial living. First-person narration is more or less nonexistent. Thus, the total speaker-audience relationship is considerably less personal than in *Our Southwest, Dancing Gods,* or *Albuquerque.* In this respect, *New Mexico* is closer to the "authority of Clio" as adopted in *Murder and Mystery.*

One might readily conclude that Fergusson grew more philosophical and thus more omniscient in her later books when, among other things, increasing age and painful bone surgery cut down on the feasibility of extensive travel. What trips and interviews she did engage in now merged with past trips and experiences. Whatever the reason, *New Mexico* reads more like philosophy than her earlier books—not that a philosophical element is not present in all of them. Even so, she still includes enough descriptive and dramatic "showing" to mark her final say about the Southwest as distinctively her own blend of history and story, exposition and argument.

She begins her story/history/pageant of *New Mexico* with imaginative speculation about the view that Sandia Man and Folsom Man (early hunters from the Clovis and Folsom periods and traced by archaeologists through kill sites, dart points, and other artifacts) might have had of New Mexico some ten thousand to twelve thousand years ago (an unverifiable speculation and, thus, essentially fictionalizing). And after taking the reader on a chronological, historical trip from New Mexico's cave-dweller past, the past of cliff dwellers, to its atomic bomb–present of Los Alamos, she merges her own perceptions as author/narrator with the enchantments of time travels in the past. She uses an elevated, omniscient, narrative vantage point, akin to that employed in *Our Southwest* and in *Albuquerque,* which follows quite naturally from the topography she is describing—the topography of heights and distances, time and space. Like the numerous travelers and discoverers before her, she ends her backward glance at New Mexico, seen through her "book," with these words—words that again have a familiar, transcendental "New Mexico baroque" ring about them: "Those who will find something for them in New Mexico come soon to a promontory on which to stop and breathe deeply. They look far across immense, silent emptiness, shadowed by dark rocks or river courses marked by trees, and their eyes rise to mountains massed against the overpowering sky. Looking, they feel the long, thin procession of human beings which has moved slowly across this land, working and worshipping, and in passing leaving many traces of the ways they found."[26] Such is the "pageantry" which provides the controlling image of the book. This expansive, bemused ending shows little direct, surface presence of the author. But, by implication, she is both one who, like Oñate, Franz Huning, and countless others, "passed by here" and one who, objectified, finds something in New Mexico to stare at, to wonder about—just as so many American writers before her (Crèvecoeur, Cooper, Irving, Emerson, Thoreau, Hawthorne, Whitman, Adams, Parkman, Twain, Garland, Crane, Fitzgerald, Faulkner, D. H. Lawrence, William Carlos Williams, Stegner, Horgan, Momaday, Anaya, Doig, Lopez, McPhee, Zwinger, Terry Tempest Williams, and countless others of diverse ethnicity and gender) have sensed in their engagement with the American landscape and particularly American regionalism and the American West. She is the observer and the observed, one who, among many, has felt the startling dimensions of the journeys of cultures, societies, individuals across the land, felt the epiphany of landscape, the spirit of place. Assuredly, Fergusson expresses, as travel theorists suggest, her outright compulsion to describe her own individual journey as being embedded in the larger journeys of lives and landscapes and her inadequacy as one mere traveler to assay (and essay) it.

In *New Mexico*, as in her earlier Southwestern writings, such metaphysical, lyrical, musing passages are found in beautiful relief to more mundane prose. They are evidence of certain epiphanic realizations by an author who is accustomed also to deal in catalogues, lists, definitions, and directions—someone caught up in ordinary, down-to-earth matters and obliged to offer pragmatic and socially scientific explanations, obliged to offer "arguments" which will help diverse peoples adjust and orchestrate the pageant into a harmonious blend of diversity.

Fergusson's lyricism and her redirecting, if not softening, of the male "dominant gaze" does not deny or undercut her advocacy; rather it is a part of it—something of the spirit to motivate the flesh. Her rhythmic juxtapositions of historical/cultural concerns are part of both Fergusson's artistry and her advocacy of New Mexico and the Southwest, her attempt to express the ordinary and the extraordinary aspects of her subject. As a modern "new" woman and budding "new" journalist, Fergusson gives the reader the feeling that she is wholly justified to wax lyrical about the places and persons, the pageantry she describes and contemplates, sees and imagines—especially since she knows her subject in everyday terms as well.

She is capable of the run-of-the mill, the routine classifications, processes, and comparisons/contrasts—similar to those theorized by Wayne Franklin earlier—involved in the journeys of humanity through that time and space called "West." And this capability becomes even more obvious in a book like *New Mexico* which, in addition to mundane-seeming lists of books consulted and personages interviewed and cited, also offers an appendix of books recommended and American Indian and Spanish/Mexican words defined in the text proper and in a glossary of foreign words. Moreover, Fergusson's scheme for rendering the successive racial and cultural conquests of New Mexico and their resulting interrelationships and laminations (e.g., Indian, Spanish, and gringo) is, on the surface of things, too simple, too reductive. As if such gigantic forces as rivers and mountains, exploration, settlement, wars, and governments—all that is suggested by the word "pageant" (still, seemingly, a rather too genteel word)—could be confined to categories, to colloquial and loaded words like "gringo."[27]

Were it not for her juxtapositioning of prosaic and lyrical styles, her travel, history, and advocacy would be considerably trivialized, one-dimensional, flat. Taken all in all, however, what Fergusson attempts to impress upon her reader goes much beyond surfaces, beyond cataloging, beyond a mere tourist's superficial acquaintance with a place only visited. She does not suffer fools gladly and has little patience with unmindful, uncaring tourism: "In winter, as always, most travelers drive quickly through New Mexico. The roads are black and smooth; they lead to places beyond. Such travelers see only a treeless land with funny flat-topped houses, and they hurry eagerly on to something more familiar"(*NM*, 394). These are the very kinds of individuals who need persuading that something of greater significance is facing them—something of considerably more pageantry.

In her chapters on "Artist Discoverers" and "Land of Enchantment," which conclude *New Mexico*, Fergusson dramatizes herself as a pioneer New Mexican who, almost in spite of herself, identifies with "Gringo" settlers, especially artists like Witter Bynner who chose not only to accept New Mexico's diverse cultures but also to identify particularly with the state's Native Americans. Fergusson clearly is proud of her affiliation with the painters and writers who banded together in political action groups of the day as part of the Santa Fe Association on Indian Affairs, an organization formed to lobby Washington in order to defeat the perceived injustices of the Bursum Bill.

New Mexico thus becomes the platform from which she can again speak out on what she believes to be the inherent rights of Native Americans. Not only was she a supporter in the campaign to defeat the Bursum

Bill at the time of its proposing, including writing essays of explanation in the 1930s, she continued the campaign supporting Indian rights into the 1940s and 1950s. *New Mexico* allowed her yet another opportunity to spread the word, in part by incorporating some of her earlier essays into this later book, almost by way of revisiting those younger, activist years, as well as by carrying on the democratic allegiances and traditions of her politician father, H. B. Fergusson.

In her acknowledgments which preface *New Mexico*, Fergusson lists four journals which ran essays now reworked and included in the book: *Americas, New Mexico Quarterly, Think,* and *American Indian* (*NM,* xxiv). In addition to "The New New Mexican," which appeared in *New Mexico Quarterly* in 1949, she also presumably reworked from that journal the following essays for incorporation in *New Mexico:* "Navajos: Whose Problem?" (1948), "John Collier in New Mexico" (1936), and "The Coronado Cuarto Centennial" (1940). The *Think* essay is entitled "New Mexico—State of Many Ages," published in 1950 during the time she was preparing *New Mexico;* "Modern Apaches of New Mexico," which first ran in *American Indian* in the summer of 1951, becomes an entire chapter in *New Mexico.* One early essay which also finds its way into the book is "Crusade from Santa Fe," first published in the *North American Review* in 1936.[28] In all of these essays—to one degree or another—she assumes the same position of "mending ways and manners" adopted in *New Mexico.*

She repeatedly endorses the sense of identification, felt by Bynner and the fifty or so other writers and painters she lists, with Native American artists of the Southwest. She recounts those times of political and humanitarian activism and those artists—implicitly identifying with them, too, as the author of *Dancing Gods* and other books on the peoples and pageantry of New Mexico—and states proudly what these Anglo "artist discoverers" accomplished:

> Indians for the first time met respectful comprehension. After centuries of the white man's scorn, smug superiority, or condescension, their dances were witnessed by quietly attentive people who recognized their artistry and religious content. Their handiwork was judged with artistic discrimination. Naturally Indians responded eagerly to strangers who advocated the revival of old pottery forms, old dyes in weaving, old techniques in basketry, and ancient and significant designs. (*NM,* 371–72)

Mary Austin, Oliver La Farge, B. G. O. Nordfeldt, Russell Cowles, Will Shuster, Lynn Riggs, Alice Corbin Henderson, Donald Beauregard, Ernest L. Blumenschein, Walter Ufer, Victor Higgins, Andrew Dasburg

—all these and numerous other Anglo artists are cataloged as friends and allies of art and of Native Americans. As "artist discoverers" they were much more than tourists and, in the end, "strangers" passing through New Mexico. They adopted and then attempted to absorb Native American and Hispanic cultures, crafts, and costumes. Ultimately, their efforts seem those of mimics.

Ironically, many of these early New Mexico Anglo artists now seem oddly patronizing in their enthusiasms for American Indian art and ritual. Even so, U.S. government Indian policy would be different throughout the Southwest today had it not been for, among other things, the efforts waged to defeat the Bursum Bill and bring about the so-called New Deal of the Roosevelt administration and the appointment of John Collier as Indian commissioner in 1933. And in Fergusson's estimation it was the Anglo artists who recognized "the value of the dying Spanish culture": "Shy old men, who had hidden the old plays, now had auditors who recognized a medieval folk-art. Old women, who had been ashamed of their wool embroideries, saw their *colchas* respectfully handled by artists who recognized the old patterns. *Santeros*, whose holy figures had been repudiated by the devout in favor of plaster saints . . . , found their carvings in cottonwood and their paintings with earth colors in demand by collectors" (*NM*, 372–73).

In her three-part account of the pageantry of "Indian, Spanish, and Gringo" cultures Fergusson works from the assumption underlying her *Think* essay, "New Mexico—State of Many Ages." In that essay, published only a few months before *New Mexico* appeared, Fergusson argues light-handedly that "[n]othing is too modern for this state with its past of stone axes and cave houses."[29] She knows firsthand that the assembling and testing of the first atomic bombs turned the sun-basking river town of Albuquerque into a city of "hush-hush developments," and "one of the nation's best-guarded spots." The two constants in a historical process of such extremes and such changes, she asserts, are New Mexico's ability to adapt to change and the constant influx of visitors—whether as explorers of historical moment or as modern tourists. Thus, the modern era witnesses not only four centuries of Spanish and Anglo history but also centuries of American Indian presence stretching back into prehistory.

One of her early essays, "The Coronado Cuarto Centennial," deals with the planning and the celebrating of the four hundred years of the presence of "white" men and women in the state. That essay, too, informs much of what Fergusson says in *New Mexico* about Hispanic, Native American, and Anglo interrelationships. In that early, 1940 essay and its account of the celebrations in honor of Coronado as "the first white man who crossed New Mexico four hundred years ago," Fergusson's pride in her home state and region is apparent in numerous comments which assess modern New Mexico in the light of its past. She says, for example, "This year is as good a time as any to look back over the way we have come, to see ourselves in our many complications and conflicts, in the ways we are working out into a unified people proud of a long and difficult history."[30]

It was just such a celebration—an all–New Mexico celebration—and particularly the dramatization of the Coronado Entrada by Thomas Wood Stevens, "acknowledged master of pageantry," which in all likelihood inspired the organization of *New Mexico* when Fergusson came to write it a decade later. The Coronado Cuarto Centennial celebration was based on the centuries of pageantry in the state—fiestas, American Indian dances, Anglo rodeos, and parades—all of the multicultural pageantry of the state. It was precisely this dedication to constancy of geological "place" amidst diversity of culture which Fergusson advocated throughout her New Mexico and Southwestern writings.

Fergusson's updating of the influences of the Spanish presence in New Mexico, and the notion which in a sense proved to be the cornerstone for her discussions of intercultural relations in *New Mexico,* is found in "The New New Mexican," the essay which occupied the attentions of more than one letter in her correspondence with Herbert Weinstock during the planning, writing, and editing of *New Mexico.* As chapter 16, it closes "Part Two: Spanish" of the book, but it first ran in the winter, 1949, edition of *New Mexico Quarterly.* What Fergusson assumed to be one of the state's most pressing problems, and anticipated as one of the country's issues as well, was the Americanization of New Mexico's Spanish-speaking citizenry. In the light of recent debates and legislation concerning bilingualism, English as an official language, and the rising sense of cultural *raza* solidarity and *carnalismo* rising from the Chicano/Chicana movement of the 1970s, much of her commentary and many of her assumptions and points of argument seem ethnocentric and paternalistic. But Fergusson's heart was very much in the right place as an advocate of equal rights for all races and cultures. In general she seems to assume that the problem is felt almost entirely by Hispanics and, as a one-sided problem, is one not mutually shared and felt by Anglos. But this "strategy" is subtly deceptive, and even though it is an accurate portrayal of the Anglo attitudes of her times, she uses it to give credit to the efforts of the new generation of Hispanics to move ahead to their own solution of the problem of second-class status: ". . . its solution, going ahead rapidly but so quietly as to be generally unnoticed, gives evidence of rare and intelligent effort."[31] In any event, Fergusson points to a problem overlooked by most Anglos, a "problem," like the perennial "Indian problem," very much alive, and, as a cultural and political issue related to multiculturalism, importantly so, oftentimes befuddled behind the picturesque tourist-conceived superficialities of adobe dwellings and perceived quaint speech patterns.

Fergusson centers her account of the disadvantages met by Hispanics on one event, the taking over of New Mexico by the United States after the Mexican War. She focuses on the provisions (ideally stated by the United States government) of the Treaty of Guadalupe Hidalgo, which gave all New Mexico's citizens the full rights of United States citizens, and the determining fact that the "United States made no provision to teach English to the new citizens, and English was the basic need—the tool for building a new life, the weapon and shield against dishonorable men who followed the honorable government" ("NNM," 417).

The metaphors Fergusson uses—language as tool, weapon, and shield, and the inherent building of emotional intensity in the sentence—give testimony again that Fergusson was an impassioned advocate not just of the landscape and history of the region but of the peoples themselves and their struggles for individual and cultural parity with the controlling Anglo culture. She notes that the "foreign in language and culture" were in New Mexico first and in large majority. This premise makes the slighting of Hispanic peoples and language all the more unjust. And it is from these two premises that she builds her argument, structuring it around historical, causal developments and forces. The points of argument in favor of Anglos learning to speak Spanish are not raised, although Fergusson prided herself on her own use of Spanish in lectures and correspondence.

The onslaught of the American pioneer rushed across Spanish and Mexican land grants without any acknowledgment—a pageant which Fergusson chronicles more dramatically, more melodramatically but just as sympathetically, in *Murder and Mystery in New Mexico*. But in her essay, the prose of her account is nevertheless dramatically stirring: "The American pioneer, rushing across the continent with his gun, his axe, his courage, and his greed, brought the simple faith of the frontier. God was his white-bearded prototype, his language the only sensible one, his ways forever best, his country forever right, and his morals the only true ones. In New Mexico this unlettered frontiersman came suddenly upon a wide fertile valley that cradled a relic of the Middle Ages" ("NNM," 418).

She portrays the development of the nineteenth-century *rico, patrón,* and *peon* class system, which many gringos relished and furthered, with indignation and regret but with a matter-of-fact acceptance to the workings of history. Indians were caught in raids and held captive just as slaves were in ancient wars. But Fergusson is able to discuss this kind of society with her characteristic sardonic humor: "Peonage and slavery, rather than

the distinction between hacienda and village, were the basis for the snobbery which seems essential to every society. A certain lady still tickles her
ego by referring to people of her surname but of humble origin as *'esos
indios'* ("NNM," 419). The Hispanic *rico* thus became, by nature of the
system, oftentimes the best ally of the acquisitive incoming gringos. Her
brother Harvey was fascinated throughout his lifetime with the *rico* culture
and wrote more than one fiction—long and short—about it. No doubt his
sister shared his interest and learned from his writings; however, her own
knowledge of the *rico* culture suggests that perhaps Harvey learned much
in turn from her. In any event, the *ricos*, in their alliance with gringos, were
assimilated relatively easily into American culture. *"Esos indios"* had a more
difficult time of it. Even the Catholic church, she says, in her continuing
indictment of the system which fostered class superiority by language bar-
riers, ignored its responsibility to teach English. She does concede that
Bishop Lamy made efforts in that direction with his schools but argues that
only the wealthy could afford such schools. Fergusson does not mention it,
but her own mother was just such a privileged student, for a time, in one
of Lamy's Santa Fe schools.

As a teacher herself and one long interested in public education, Fergusson extends her argument by leveling accusations of inadequate funding
and overall inattention to the teaching of English to the state's public
school system: "New Mexico today spends proportionately more on education than any other state in the Union, but its illiteracy rate is one of the
highest; high school and even college students have difficulty with English,
are still refused jobs because of a Spanish accent" ("NNM," 420–21). And
it is at this point that she crystallizes her thesis in the most forceful of
terms: "This is New Mexico's great tragedy. Citizens of the United States
have been denied their right to its language. Its mark remains, a hundred
years later, on every phase of the state's life. Lack of the language has served
to perpetuate many old ways of thinking and thus to corrupt politics, to
make it easy to maintain an underprivileged class of Spanish-speaking folk,
and to hamper assimilation and adjustment" ("NNM," 421). Her assumptions are clearly, unquestioningly in favor of assimilation and adjustment,
and her point of argument (at least up to this time in her argument) is
reductive—that facility with English is all-determining; however, her advocacy is cogent, and she speaks with an urgency for her time, broadening
our understanding of the complex network of cultural cause and effect and
the issues surrounding bilingualism.

Politics, she next asserts, is the key to the whole problem. The *ricos*
acquired the new language, held onto their land, soon went into business,
and then into politics. Spanish *patróns* soon became political bosses, deliv-

ered the vote, and, in turn, were rewarded with political offices. In what amounts to a synopsis of her brother's first novel, *Blood of the Conquerors* (1921), she then profiles the decline of the "old hidalgos," as young sons soon gambled and variously squandered away their own birthrights, usually their land grants. Even village land grants, such as that of Chilili in the Estancia Valley east of Albuquerque (also dramatized in *Murder and Mystery in New Mexico*), soon disappeared in the face of frontier lawyers (a class, like her father, H. B. Fergusson, which she still holds forth in admiration as men "with their tradition of hard work, canny trading and long saving").

Hope resides, however, Fergusson believes, in the efforts of the new New Mexican who is resolved to work hard, and stay in school, and in general follow the Anglo system from within. (Again, the assumption is ethnocentric insofar as Fergusson believes in assimilation and adjustment, certainly not the assertiveness, protests, and acts of violence which were typified by such culture heroes of the 1960s as Reies López Tijerina and his disruptive, but in the end short-lived, northern New Mexico rebellions.) Her assumptions include, it should be noted (what by today's majority values is a given), the social involvement of women as well as men, although today the woman might well be the leader. Perhaps Chicanos and Chicanas still in the wake of the fervor of the 1970s' Chicanismo movement, and possibly an old hippie or civil rights activist, might wince at Fergusson's words of forty-odd years ago. Nevertheless, the humane heart and humanitarian motive behind them still ring true:

> New Mexico is fighting a battle for decency. The questions are: will the old easy friendliness of the Rio Grande region be strong enough to withstand the hordes of newcomers? or will there be, among the newcomers, enough people of good feeling and good sense to offset the prejudice of those who know no better?
>
> Despite these manifold handicaps the young Spanish-speaking citizen is forging ahead, becoming a new New Mexican. And he is doing it—with her help—in the best American style of individual initiative, courage and brains. This is not new. Always the class that seemed doomed to be forever poor and ignorant has produced a few individuals who could force themselves up and out. ("NNM," 423)

In her attempts to portray the amount of discrimination and its effects on the younger generation of Hispanics particularly (she consciously and carefully refers to them as "American citizens of Spanish background"), she repeats several fragments of conversations—possibly the results of "interviews" of the most casual sort—and concludes that considerable effort is made by new New Mexicans not to place themselves voluntarily in situations which would make for possible prejudicial judgments by Anglos. A mother says: "Never marry a gringa. . . . She will only take you for what she can get out of you. A girl of your own people will be a real help"; a university girl says, "I refused the sorority invitations; I'd never give anybody a chance to discriminate against me"; and "boys sometimes are too stand-offish to attend fraternity smokers" ("NNM," 423). If these are the techniques of "fiction" like those which Herbert Weinstock counseled against, they no doubt still have their own special truth.

Part of her strategy is to pose her argument as an ironic one, playing off the new New Mexicans—who are actually the old New Mexicans of a lineage which dates back to the Spanish colonization of New Spain—against the other new New Mexicans, the truly recent gringo arrivals. And she does it not only by playing up this irony but also by introducing humor into what is essentially a serious topic. She credits new New Mexicans with using their own kind of humor in dealing with insensitive new gringo arrivals, for "[t]hey are talking frankly and easily without fear of the taboo words, and they have quite completely got the number of the stupid newcomer who considers himself superior" ("NNM," 424).

This change in attitude among the new New Mexicans—from feeling inferior to feeling equal if not superior—she traces to such forces as the depression and the opportunities afforded by C. C. C. camps, which allowed Hispanic workers to learn the language, and W. P. A. projects, which preserved old arts and crafts and approved Spanish folkways. She also argues that higher education and politics have allowed opportunities for the new New Mexican to excel.

Given her own membership in the sorority system while in college and her lifelong support of the concept, it is not surprising that she offers at least a partial defense of its inherent snobbishness by appealing to "the record," which she says "reveals that those whose families can pay the assessments and contribute social glamor are 'Greeks'" ("NNM," 425). War veterans in particular are singled out as individuals who are indifferent to the hobbles of discrimination. She quotes one anonymous political candidate who viewed his defeat with "maturity and balance," admitting that in politics he had to be ready to deal with appeals for and against his "Hispano" heritage.

In a closing peroration, she concludes her argument by placing her own views in favor of assimilation and adjustment into the minds—the attitudes and perspectives—of the new New Mexicans: "These new New Mexicans, of both sexes, ask no special favors; they want only the chance that any American has. They are turning what used to be a language handi-

cap into an asset as they enter the teaching profession and the foreign service, and perform brilliantly in both fields. They find their dual culture an
enrichment of life wherever they are, and a widened opportunity. They
are beginning to talk about how they, as the more developed and understanding citizens, may cure certain ignorant gringos of intolerance and
prejudice" ("NNM," 426). Her role as advocate was always the role of a
spokesperson who was a member of the economically dominant Anglo culture who welcomed and encouraged the Americanization of Hispanics and
American Indians. But she never lost sight of the original and passing
dominance of both groups—first the Native Americans, and then the
Spanish/Mexicans—and of their continuing and real claims of differing
kinds of cultural, religious, and ecological dominance, or even "superiority,"
over the newest of newcomers, the "Gringos." Her personal and rhetorical
stance as advocate, thus, was a collective one, one that stressed in writing
after writing, the notion of "our" Southwest—a place where the best of
all three traditions known to New Mexico could combine, allowing each
individual to get ahead on his own initiative and power, with freedom and
dignity.

Fergusson's interest in the Hispanics of New Mexico is traceable in her
writings all the way back to her early essay in *Century Magazine,* "New
Mexico's Mexicans" (August, 1928), and beyond that to the speeches of her
politician father before Congress and while campaigning in New Mexico.
The influence of her father's series of speeches on the need for New Mexico
statehood, delivered before Congress in the first months of 1898 and recorded in the *Congressional Record,* carries through in both "New Mexico's
Mexicans" and "The New New Mexican."[32] Not only does Fergusson argue
some of her father's same points, she also adopts some of his impassioned
oratory so that her essays have the ring of political polemic.

Fergusson's father, in his speeches before Congress, also takes the occasion to attack W. W. H. Davis's account of the Southwest, *El Gringo* (1857),
as a "shameless libel," "beneath contempt" in its treatment of Spanish
Americans. Ironically, H. B.'s son, Harvey Fergusson, in his introductory
commentary on a 1938 edition of *El Gringo,* stated that although Davis was
a Victorian and a bit of a prude, shocked by much of what he saw in the
Southwest, he nevertheless compiled an amazing amount of cultural detail
for posterity and thus wrote "one of the best books about nineteenth century New Mexico."[33]

What specifically stirred H. B.'s ire about *El Gringo* is that in 1888 the
Committee on the Territories of the Fiftieth Congress, in its minority report made by the Republicans, had entered into House Report Number

1025 a quotation from Davis's book which portrayed New Mexicans as immoral. H. B. quotes two long paragraphs cited by the Committee on the Territories and denounces the Republican congressmen who introduced such slanderous words into the permanent record. And again his strategy is that of paralipsis; by the pretense of passing over an idea, he presents it in great detail. He claims proudly to be one of the permanent settlers of the "great West" who went to New Mexico to make his home and insists that he knows firsthand that his constituency of Spanish Americans in New Mexico is nothing like Davis's description. Such a malicious portrait, he contends, could be written by no one less than "an irresponsible scribbler": "I have known the Spanish-American citizens of New Mexico for fifteen years, and I tell you, Mr. Chairman, it is utterly impossible that their mothers and fathers were the moral lepers pictured in that minority report."[34]

Good intentions notwithstanding, there is a lingering aura of paternalism in H. B.'s speeches about the Spanish Americans of New Mexico. And that well-intended paternalism carries over in his daughter's essay/defense of "New Mexico's Mexicans" thirty years later in *Century Magazine*. In that "defense" she acknowledges that it would be more "politic" to refer to them as "Spanish-Americans" but chooses the word "Mexican" in order to highlight the changes of New Mexico history now centuries removed from Spain:

> I use it, intending no disrespect. They are Americans and have been citizens for three generations. They are not immigrants. Their ancestors came to New Mexico and established homes three centuries ago. In 1846 they welcomed the American army of occupation, for they were glad to leave the slovenly rule of Mexico for the firm blue-coated administration which promised them protection from Indian depredations. They eagerly enlisted in the American army, they adopted the flag and the Constitution. They were and are the most loyal of patriots. They have fought in every war since 1848, and they have always performed creditably.[35]

Her tone and her statistics echo her father's speeches before Congress in defense of "Spanish-Americans" in the Southwest. By the time she came to write "The New New Mexicans" and revise it for *New Mexico*, Fergusson had more or less rid herself of the paternalism evident in her attitude toward Hispanics, but in her early *Century Magazine* essay and despite her sincere "defense" of her state's "Mexicans," what now reads like embarrassing stereotyping abounds. Fergusson's central point is that these people are progressing, in a "picturesque process," toward Americanization but that problems exist in the areas of language (their need to be taught English) and politics (a more educated electorate is needed). They are assumed to hate work and admire authority, to vote as their political bosses command, and to be naively influenced by patronage and empty titles: "Spanish pride seems to rest on ancestry, on offices or titles more than on the individual's achievement" ("NMM," 440). Fergusson traces the "process" of Americanization, underlining its political cause and effect from the days of the *ricos,* the *dons,* and the *patróns* up to the twentieth-century present. In Fergusson's schematic reduction the government which promised the Mexicans so much was Republican, so the *dons* became Republican and the *peones* followed. She follows the history of "American" conquest and its effect on the "Mexicans." Although the first Yankee pioneers rode roughshod over the Mexicans, taking not only their lands but also ignoring their customs, Fergusson credits contemporary artists with restoring respect for old crafts, customs, graciousness, and hospitality. Although she concedes that "exquisite manners" and "fine old courtesies" were almost lost in the Americanization process, she observes that they are now on their way back—thanks not just to empathic Anglo artists but also to the new generations of modern Spanish/Mexican Americans: "Most of the old families have lost, but probably for every such one there is a new Mexican family coming up" ("NNM," 443). She credits, without mentioning him by name, her father's legislation at the turn of the century which protected lands for public education and the public school system, established in 1890, which allowed the "natives . . . to learn the language of their new country." Regrettable and clumsy as much of the process of Americanization has been, Fergusson believes it is inevitable, and the Mexican "will work through": "Reluctantly and sadly they see that in adjusting to the new he is losing much of the grace and charm of the old. However, he is coming. Perhaps his warm black eyes, his gay spirit, his love of play and his gift for beauty will bring into the life of New Mexico something which the rest of the country may well envy" ("NNM," 444).

Taking up the same kinds of argument with the same kinds of assumptions (but progressively less ethnocentric than her earliest essays), Fergusson also fought for the new generation of American Indians. She never succumbed to the prevalent thinking of the late nineteenth and early twentieth century about either the "vanishing" Indian (i.e., assimilated) or *the* American Indian (all Indians stereotyped as one)—as if the great variety of Native Americans could be lumped together as only one kind of person. She assumed Americanization was a good thing—but not at any price, not at the price of the obliteration of Native American cultures. In her early and late essays, as in *New Mexico,* she spoke frequently about "Our Modern Indians," "Our Indian G. I.," and "Navajos: Whose Problem?"—titles and approaches which indicated two of her main thrusts: collective responsibility and contemporary concern.

One of her most significant and lasting essays, "Crusade from Santa Fe," reveals not only her advocacy of Indian rights but also the difference that joint Anglo–Native American efforts made in the history of the U.S. government's Indian policy.[36] Anyone interested in the Indian New Deal of John Collier and the rise and fall of Holm Olaf Bursum's bill owes no small debt to Fergusson's account of the role played by Santa Fe and Taos artists in bringing about not only defeat of Bursum's bill but also subsequent reform of U.S. Indian policy. Bursum's bill, as introduced to the New Mexico Senate, would have, in effect, resulted in the loss of significant acres of tribal lands by confirming non-Indian claims to Pueblo lands. Very much an advocate of Indian reform, Collier, with the help of the Indian Rights Association and the General Federation of Women's Clubs, crusaded against the bill and Bursum's assumptions. Collier created the Indian Defense Association to focus and further the fight against such usurping legislation.

"Crusade" is, again, although about a very serious topic—namely, the then latest chapter in the history of the "Indian problem" in the United States—a humorous, even satirical, essay offered to give needed perspective to a much publicized, often emotion-laden national debate. Fergusson's strength is in her blending of respect and irreverence for all sides. Her brother Harvey satirized rather playfully what he referred to as the worship of the primitive in *Footloose McGarnigal,* and although "Crusade" is by no means a full-blown satire, it does share some of the novel's targeting of the extravagances of the Taos and Santa Fe artists of that era.

She begins her essay by combining the metaphor of travel with a breezy tone which makes fun of the capriciousness of Anglo attitudes toward *the* stereotypical Indian and the modern Indian's ironic ability to adapt to Anglo ways, thereby fighting stereotypes not with outdated weapons but with words:

> There is no getting through New Mexico, by whatever route, without running onto the Indian problem. The Indian, at different times a savage to subdue, a little red brother to convert, a government ward to civilize, is now a problem. He is even becoming a problem able to stand on its own feet and make its own fuss, as witness several recent

monographs submitted by western tribes, organized and represented by committees to tell Congress what they think of their white guardians. To each age its own Indian. ("CSF," 376)

After cataloging various versions of *the* Indian in literature and in the movies as savage and salacious and after poking fun at the puritanical investigations and allegations of the Indian Rights Association and Philadelphia Quakers, represented during the Coolidge administration by Matthew K. Sniffen (caricatured as a Dickensian figure), Fergusson takes on the Santa Fe and Taos artists who flocked to those places after World War I, making them "colonies." Although she was friends with many of these individuals, throughout her description reigns her respect for the unselfconciousness of the Indians, whom the artists imitated, as well as her own preference for residing in Albuquerque with its bourgeois, merchant ambiance over and above the artsy-craftsy "extravagances" of the two northern sister towns:

> Meanwhile New Mexico had been discovered by artists. In frenetic effort to escape the complications of eastern cities, they were seeking not only the peace of the desert, but the refreshment of primitive life. What a relief to turn from the War and its drives to softly mellowed pueblos where brown men raised what they ate in peace. From feminism, free love, and flaming books to a sanely humorous people who took sex as simply as weather. From anguished searchings for something to replace religions proven sterile, to sunlit ceremonies worshipping nature with both beauty and intensity. Jaded and nerve wracked aesthetes plunged into it as into a refreshing bath. Nothing was too extreme to express their desire to go western, Indian, to live simply, to be part of the country. ("CSF," 377)

There is more of the sense here of laughing at one's own kind than there is of malice in her descriptions of individual artists and their attempts at costuming; however, aside from her Koshare and Fred Harvey courier days, she was never one to affect stylized western dress. Her claim to being a native-born daughter went much deeper than the superficialities of clothes, her uniforms for "tours" notwithstanding. She took pride in being there when the "tourists" came and advertised their wish to belong:

> Witter Bynner bought and wore and hung on his friends a famous collection of Indian jewelry. Alice Corbin introduced the velvet Navajo blouse. Stetson hats, cowboy boots, flannel shirts, even blankets were the approved costume. Everybody had a pet pueblo, a pet Indian, a pet craft. Pet Indians with pottery, baskets, and weaving to sell were seated by the corner fireplace (copied from the pueblo), plied

with tobacco and coffee, asked to sing and tell tales. Jane Henderson made a record by living in Santa Clara all winter and learning a whole repertoire of Indian songs. Mary Austin discovered and ordered her life to the beat of the Amerindian rhythm. Carlos Vierra and Jesse Nusbaum designed the state museum along lines of the pueblo missions: poems and pictures were Indian strained through such diverse personalities as Parsons, Cassidy, Baumann and Nordfeldt. It was obligatory to go to every pueblo dance. Failure to appear on a sunny roof on every saint's day marked one as soulless and without taste. ("CSF," 377–78)

In Fergusson's ostensibly playful but nevertheless serious account, if the Bursum Bill sought to alter the Indians and their land claims, it also changed the artists who "organized" to preserve the Indian's "primitivism." Ironically, in organizing, the artists lost some of their own "fine, free, individual frenzy" which they first felt when they came to New Mexico.

In the remainder of her essay Fergusson serves up a delightfully interesting "history" of the stir caused by the introduction into the U.S. Senate of the Bursum Bill by New Mexico's senator Holm Bursum. In her account, although told more or less "impersonally," much of her own advocacy creeps in by means, again, of mild sarcasm, irony, humor, and Southwestern wit. Fergusson portrays Bursum as an unsuspecting sheep rancher from Socorro County who believed that all his bill did was "to settle land claims of persons not Indians within Pueblo Indian lands" ("CSF," 378). She also depicts him as acting on his own, avoiding the counsel of his more astute colleague, Albert Bacon Fall. In fact, Fall had much more to do with the whole affair—including instigating an attempt to resolve Pueblo and Spanish/Mexican land-claim conflicts as secretary of the Interior—than she implies. Perhaps Fergusson's elision is due to her respect for her father's professional and personal association with Fall, going back to early times in White Oaks and later as fellow defense counsels. In any event, she simplifies the specifications of the bill and merely observes that when someone in Santa Fe pointed out that the bill might well leave the Pueblo Indians with no land at all, the artists organized their lobbying efforts into an inevitably victorious force: "Never did a more articulate, vociferous, propaganda-minded lobby descend upon the Congress of these United States for any cause" ("CSF," 378).

The list of individuals who lobbied against the Bursum Bill is a long and luminous one, which includes just about every artist living in Santa Fe and Taos at the time. The lobbying, however, was a national effort as well, and Fergusson's account includes mention of a number of nationally distributed articles by distinguished writers: Alice Corbin Henderson (*Nation*), Elise Sergeant (*New Republic*), and Witter Bynner (*Outlook* magazine), all joined the fray. Harvey Fergusson—then a newspaperman in Washington—wrote for a capital paper which she does not specify; Mary Austin, Harriet Welles, and Eugene Manlove Rhodes all put fiction aside for polemic; Dana Johnson, editor of the Santa Fe *New Mexican,* made himself heard all the way to New York. But it was Mabel Dodge Sterne, not yet married to Tony Luhan, who brought more focus to the movement through her contacts with Stella Atwood, then heading the Indian Welfare Committee of the General Federation of Women's Clubs, and her protégé, John Collier.

Collier, working with Francis Wilson, Santa Fe lawyer and United States attorney for the Pueblos, prepared a careful analysis of the bill and sent a published assessment of the implications of such legislation to every member of Congress. Through the network of Atwood's committee, Collier's report was disseminated nationally. By that time the artists had organized as the Santa Fe Association on Indian Affairs and lobbied with even more weight.[37]

Fergusson's explanation of the causes leading up to the Bursum Bill and of its potential consequences on the parties involved shows again her prowess not just as a writer of history but as a rhetorician, able, like her father in his Congressional speeches, to command an edge of satire and persuasive argumentation. The thousands of claimants to the lands originally owned by the pueblos she places in three categories: (1) towns like Taos itself which were settled early in the eighteenth century on the invitation of Pueblo Indians wanting protection from other hostile Indian tribes; (2) squatters who, whether with deeds or not, had bought their land in good faith from white settlers; and (3) "the inevitable bright boys," as she calls them, "who had found that the government took little note if they moved their fences to include bits of pueblo acreage" ("CSF," 380). (More caustic accounts at the time referred to these "bright boys" as, for example, "New Mexico land-grabbers.")[38]

Citing the neglect of minorities' rights throughout "The New New Mexican" and *New Mexico,* Fergusson portrays the prime cause of the conflicting and varied land claims as the federal government and its failure to enforce its own laws and treaties: "The treaty of Guadalupe Hidalgo guaranteed the Pueblo Indians their lands held under Spanish grant, and so saved them from such exploitation as Indians suffered in other states. But the federal government, always responsible for the Indians as wards, minors, had been so lax in guarding the interests of the Pueblos that they were in danger of losing more than ninety thousand acres of valuable lands, their principal source of income" ("CSF," 380). In the Bursum Bill all land disputes and associated water disputes would be turned over to the state courts. Moreover, the bill proposed that a survey which showed where the opposing claims were would serve as proof that contested acres belonged to white claimants—allowing the Pueblos no right to defend their claim.

The battle against the bill took over two years and as in all such fights left many casualties. The Pueblos sent delegations to Washington, and the Santa Fe Association on Indian Affairs gained the support of monied groups in the East. The original bill was defeated, a substitute bill was temporarily stalled, and then finally passed as a compromise, which satisfied the New Mexico artists, Fergusson, and, on certain levels, the Indians. Although Collier and Wilson came to a disagreement, the Santa Fe Association on Indian Affairs was lastingly strengthened and enabled to turn to other aspects of the continuing "Indian problem," such as poor health conditions and the dying out of Indian arts. Herbert Hagerman, a Pecos rancher and former governor of New Mexico and, because of the modified Bursum Bill, a member of the Pueblo Lands Board, was appointed U.S. commissioner to the Navajos and gained the support of the Santa Fe Association. Soon Hagerman and the Pueblo Lands Board squared off against Collier and the Indian Defense Association, and a new chapter was opened—not just in U.S. government Indian policy but also in the social history of Santa Fe. Fergusson recounts it in her own unique way, finding the humorous and the human in the midst of the melee.

She portrays Collier as a zealous crusader—"a truculent fighter for whatever could be got or claimed for the Indians, an unrelenting critic of the Indian Service, aggressive, quick to catch a weak point, often violent" ("CSF," 383). Stella Atwood and the General Federation of Women's Clubs followed him with unified conviction. The Indian Defense Association, under Collier, started a policy of financing litigation and hired a firm of Albuquerque attorneys to monitor the Pueblo Lands Board. The scrap which ensued became the only topic of conversation in Santa Fe. As the Pueblo Lands Board made its rounds from pueblo to pueblo hearing testimony and settling claims, Collier and the Indian Defense Association denied any responsibility for fees and held that any Indian who lost his land originally through governmental indifference or later through settled claims was defrauded not just of land but of water rights—and the association demanded compensation for land *and* water. Collier organized the All Pueblo Council and was countered with a Government Council. The dividing line became more pronounced: "There were 'our Indians' and 'Collier's Indians.' White people and Indians gathered in tight little bunches shooting venomous glances at each other. Each side suspected the other of making false representation to the Indians" ("CSF," 384).

The activity took on the aspect of sophomoric masque, and Fergusson likened it to "a college rush week." In one instance the Santa Fe crowd of writers and artists, chanting their admiration and support for Governor Hagerman and the Pueblo Lands Board, accompanied him, upon his return from a Washington trip, from the train station at Lamy into the town of Santa Fe. Artist Willard Nash rode on the top of his car dressed like an Indian and beating a drum; fellow member of "the Cinco Pintores" group, Will Shuster, carried an effigy of Collier; painters Andrew Dasburg, Gus Baumann, Nancy Lane, and Frank Applegate drove cars sporting painted signs and slogans. Witter Bynner "chanted a doxology" in ironic criticism of Collier's praise of himself above the Indians whose welfare he ostensibly served: "Love for the Indian is my boast; and yet I love John Collier most" ("CSF," 385). When the retinue arrived in Santa Fe the artists hanged Collier in effigy on an infamous cottonwood near the Old Palace.

That particular parade was carried further when the annual Santa Fe fiesta was revived and new encouragement was given to the region's Indians to display their pottery, jewelry, baskets, and weavings. Indian dances were staged. "Indians were given prizes for doing their own things in their own way," and thus was born a modern mecca for tourism. The Atchison, Topeka, and Santa Fe discovered the "gold mine" of Indians and artists as dual attractions and launched the Harvey Indian Detours. Fergusson quotes key personages in their response to it all—"'So,' said Alice Corbin, surfeited with the whole thing, 'so we've saved the pueblos for Fred Harvey'" ("CSF," 386). The ironies were elevated to another level of pageantry, this time bureaucratic pageantry, when Collier, ever the enemy of the Indian Bureau, was appointed Indian commissioner.

Events catch up with her panoramic telling. The whole ruckus affirms—albeit satirically—not just human effort (and the workings of luck and folly) but the possibility of intercultural and interracial cooperation. Collier's handling of his appointment proved to be a credit to all factions, and a new synthesis was shown in smooth operation: "Day schools and better architecture. More hospitals. Encouragement of dances. Modern methods of education, including the teaching of Indian arts and crafts. Action against sweat shop methods in the making of Indian jewelry, and the selling of fake as authentic Indian handiwork. And a violent transfusion of new blood into the whole dusty bureaucracy. Everybody, naturally, takes full credit for everything" ("CSF," 386–87).

The construction of her sentences mirrors their meaning. Questions are simplified. Issues are resolved. Even so, she reserves judgment as to whether conditions are on the whole better or worse, saying only "they are certainly different" ("CSF," 387).

Fergusson's support for Collier's role as Indian advocate is subtle but noticeable in her telling of the "Crusade from Santa Fe." She wrote, for example, a favorable account of Collier's participation in the Committee on Cultural Relations with Latin America during the summer of 1936. She, too, was in Mexico for the committee meeting and offered a firsthand testimonial to Collier's tact: "As an ambassador of good will, John Collier is a success. Intense and serious, eager to learn and quite without bombast or what Mexicans consider typical Yankee conceit, he makes friends with Mexicans and convinces them that at least one gringo thinks they are doing worthy and significant work."[39] Her comments on Collier as Indian commissioner appeared in the *North American Review* the next winter.

Oliver La Farge took over as president of the Santa Fe Association on Indian Affairs and corresponded with Fergusson from time to time over many years. In January of 1951 La Farge invited Fergusson to become a member of the board of editors of *American Indian*, "a forum for discussion of the background, conditions and prospects of the Indians of the United States and Alaska."[40] Her "Modern Apaches of New Mexico" first appeared in La Farge's Association on American Indian Affairs publication and was also included in *New Mexico*. That essay proved to be especially noteworthy because it underscores the dangers of Anglo advocacy of American Indian peoples and rights, namely the danger of presuming to speak on behalf of "minorities" who would, in more cases than not, just as soon speak for themselves.

Fergusson was aware of such dangers and some years after her Apache essay first appeared conferred in a belabored letter to La Farge about the semantic distinctions that should be drawn between the terms "integration" and "assimilation" and the ideas behind them. Trying to decide on both a topic and an arrangement for a lecture-under-the-stars at the University of New Mexico, Fergusson said:

> . . . I am trying not to use any taboo words. I certainly do not wish to offend any Indians, but it is difficult to get things said without using words in current use. . . . But there must be a word for both of these ideas that will put me in the clear with Indians and their friends and still give my audience a notion of what I mean to talk about. . . . My personal belief is that Indians are on the whole a remarkable people

who can do, as they have always done, a lot for themselves. In too many cases they have been hampered rather than helped by even well-meaning people."[41]

The Jicarilla Apaches were one group which felt, especially when *New Mexico* was reprinted in 1973, that Fergusson might well have "helped" someone else. Invariably throughout her "Indian" writings she focuses on three categories of peoples: Pueblo, Navajo, and Apache. Her bias tended to favor the Pueblos and, among them, the Zuni. Presumably she favored the Navajos next, and then the Apaches. The Apaches, subdivided into "Warlike" and "Modern," "Mescalero," and "Jicarilla," are invariably discussed last, and although she attempts to empathize with them as a defeated people and presumes to argue for them, her portrayal of the Apaches is the most ethnocentric and least effective of all her attempts, if for no other reason than her goodwill toward the Apaches of the Southwest dramatically backfired.

In part, the vehement objections of the Jicarilla Apaches to Fergusson's account of them in "Modern Apaches of New Mexico" and in *New Mexico* illustrate that the very cause to which she was dedicated—American Indian self-reliance and self-respect—passed her at one time avant garde and, then suddenly, old-fashioned views. The crusades of the 1930s and even the 1950s were not those of the 1970s.

Fergusson died before the anger of the Jicarillas erupted into a protest that *New Mexico* was an untrue, degrading, and offensive portrayal of them, and a demand that such "lies" be retracted. An anthropology class at Dulce High School brought Fergusson's account to the notice of the Jicarilla Tribal Council. In 1973 the council president, Hubert Velarde, demanded apologies on several counts, saying that Fergusson's "facts are misleading and her conclusions are totally tasteless" and insisted, to list just a few of the council's numerous points, that:

the Jicarillas observe a high moral code both as a matter of law and social tradition;

the Jicarillas are not on the dole but are a self-sufficient people who govern themselves and take care of their own, despite a long and determined effort by white people to extinguish them from the universe;

the Jicarilla population has nearly quadrupled since 1921, and the people live in modern housing adapted to the terrain of their reservation land;

> the Jicarillas are an intelligent, sensitive, and brave people, as wit-
> nessed by the vale of tears of their suffering, and their ability to
> survive the genocidal onslaughts of the white invader.[42]

The rhetoric and tone of Velarde's demands bespeak the temper of the
1970s truly enough. And, by current standards in the politically correct
1990s, it is difficult to imagine that Fergusson was oblivious to the assumptions which are implicit in much of her commentary about the Apaches.
No doubt she would have been more "bewildered" than the Jicarillas had
she lived to hear indictments such as Velarde's: "Miss Fergusson totally
ignores the tragic history of the American Indian and the courses of the
moral and economic bankruptcy she purported to find. When a peoples'
culture is ruthlessly suppressed and their homelands are viciously stolen,
there remains little wonder that a bewildered society remains."[43]

What angered the Jicarillas? Were the Jicarillas not grasping Fergusson's total context? Were they mistaking her objections to the reservation
system which brought about the results for objections to the people? Were
her quotations, her ever-present interviews somehow being mistaken for
her own personal views? And what makes a post–political correctness read-
ership today flinch at some of her obviously prejudiced, racist-sounding
comments, and compel readers to cross out angrily some of her phrases,
markings which at times are encountered in library editions of her works?

Unfortunately, some of her descriptions can tend to confuse criticism
of the system with criticism of the very people themselves and their culture:

> The Apaches live in widely scattered, weathered frame shacks
> and dusty tents. The picturesque pointed tepees of their ancestors ap-
> pear now only on ceremonial occasions; civilization seems to have
> brought ugliness with no greater comfort except that supplied by
> sheet-iron cookstoves. Other furniture consists of piles of dirty sheep-
> skins and a few pots and pans. Flies, filth, and unwashed children
> abound. Water is scarce; often it must be hauled miles from the near-
> est lake. . . . Most homes are not permanent; sheep people drift with
> the flocks.
>
> Teachers and missionaries, laboring devotedly for what they con-
> sider good for Apaches, seem doubtful of their success. A gentle mis-
> sion worker carries a bunch of keys heavy enough to brain an ox, and
> unlocks and relocks every door as she shows the clubhouse for Indi-
> ans. "They all steal; they even bring us their things to lock up." Mis-
> sionaries find immorality on the increase: more illegitimate babies,

more drunkenness. "They have lost the old taboos that kept boys and girls apart; they have not learned morality."(*NM*, 124–25)

Perhaps there is more irony intended in such a passage than comes through. Fergusson is quoting from an on-the-spot interview, presenting an anonymous, perhaps typically morally fastidious, missionary's account. The quote tells us much about missionary attitudes that do not seem all that "gentle," as Fergusson may well have intended to suggest. In Fergusson's defense it is worth noting that throughout her Southwestern and Latin American writings she decried small-mindedness. Moreover, in later comments on these missionary accounts of Apache life, she says, "This is the measure and perhaps the reason for what fifty years of civilized training has done to an Indian tribe" (*NM*, 125). Clearly she *intended* to be on the side of the Apaches, whether they took her to be so or not.

To give her the benefit of the doubt, what she intended, generally, in her account of the Apaches—Mescalero and Jicarilla—was a condemnation of the U.S. government, not of the Apaches. Her concluding comment says as much: "Perhaps these Apaches are the most instructive example of what our government has done with, or to, its conquered dependents" (*NM*, 132). But her descriptions and quotations are harsh and ultimately capable of misinterpretation as demeaning to the Apaches, an ironic and regrettable example of how even a well-meaning Anglo of deep liberal and humanitarian conviction can add to the problems of prejudice rather than diminish them and be misunderstood and denounced by the very people she sought to help. In a sense, Fergusson's Southwestern writings retain a particular interest as historical, to a degree "quaint," documents (especially in light of the culture wars, the courtroom trials, and the ethnic cleansing of the 1990s) which portray the developing but still naive, liberal, Anglo-American attitudes and assumptions of the early and mid-twentieth century. Such writings afford readers, more than a full century after her birth in 1888, genteel but still insidious glimpses into just what a knotty, deep-seated problem racial prejudice in America is, what a difficult struggle has been waged toward tolerance and equal rights, what journeys still remain for the ethnicities and races (especially American Indian, Hispanic/Chicano/Latino, and Anglo-American) of the Southwest (and, indeed, the nation and the world) to travel if such a historical pluralistic and multicultural region is to become what Fergusson at once hoped and, ironically, at times hindered. In the title of *Our Southwest*, the prototype of *New Mexico*, the "our" is not meant to signify Anglo-American possession and dominance but mutual acceptance and respect among races. That is the Southwest which Fergusson envisioned. That was Erna Fergusson's Southwest. And her Southwest, advancing into modernism, still affords guidance now at the dawn of the millennium.

Albert E. Stone makes a similar point about J. Hector St. John de Crèvecoeur: "Crèvecoeur the satirist is an authentic expression of the United States of America's first man of letters. His career's prophetic significance consists both in myth-making and in saying nay to official values and hallowed ideologies, in speaking for minorities and outsiders."[44] As New Mexico's first lady of letters, Erna Fergusson more than earned her part, not just in the literary history in the Southwest but of this same great American tradition of racial and cultural understanding and tolerance hard fought, hard won.

Chapter 5

. . . .

Friends:
First Lady of Letters

In considering Erna Fergusson and the modern Southwest it is helpful to survey what her friends and acquaintances have said about her position in Southwestern literary history. Traditionally she has been viewed more as a social commentator on the Southwestern artistic scene than a part of it. In large part this perception is due to her never having published any fiction, poetry, or drama. She was, however, nearer to the center than to the periphery of what some have labeled the mid-twentieth–century Southwestern Renaissance. And the list of writers she knew, visited, and entertained during this regional rebirth is long and luminous.

The artists colonies of Taos and Santa Fe were undoubtedly the hub of that particular flowering of painting and writing. The arts reacted to and incorporated the enchanted landscapes and lives of the Southwest as a landscape of the soul, an enchanted place, a *tierra del alma, tierra encantada* of vast geographical, historical, and personal dimensions. Although Fergusson was born in the comparatively more commercial town of Albuquerque and continued to live there, her life crossed paths with virtually every noted author of that time, including Charles F. Lummis, Mabel Dodge Luhan, Oliver La Farge, Haniel Long, Witter Bynner, Spud Johnson, T. M. Pearce, Frank Waters, Lynn Riggs, Conrad Richter, Mary Austin, Ross Calvin, Fray Angelico Chávez, Paul Horgan, Peggy Pond Church, Frieda Lawrence, and numerous other writers, editors, impresarios, and literary and artistic luminaries.

In later years she became close friends with Lawrence Clark Powell, and his commentaries on her writings (plus those of Paul Horgan; of attorney, family friend, and local historian William A. Keleher; of editor and publisher Roland Dickey; of poet Peggy Pond Church; of journalist Irene Fisher; and of academic writers T. M. Pearce, Dorothy Woodward, and David Remley) have perhaps done most in securing Fergusson's name and prominence in Southwestern literary history.

General guides to such regional literary history confirm that she is best regarded as a native New Mexican whose writing is based on firsthand experience and on deep devotion to her birthplace. The late T. M. Pearce merely alludes to four of her books, *Dancing Gods, Our Southwest, Albuquerque*, and *New Mexico* but generalizes that "Miss Fergusson wrote books about many places, but she was at her best in writing about her native, much loved state."[1] Pearce's many books about the Southwest establish him as an authority on the subject. After obtaining a Ph.D. at the University of Chicago and teaching at the University of Pittsburgh, he went to the Southwest in 1926 to teach at the University of New Mexico and soon was editing the *New Mexico Quarterly*. It was in this position, which he held nearly a decade, that he accepted and published many of Fergusson's essays and reviews and began a long friendship with her which, in addition to her status as an alumnus of the University of New Mexico, also resulted in her inclusion on a regular basis in a now legendary Lecture-under-the-Stars series which Pearce inaugurated in 1935 and administered for a time until 1941.

Fergusson joined this series of under-the-stars summertime lectures over a dozen times—from the first lecture in 1935 and including 1938, 1939, 1940, 1941, 1946, 1948, 1949, 1950, 1955, 1957, and 1959.[2] It was something of a tradition that she was the opening speaker for the series, which often drew up to 1,500 persons. During the summers in which she did not appear on the program she was, Pearce surmised, out of town collecting materials for her books on Latin America: *Fiesta in Mexico* (1934), *Guatemala* (1937), *Venezuela* (1939), *Chile* (1943), and *Cuba* (1946). Another travel book, more west than south, *Our Hawaii*, appeared in 1942. During some of these years she was also engaged in education and government service. In his remembering Fergusson's lecture topics and his introductions of her, Pearce cites the following:

"The Indians in Southwestern Literature," 1935; "Mexican Artists and the Revolution," 1938; "Interviewing Latin America," 1939; "Our Hawaii," 1941; "Latin Americans in Their Recent Books," 1946. On the card for this year [1946] I wrote that from 1934 until 1941, she was a lecturer in the Mexican seminars of the Committee on Cultural

Relations with Latin America, and in 1943–1944 she was in Washington as Program Officer for the Division of Science and Education of the Inter-American Educational Foundation.[3]

Something of what Pearce heard and saw in Fergusson as a lecturer is also implicit in her early and later voicings, her personae as a "lady" writer, dude wrangler, traveler, historian, and advocate. Pearce's description of Fergusson the lecturer is thus worthy of noting in this context: "Erna was a splendid lecturer: her voice was clear and her expression was forceful. I'd say she had a commanding personality, a fine figure, and a pleasant personality. Erna was not pretty but rather handsome. . . . To my way of thinking, she was the most important literary figure Albuquerque has produced." Pearce conjectures that at the time of Fergusson's death much of her greatness as a person and writer was her insistence on the "useness" (or usefulness), her attitude of the collective purpose of "our Southwest" as she phrased it.[4]

Fergusson's ties to the Southwest also included her graduation from the University of New Mexico, which now honors its distinguished alumni with an award in her name. She entered the university in the fall of 1910, after matriculating from the Girls' Collegiate Preparatory School in Los Angeles in 1903 and the University of New Mexico Normal School in 1906. She received her B. A. (Bachelor of Pedagogy) degree from the School of Education at the University of New Mexico on May 26, 1913. (She also attended other schools, including the University of Chicago and Columbia University from which she earned her M. A. in history.)[5]

At the University of New Mexico she also became a charter member of the Xi chapter of Phi Mu social sorority in the spring of 1911, further strengthening her ties to the institution as a member of UNM's first national sorority. Among the many honors which came to her as a New Mexican was posthumous recognition in 1965 as one of the first Phi Mus.[6] In 1958 she was presented an honorary membership in Theta Sigma Phi's Albuquerque Alumnae chapter of this national women's journalistic fraternity.

More significant than such relatively charming, if not somewhat precious, honors is the esteem with which she was held by the University of New Mexico, which in 1943 awarded her an honorary Doctor of Letters degree. Today the University of New Mexico honors distinguished alumni with The Erna Fergusson Award. Another important tie to the university was her friendship with Roland F. Dickey. Dickey first met Fergusson in the late 1930s when he was an undergraduate at UNM and interviewed her about her Latin American travels. Their friendship continued over thirty years until her death in 1964. Dickey, one of New Mexico's well-known writers and the author of *New Mexico Village Arts,* was for many years head of the University of New Mexico Press, and he aided in the publication of reissues of Fergusson's books, including *Dancing Gods,* which the press reprinted a number of times from the Knopf plates, and the still-in-print *Mexican Cookbook* (originally published in 1934 but revised and reillustrated by UNM Press in 1945). At the time of Fergusson's death Dickey was president of the Albuquerque Historical Society and helped establish the Erna Fergusson Memorial Fund for the Albuquerque public libraries.

Many close friends and a large number of Albuquerque residents mourned her death. She died in her northwest Albuquerque home at the age of seventy-six, in the early morning hours of July 30, 1964, after several years of lameness and pain from arthritis and hip surgery. But it was cancer which finally caused her death. The memorial service was held August 1 at 2 P.M., following cremation services July 30. At her memorial, held, quite appropriately, in the university's chapel, Dickey read President Tom Popejoy's address which mourned the passing of one of the Southwest's best-loved citizens, a great lady who was always interested in "the magic of learning," an educator "whose vast store of knowledge was matched by an intense interest in young people," a writer who tried to instill in her readers an interest "in their surroundings and a love of their natural heritage."[7]

Popejoy's eulogy was only one in a memorial service which also included the major, sustained tribute of attorney and fellow writer William A. Keleher. Keleher, a prominent Southwestern attorney and author of such works as *The Fabulous Frontier* (1962) and *New Mexicans I Knew* (1969) was a "historian" cut from a similar cultural cloth as Fergusson—he had grown up "Gringo" in New Mexico, had participated in the Anglo "settlement" and growth of Albuquerque as a railroad city and health sanctuary during its transition from the old Southwest to the new, from the nineteenth to the twentieth century. He had been her close friend and counselor, was close to her in age, and was from the same neighborhood around Old Town, had known her family—her maternal grandfather, Franz Huning; her father, H. B. Fergusson; knew Fergusson's mother and Huning's daughter, Clara Mary Fergusson. Keleher, too, had been involved in the purchase and demolition of Huning's historic castle on Central Avenue (originally Railroad Avenue), an ironic involvement for a man with a keen sense of the legacies of Southwestern history.

In his address, published two months later in the seventy-fifth anniversary issue of the *New Mexico Historical Review,* Keleher traced the history of Fergusson's life and listed her achievements as a prominent Southwestern author and lecturer.[8] In his emotional peroration, Keleher offered this appraisal of his friend: "Erna Fergusson's contributions to this community, to New Mexico and its people, were significant, important and of enduring quality. Active participation in civic projects spanned her zeal for saving her beloved cottonwood trees from the inroads of a bulldozer to the preservation of our heritage through the medium of the Old Albuquerque Historical Society. Her roots went deep into the soil of New Mexico. She loved it with a passion. New Mexicans were always proud of the fact that she never had any desire to make her home elsewhere."[9]

The pride which Keleher notes in the identification of Fergusson as a traveler, who, although she roamed far and wide, loved to travel best in New Mexico and to keep her residence in Albuquerque, is one she herself promulgated, stressing her independence as a lone woman, and reveals a persona worth tracing in her New Mexico as well as her Latin American writings. This identification with New Mexico went far in establishing her among the Anglo literati as the "first lady," the culturally mutated and publicity-enhanced version of the reported Indian appellation, Beautiful Swift Fox, in the minds of her mostly Anglo readers and colleagues. All of the remembrances offered about Fergusson undergird the fascination of her role as a bicultural icon—as New Mexico's Beautiful Swift Fox eventually become first lady of letters.

Pulitzer Prize–winning author Paul Horgan, like most of Fergusson's contemporaries, now deceased, was also another friend of Fergusson's who, through his own fond regard, helped further her literary reputation. Horgan moved to Albuquerque as a boy in 1915, and at the age of twelve soon became acquainted with the youngest Fergusson child, Francis. Through Francis he soon met Erna, who lived with her widowed mother. (The other two Fergusson children, Harvey and Lina, no longer lived in New Mexico.) It was at the Orchard Place home of Fergusson and her mother Clara that Horgan says he "felt most directly in touch with the graces of civilized life and the possibility of growth in those directions of the arts and ideas to which I was then aspiring as an adolescent."[10] Over the ensuing half-century, Horgan and Fergusson kept up a lively friendship, including visits, correspondence, and consultation about writing, politics, and things Southwestern and beyond.

Horgan's description of her personality and presence remains one of the most accurate and endearing:

> She was a tall person who held herself beautifully and moved with energetic grace. Her eyes were a fine sky-blue which reflected her thought with piercing immediacy. Her face had marks of great humor. It was always a delight to hear her in anecdote—beautifully

framed words, a voice of fine timbre, her hands held palms upward as if bearing her opinion and making gestures of circular support for her story, which was often droll and punctuated with little runs of laughter. One of her favorite comments on some egregious piece of idiocy was, "Isn't it simply gor-r-rgeous?" As her years went on, she grew more and more distinguished in mind and bearing, so that while not conventionally handsome, she ended by impressing everyone with an appearance as beautiful as it was civilized.[11]

Whether at home in Albuquerque, traveling in Mexico, Central America, South America, touring the Southwest, or visiting her brother Harvey and other relatives in California, Fergusson wrote to Horgan— while he was in Roswell as librarian at the New Mexico Military Institute, when he was in Washington during World War II, and later when he headed the Center for Advanced Studies at Wesleyan University in Middletown, Connecticut. Their extant correspondence runs to scores of letters of the liveliest, most urbane, at times biting and satirical but always sincere and honest sort. Impressions of her travels invariably found their way into her letters to Horgan—almost as if by epistolary trial run she first sketched out her word "photos" of what she saw and felt.

Prior to the Japanese bombing of Pearl Harbor, for example, Fergusson described Honolulu this way in the fall of, presumably, 1940, as she was gathering materials for *Our Hawaii* (1942). Correspondence indicates she sailed for Hawaii in September and wrote to Horgan in October: "A ride in a white-lined launch manned by sailor boys across Pearl Harbor which (hate military preparations as much as you like) looks like all the fairylands and all the Christmas trees put together. Ships of all sizes outlined in red and white lights which stab the smooth black water and wink messages at each other, and that pattern cut across a hundred ways by scooting little launches with red stars and beyond all that the city climbing the hills in pyramidal and bowknot designs of light. Lordy, lordy, what a sight!"[12] Beyond their visits and exchange of letters, Horgan remembers that it was Fergusson's habit to ask him to read chapters of her ongoing work—"Not in every case, but many of her books I saw chapter by chapter."[13] It was Fergusson's custom to write on rough yellow paper, the kind used in newspaper offices, and to pin revisions onto her manuscript with straight pins, a habit which caused some amusement between the two friends. "She said, drolly enough, that she thought rather than glue or any other staple procedure she thought a lady author was quite proper in using dress-maker pins in pinning her manuscript together."[14] Concerning her writing, Horgan observes, "Erna was very receptive to critical discussion of her work. And she always was able to count on my admiration and sympathetic reception of her work because I truly admired . . . her general approach and prose style."[15]

Fergusson, apparently, would often take strong specific exceptions to some of Horgan's writings—particularly regarding the conquering Spaniards and Indians in New Mexico history. Horgan's method was to attempt to present what happened as closely as possible to what he regarded as "historical fact," and although he insisted that he did not in every case strike an attitude in favor of one against the other, Fergusson often found him an obvious partisan. Such resultant biases in favor of the Spanish or Catholicism, for example, offended what Horgan characterizes as Fergusson's "liberal point of view," but Horgan insists that "I honored her responses . . . without necessarily being persuaded by them."[16]

Horgan's visits to Fergusson's and her mother's Orchard Place home in Albuquerque he remembers as "extremely congenial, beautifully hospitable." If he stayed overnight in the guest house to the rear of the residence, everything was "beautifully arranged, quite simple, but in perfect taste." The whole feeling was "undemonstrably intelligent and civilized. It was a great joy to be in such a household as charmingly ordered, as simply conducted . . . so that going there was always a great joy to me." Both in his conversation and in his introduction to *New Mexico* Horgan remembers that "no one ever lived in greater harmony with the immediate environment than she": "I particularly remember the tone of Albuquerque, which I love as much in retrospect as I did at the time, of their small house sheltered under towering cottonwood trees. The gracious and commodious shade of the trees always seemed to me and still suggests to me something of the spirit of the whole household—the encompassing grace which you felt when there, the grace of the shade of the tree, the grace of the overarching charm and consideration of their presence together."[17]

In 1962, just two years before her death, Fergusson's prominence was most explicitly described in an article by Lawrence Clark Powell in *New Mexico* magazine.[18] Powell was then dean of the School of Library Sciences at the University of California and later head of the University of Arizona's library in Tucson. He was the author of a regular column, "Western Books and Writers," in the travel magazine *Westways* as well as numerous other essays and books about the Southwest and its literature. He knew the region intimately from his many automobile journeys through it. And he knew Fergusson; he had arranged a lecture for her at UCLA in 1955 on the establishment of library service in New Mexico and had, in turn, visited her in her Albuquerque home.

In his "First Lady" essay Powell interviewed his friend and found her, although in her seventies, still alert and interested in issues and people. She was reconciled to the changes "progress" had brought to her Southwestern home on the cultural and geographical crossroads. The one thing which troubled her then was the discrimination against Spanish Americans, a people for whom she always was an advocate but, inadvertently at times, a paternalistic, even patronizing one. After a brief biographical sketch Powell states his appraisal of Fergusson: "The deep attachment she feels for New Mexico, and her ability to reconcile herself to the profound social changes it is experiencing, as well as the tempered affection with which she expresses her self, have earned for Erna Fergusson the title of New Mexico's First Lady of Letters."[19]

Powell's impressions of Fergusson register his respect for her not only as a writer but as a congenial impresario whose home functioned as a kind of "river road salon" where she planned porch parties and received callers ranging from Los Alamos scientist Robert Oppenheimer to writers, artists and editors, to local American Indians, neighbors on horseback, booksellers, politicos, teachers, or priests. Powell assumes that everyone saw in her the same characteristics he did, the characteristics of "a woman who, if she had chosen politics instead of writing, could have ably represented her state on the highest level, for she has the qualities of politician and diplomat: liking for people tempered with shrewd judgment, energy, and a sense of humor."[20] For Powell, New Mexico and Fergusson were synonymous. Powell contends that Fergusson's love for New Mexico land and sky and her passion for the state's people is why she remained in Albuquerque and what inspired her writing and gives her writing its charm and value. According to Powell, her books satisfy a middle ground between the extremes of academic treatise and inspired journalism. He views her as a complete scholar and reporter, with a clear and simple style which every now and then lights up into passionate, transcendent writing.[21]

A year after his 1962 essay on Fergusson, Powell dedicated *Southwestern Book Trails* (1963) to her and was in attendance at an autograph party in Old Town as part of the festivities honoring Fergusson during New Mexico Writers' Day (proclaimed by then-Governor Jack M. Campbell, who singled her out for that particular observance). Two months following her death, Powell devoted his October "Western Books and Writers" column to Fergusson and her writings, then remembered her again in his November column, since the intervening time had also brought the death of the flamboyant University of Texas writer and professor J. Frank Dobie, also a friend of Fergusson's. Powell's suggestion that a memorial be established in Fergusson's name was taken to heart by the Albuquerque Historical Society and its chairperson, Fergusson's friend, Roland Dickey, who established a

Southwestern book fund in her name for the Albuquerque Public Library. Some years later a branch library on San Mateo Boulevard in the northeast heights was named the Erna Fergusson Library.

In 1971 Powell wrote his longest essay on Fergusson when he "reread" *Dancing Gods* in a series devoted to "Southwest Classics Reread" for *Westways*.[22] Much more than a commentary on her first and most famous book, Powell makes an eloquent case for his friend's status as a major Southwestern writer—"remembered because she was . . . a writer, a creative woman unneedful of marriage and children, who left a heritage more widely meaningful than her own flesh and blood."[23] Powell's interest is to discover what contributed to Fergusson's writing of a work which, in his estimation, surpassed all others on the subject of ceremonial Indian dances. His answer is based on the deductions of biography in their most overt outlines and his tracing of her burgeoning interest in writing—"An interest and training in history, a passion for the peoples of her own land, and a compulsion to communicate were the elements that gradually coalesced in the making of Erna Fergusson as a writer."[24] Powell judges her writings as more than guide books and something less than histories—but clearly "literature." One criterion qualifies her books as literature for Powell: "What lifted her books to the level of literature was the personal vision which illuminated her material."[25]

Powell concedes that spotting the literary qualities in Fergusson's writing is indeed a subjective enterprise. She was essentially a journalist in his estimation. Her early newspaper pieces for the old *Albuquerque Herald* were what led her to her career as a writer. But finding the literary, aesthetic quality of her books is a matter of personal taste: "You have to sense it. It's like Frost said, if you feel like the top of your head's just been taken off, that's poetry or when Housman saying when he was shaving and his skin begins to bristle, well, that's poetry."[26] In Powell's estimation she rose to her subject in two of her books, *Guatemala* and *Dancing Gods:* "I think the whole idea of Indian ceremonials excited her imagination, and she took fire more; her prose reflects this. But this is a personal literary judgment."[27]

Powell's definition of literature as writing with a "personal vision," an ability to feel something special in the words—"after a hell of a lot of reading"—remains rather impressionistic and abstract. Like his definition of "classic" literature as that which resists "going out of date," his assessment depends on his specific conception of the author's particular way of "seeing, sensing, and saying." Not fully satisfied that he reaches the essential truth of Fergusson's achievement, Powell cites, somewhat ambiguously, her "womanly" quality, her first-lady status as a factor which contributes to understanding her essence as a writer. He does not, however, go so far as to say that gender is the key to understanding her way of seeing, sensing, and saying. She appeared to Powell as a "down-to-earth writer, . . . so simple and uncomplicated, apparently."[28]

Peggy Pond Church first knew Fergusson as a friend of her mother. In the early 1930s whenever she went to Santa Fe she would stay in the family guest room. Church was living at the Los Alamos Ranch School until 1934, when she moved back to Santa Fe. And through her friendship with Haniel Long she grew to know Fergusson. She met her again in the 1950s in Berkeley when Fergusson was there for a hip operation. After that, in 1958 Church took her manuscript of *The House at Otowi Bridge* to Fergusson to read in Albuquerque. Fergusson, in turn, contacted Roland Dickey, then editor of the *New Mexico Quarterly*. According to Church, "Perhaps Roland was the godfather, and Erna was the godmother."[29] In Pond's assessment, Fergusson "wasn't a poet. She was a very extroverted person who saw life in its complete reality and didn't look at it symbolically as poets do."[30] But Church and Fergusson shared an enthusiasm for New Mexico, the Southwest, and all the trips that she took. When Church returned to New Mexico from California in 1959 that winter she wore Fergusson's raccoon coat to the Shalako dance at Zuni Pueblo and found it "full of mana." Fergusson knew the Southwest historically, geographically, and personally—and this made up her enthusiasm for New Mexico and her ability to write about it. Church sees Fergusson's relationship with the Indians of New Mexico as rather superficial but broad. "She noticed the detail and how the dances fit into the country, and she had, as we all had, a feeling of the Indians as part of the environment." But Fergusson's perspective, like Church's, was from the outside looking in. Fergusson's involvement with New Mexico was, according to Church, more with people than with the land, having never really been involved with it in a solitary, introverted way. "She was gregarious and friendly and warm and had a way of putting all kinds of people at ease."[31]

Her friends, if they felt they "knew" her as a straightforward person, apparently never really fully fathomed, or at least have never thoroughly expressed, her versatile and many-faceted voicings. This task has been left for others beyond her personal acquaintances to attempt, as I have in this study, and to a few other individuals whose accounts attempt to analyze critically and assess her achievement as a regional writer of the American Southwest. One such critical work is Remley's *Erna Fergusson,* a pamphlet in the Steck-Vaughn Southwest Writers Series. Following the set format of the series in which he is writing, Remley offers a brief biographical sketch of Fergusson, then considers her "foreign travel" books in chronological sequence (e.g., *Fiesta in Mexico,* 1934; *Guatemala,* 1937; *Venezuela,*

1939; *Our Hawaii*, 1942; *Chile*, 1943; *Cuba*, 1946; *Mexico Revisited*, 1955), leaving her "Southwest" books and selected articles for final consideration (e.g., *Dancing Gods: Indian Ceremonials of New Mexico and Arizona*, 1931; *Our Southwest*, 1940; *Erna Fergusson's Albuquerque*, 1947; *Murder and Mystery in New Mexico*, 1948; and *New Mexico: A Pageant of Three Peoples*, 1951).

In Remley's opinion, similar to Powell's, Fergusson's first book, *Dancing Gods*, succeeded in stimulating wide public interest in Southwestern Indian dances and secured her claim to being a Southwestern writer. But her start as a writer is traceable to her beginning as a journalist for the Albuquerque *Herald*, the New Mexico *Highway Journal* (later *New Mexico* magazine), and then in *Century Magazine* and other periodicals of the time. In Remley's estimation her experience as a tour guide and operator of Koshare Tours had given her the impetus for *Dancing Gods*, and "her childhood in a territory only recently saved for 'progress' from the Indians and Spanish Americans had provided the enduring interest from which all her writing would follow."[32] Fergusson's merit as a Southwestern writer, says Remley, is not her social criticism, necessarily, but her ability to offer a balanced view of both the good and the bad aspects of the Southwestern region, resulting in a final product which is "an affirmative description of a heritage she felt positively about" (*EF*, 2).

Remley theorizes that Fergusson more or less inherited her egalitarian views and her passion for the oppressed peoples of New Mexico from her father. Although she was a fierce individualist, she was a loyal Democrat all her life, supported Democratic causes and politicians like Bronson Cutting, Clinton P. Anderson, John F. Kennedy, and others—and took pride in her father's legacy as a New Mexico politician and friend of such regional cultural heroes as Elfego Baca. Remley only hints at Fergusson's strong sense of pride in not only her father but her pioneer grandfather, German immigrant Franz Huning, who became an early legend in old and new Albuquerque around the time of the coming of the railroad in the 1880s, and, indeed, her grandmother and namesake, Ernestine Franke Huning, and her mother, Clara Mary Huning, for whom Fergusson cared in her later years. Remley further speculates Fergusson inherited from her grandfather "her fundamental distaste for the new society the railroad brought in and her love of the old Southwesterner of the pre-railroad days," even though she thought of herself as a modern woman ready to meet the future (*EF*, 7–8).

Remley also singles out her early narrative, "Justice as Interpreted" (1933), and her essays, "Crusade from Santa Fe" (1936) and "Navajos: Whose Problem?" (1948), as examples of her concern with the Southwest's "explosive problem" of race relations. In this regard Remley says: "It is com-

monly said that no white man will ever understand 'them' [American Indi-
ans]. Probably Erna Fergusson comes closer to it than most of us do" (*EF,*
16). Her own Anglo-American status aside, Remley finds that, if anything,
Fergusson in her "Indian" writing is "completely in sympathy with the Indian and his threatened way of life, and she occasionally seems to practice
an inverse discrimination against the Anglo intruders. She is down on Indian agents and the efforts of government bureaus to educate the Indian
for assimilation" (*EF,* 30).

Remley goes far to say that Fergusson "knew" the Native American
Southwest better than any Anglo writer who attempted descriptions of ceremonials. Peggy Pond Church would, as explained earlier, stop short of
such a sweeping generalization—as would noted American Indian authority Frank Waters (who, coincidentally, died in 1995, the same year Horgan
died), who knew Fergusson during World War I when they both worked
for the Office of the Coordinator of Inter-American Affairs and later when
they both returned to New Mexico. Waters observes: "She wrote a series
of popular guide books. One of them was *Dancing Gods,* a superficial,
somewhat sentimental look at Indians. As I was doing research at depth
for my *Masked Gods: Navajo and Pueblo Ceremonialism,* I was quite disap-
pointed in it."[33]

Others, namely Lawrence Clark Powell, see Fergusson as a more authentic commentator on Indian ceremonialism than did Waters.[34] Herein
resides an issue clouded by considered judgments and opinions as well as
personal allegiances and friendships. Invidious comparisons between Fergusson and Waters are ultimately of little real profit, but consideration of
the "truth" and "accuracy" of her accounts of Pueblo dances does lead to a
better understanding of her social attitudes and her aesthetic as a traveler/
journalist/historian/advocate. Close reading of *Dancing Gods,* for example,
goes further in evidence of Fergusson's ethnocentrism, however well intended her accounts and observations, than Remley would allow in his ar-
guing that she was "completely" in sympathy with the Indian's way of life.
She held out for a greater degree of accommodation and assimilation than
such a sweeping assertion permits. It is, however, precisely here—in her
Anglo attitudes and assumptions toward American Indians and Hispanics,
their lives in relation to landscape and encroaching Anglo-American culture—that her overriding contribution as a writer is found. She dared to
attempt to come to terms with the knotty cultural and racial issues of her
day, issues still with us; and out of her empathetic zeal for "otherness" came
her "classic" books.

Remley finds *Our Southwest, Erna Fergusson's Albuquerque,* and *Murder
and Mystery in New Mexico* flawed and lesser works than either *Dancing*

Gods and *New Mexico: A Pageant of Three Peoples*. *Our Southwest* he finds the least satisfying because of its overly ambitious scope, although he concedes that "her observations and her pattern for touring the Southwest are interesting in themselves" but neglects to elaborate on just what he means by such a statement (*EF,* 32). *New Mexico* he judges her best book, and the culmination of a lifetime spent living, studying, and traveling in New Mexico (*EF,* 34). All in all, Remley finds Fergusson a difficult writer to place, a difficulty complicated by what he views as her eclipse by the achievements of her grandfather, father, and her brothers, novelist Harvey Fergusson and critic/professor Francis Fergusson. In this judgment and in the following summary assessment there is room for debate: "Her work is not a part of a literary tradition, but essentially an isolated phenomenon in the Southwest (she wrote fifty years later than the first great popularizer, Charles F. Lummis, and her work is very different from that of Mary Austin and Paul Horgan). She wrote little fiction and no poetry. Hence, she cannot be treated with the usual devices of literary criticism" (*EF,* 36).

Assuredly, there is much validity in what Remley says. And friends like Powell tend to agree in not regarding Fergusson as actually at the center of the Southwestern literary establishment during her lifetime. But what is the distinction between "letters" and "literature"? In part, the distinction depends on the identification of travel literature and journalism adjudged, even to this postmodern time, as decidedly lesser literary enterprises. Such assumptions deserve greater questioning, especially in relation to the tradition of Southwestern literary history, regional writing, gender theory, American, comparative cultures, and ethnic studies.

Travel narratives and "reports," discussed earlier, are at the center of writing about the Southwest, intrinsic to its very history. Even Remley seemingly contradicts his assertion by alluding to Lummis as the first great popularizer. A half-century gap notwithstanding, Fergusson nevertheless does fit into a tradition of Southwestern writers who were indeed popularizers. Moreover, her residence in Albuquerque rather than the artist colonies of Taos and Santa Fe in no way places her outside the tradition of the Southwest Renaissance as it occurred in New Mexico in the 1920s and 1930s.

This book attempts to reevaluate Fergusson, her identities, reputation, and her legacy as Miss Fergusson, Beautiful Swift Fox, and first lady of New Mexico letters. Fergusson's personae go much beyond any one, simplistic, isolated ingredient. The lives and the landscapes of her environment affected her in quite complex ways, ways which allowed her, perhaps compelled her, to express herself in writing. At this point, a few years from century's turning and more than a century after her birth in 1888, as interest grows in such areas as "new history," "new ethnic studies," and "new journalism," in travel narrative, the poetics and aesthetics of regionalism, semiotics, deconstruction, the artistic and scientific relationships between history and fiction, Erna Fergusson's perspective on the Southwest gains in its fascination—and its enchantment. Eventually, and perhaps more so now in the feminist nineties, most who approach her through her writings find her a friend, flawed in many of her views and pronouncements, determined by place, gender, and ethnic heritage but wanting to transcend those "limitations." Many past readers, consequently, found her very human in her love for lives and landscapes and never misanthropic. So perhaps new readers can come to agree with Lawrence Clark Powell that in her warmth for living and her tolerance for the many forms it takes, Erna Fergusson's books were indeed her monument, and through them she remains "Shikya-wa-nim," Beautiful Swift Fox.

Appendix

. . . .

South and West:
Fergusson's Latin American,
Caribbean, and Hawaiian Travels

Fergusson's Southwestern travel books provide only one focus, albeit a major one, in understanding her complex and multifaceted roles as Beautiful Swift Fox, Miss Fergusson, first lady of literature, and woman writer—a traveler, historian, advocate, and "new" woman in not just a new West but a new world which opened to her through her travels and writing about them.

It is important, however, to pay some attention here to her other travel books and her vista farther south, farther west into Latin America and Hawaii. Her Southwestern and her South-West commentaries—both thematically and stylistically—evidence her dedication to discovering not only her identity as a privileged Anglo–New Mexican woman in the twentieth century but also her attempts at understanding other cultures. These other cultures, largely Hispanic, were defining and determining both continents of the Americas, north and south, and directly influenced the history of her New Mexico home and her modern Southwest. They also reciprocally influenced the Southwest's and America's influence on the ancient but new, democratically developing "modern" countries of Mexico, Central and South America, Cuba, and the imperialism, or the territorial and military imperative and extension of American manifest destiny, which had propelled the Anglo-American settlement of the Southwest far across the Pacific to the Hawaiian Islands (and farther), to a west much past her own immediate Albuquerque horizon.

Fergusson's grandfather, Franz Huning, had settled in Albuquerque's Old Town and developed New Town as early Albuquerque burgeoned with the coming of the Santa Fe railroad. Erna Fergusson, like her brothers, Harvey and Francis Fergusson, all of them born at that transitional time at the end of the nineteenth century and the beginning of the twentieth, awoke to a morning after. It was a time when the alleged closing of the frontier and the coming of more than just the railroad signaled both technological promise and paranoia, the anxiety of many and severe machines in the garden, from the automobile to the atomic bomb.

Her mother, Clara Mary, had pioneered as well as persevered as a daughter, wife, and mother through the rise and fall of the Huning-Fergusson dynasty and through the tragedy, depression, and despair of her husband's suicide. She, too, awoke on a morning after in that once idyllic and soon most ironic of haciendas, La Glorieta, to find her prominent husband dead beside her with his throat slit by his own hand. Perhaps Erna Fergusson's travels were largely determined by those ghosts, and perhaps that is why she remained "Miss Fergusson" and never married, choosing rather to run with young Hopi girls as Beautiful Swift Fox and, in passing, to observe and to engage the many families, cultural and national, she sought to understand and explain.

Whatever her psychological identifications and motives, Fergusson realized early on that the Hispanic and Latin cultures which had helped make the cultures, the places, and the spirit of the Southwest, were far from static. Indeed, they were evolving and dynamic, living cultures and countries which were still in a very deep and protracted partnership, linked by language as well as by certain cartographies of longitudes and latitudes. The relative location and boundary of "Southwest," Fergusson soon realized, is contextual and variable—as much recognizable by north-south forces of settlement and empire as by east-west. She traveled little north, in Canada or Alaska. And she cared hardly at all for her European, Germanic roots, if we are to infer interest and importance from those places about which she wrote.

Her compass was pointed south and west, and in traveling those directions she also traveled along parallel paths and routes familiar to her own home in the American Southwest. Her Southwest informed her perception of Mexico and Latin America, Cuba and Hawaii—and those disparate yet kindred places informed and gave meaning to her central demarcation point, her New Mexico home, her *tierra encantada.*

All of which is to say that ultimately Fergusson's travel writings are of a whole and reinforce our own almost desperate postmodern need also to look south and west, all along Mexico, all through Central and South

America and the whole Pacific Rim to the large world suddenly come home again, and with new imperatives, to our Southwest, to our global village. In this sense, Fergusson's Latin American and other non-Southwestern travel writings, albeit at times seemingly quaint and naive in certain respects—both historical and technological—are in actuality fascinating and full of meaning. And that meaning, if not prophetic, is astute and prescient, and most enjoyable and entertaining.

Interwoven with the publication of her Southwestern writings, Fergusson's books on Mexico, Guatemala, Venezuela, Hawaii, Chile, and Cuba are essentially windows on the 1930s, 1940s, and early 1950s—the era and legacies of Franklin Roosevelt, World War II, and New Deal, liberal Democrat attempts to strengthen good neighbor, Latin American, and world policies. In this respect, in these books about the wider southern continent Fergusson's tendency toward advocacy of the downtrodden, be it American Indians or Spanish Americans or Mexican Americans in her Southwestern writings, turns against tyranny and dictatorship to champion heroes and heroines of political liberation and intercultural understanding. Writing, characteristically, from a perspective of at times bothersome paternalism and Yankee jingoism, Fergusson nevertheless empathizes with Latin disdain and intolerance for pushy and domineering Ugly American tourists and politicians. Although empathetic and tolerant of such reciprocated intolerance, Fergusson never misses a chance to fire back at either the defensiveness or the arrogance of nationalists and, at least in the instance of *Venezuela* and *Chile,* at displaced and hostile Nazis.

Always sensitive to her role as outsider, often perceived as a know-nothing gringa visitor herself, Fergusson is always gracious, always demonstrative of both pluck and charm, anxious to try her self-deprecating fluency in Spanish with peasants and aristocrats in seedy as well as first-class hotels and homes. She seemingly adapts as easily to comfortable cruise ships, sleek and smooth-flying airplanes, and powerful touring cars as she does to sputtering boats and rattletrap buses and taxis. A few minutes freshening up with cold cream and a washcloth or drinking a cup of tea or a cool native beer or beverage and she's ready for the next phase of her journey—seeing historical towns and monuments, talking with people of all classes and occupations: educators, radical reformers, old-guard protectionists, young Turk idealists. Whether engaged in deliberations and discussions about democracy, art, life, or comparative cultures, Fergusson is always vibrant, engaged, and engaging.

Her method is generally to describe her mode of travel, her route, and the geographical locale as she first experiences it, laced through with personal anecdotes about friends or guides, women, children, and men of various degrees of talent and intelligence. Then she offers a historical overview of the country, narrowed first to great leaders, both male and female, widening out to a discussion of folkways and mores, customs, ceremonials, and celebrations which are intrinsic to the respective cultural identities of the people and countries she visits and of significant interest to her and, she naturally assumes, to her readers. In this respect she is seldom wrong. She almost always summarizes recent key books and readings which have given her insight about her destinations and often schedules an audience or a chat with those very same intellectuals, authors and artists and politicos, who have stimulated her thinking about their countries. Never fully accepting of their writings, always critical and inquiring, Fergusson involves her reader in the various important and pedestrian dialectics of the day.

If there are key Americans living in the cities she visits she usually has contact with them and benefits from their advice and counsel. Her itineraries seem simultaneously planned and spontaneous as does her role as a lone female tourist but also a kind of emissary, representative of larger American group or organizational interests.

She pauses often to tell an interpolated story or two, be it myth or legend or gossip somehow become crucial, transcendent. And, as is the case in her Southwestern writings, her descriptions of various events and places, recreations or worships, offer the highest of rewards to the reader, topped only by her strategically placed, perfectly apt turns of phrase which usually get their kick from the ironic or anticlimactic rhetorical flourish she gives them. If style is best described as the total way in which an author dramatizes herself or himself, Fergusson's style is determined by her good humor, her lightly barbed sarcasm, and her overall tone and voice of personableness. Readers—her contemporary readers and latter-day readers—come away convinced that she would make a fine traveling companion—always the sport, never the wet blanket, redoubtable in her ability to find and to attribute the best possible interpretation to even the most disappointing of plans gone awry. One always feels Fergusson applies her own experiences as a tour guide to project on herself the best possible role of the tourist who is being guided and shown around someone else's very beloved country. In this sense Fergusson's books prove that the best tourist is an experienced tour guide.

This is not to say that Fergusson comes across as some Polyanna dogooder and blind optimist. Quite the contrary. Although seldom pessimistic or cynical, even in her sanguinity she is at times painfully truthful, even to the point of embarrassment in certain of her judgments and observations about race and class.

More than once she breaks over into what today would be bothersome, even offensive, generalizations about physical beauty or ugliness, about sanitary conditions, about overall backwardness of deprived individuals, bloodlines, and groups. So that, as in her Southwestern writings, what for her time was no doubt a vanguard position in relation to issues of class, gender, race, and ethnicity are now often awkward and seemingly tactless. Various discussions about breeding and eugenics, even the ironically proposed need to thin out the Germanic strain in South America, strike one— although admittedly much a part of her times of world war and proposed in honesty—awkward, ill-advised, and upsetting in the reading.

A classic instance of this is in the following sentences from her generally delightful chapter entitled "Children's Fiestas" on, most specifically, San Juan's Day in *Fiesta in Mexico:* "It used to be said that every Mexican bathed then [San Juan's Day] whether he needed it or not. But this is just another of the many silly misconceptions about Mexicans."[1] One anonymous reader has crossed out these sentences in heavy ballpoint ink, evidence of some significant discomfort and disagreement, maybe either hurt or anger. Thus, even in her attempt to correct one of the "silly misconceptions," as if protesting too much, Fergusson's effect is opposite of her intention. Many such instances appear in her writings and particularly evidence the difficulty of her mission across more than national boundaries to bring about greater intercultural understanding and communication. Fergusson remains undaunted in the enterprise, however, in her resolve to improve cultural relations with Latin America and Hawaiian cultures, and more than a half dozen such books offer her testimonial to this cause.

In *Chile* Fergusson devotes an entire chapter to "Cultural Relations," discussed explicitly and directly. The entire book began as a result of a trip, sponsored by the U.S. Department of State and the Committee on Cultural Relations with Latin America, which was to introduce Fergusson to South America as a kind of envoy who might help introduce Latin America to other Americans—and to each other.

Whatever the governmental presumption, or benevolent intent, or ignorance, or pragmatism in the face of world war and needed hemispheric allies in 1938 when the Committee was established, Fergusson was a willing partner in the big Uncle Sam mission of the moment: "What a historical irony if the function of the United States should be that of introducing Latin Americans to one another."[2]

As usual, she is humble in insisting that she knows relatively little about Chile specifically or South America more generally (although she had traveled in and written about Venezuela five or so years earlier), but she is confident of her way with people and shines in self-confidence of much travel into foreign and exotic lands.

In her explanations about the nature of cultural relations she does her best to speak like a governmental envoy. Even here, however, she retains her independence and healthy individualism. Cultures meet either to clash or fuse, she insists, and, as such, cultural relations are not always jolly good tourist fun. Fergusson sees person-to-person relations at the heart of all nation-to-nation relations, and this functions as the baseline for all of her Latin and other travels:

> Perhaps it is typical of the idealistic United States to use the phrase as connoting only good and of our gift for organization that we have set up a division under the Department of State to foster more and better cultural exchange with the whole world. It always seems to us that anything well done by individuals could be better done on a large scale by trained and organized groups. This may be true, though it would be truer if the original man to man aspect of human relations were never lost sight of. (*Chile*, 329)

That Fergusson saw her role as envoy secondary to her role as personal ambassador and writer is apparent. Each of her Latin and Hawaiian books is replete with her self-identification as a writer, come to see, to try and understand, and to assimilate and communicate what she does find for those travelers who will follow her, either vicariously through her books, or who might place more practical utility on her books as actual cultural "maps" of their own replicated journeys. And in *Chile* she sets forth the catechism of questions and expectations with which she is confronted by local citizenry who often seek to wrap up their impressions in as short a time as possible before confusion and complexity—and true knowledge—overwhelm them. Fergusson speaks generally about "foreign," and especially Yankee, writers, but she holds up the mirror of suspicion to herself as well:

> Writers are looked upon with suspicion. As why should they not be? There is something impudent about bouncing into a country, un-invited, to write about it. A citizen might reasonably inquire "Who are you, anyway? How dare you assume that you are fitted to write about us? Why should we who live here suffer being presented to your countrymen as we happen to strike you? Is your judgment any good? Is your heart in the right place? Can you speak our language, appreci-ate our point of view? Do you know our history, our literature? Are

you going to stay long enough, study hard enough, to qualify on any
of these points?" (*Chile*, 136–137)

And herein is the crux of what Fergusson tries to accomplish in her travel
writings, Southwestern and South-West. She seeks to "run the race," become the Beautiful Swift Fox which those legendary Hopi girls reputedly
named her. She seeks to establish her credibility by working hard to see the
point of view, know the hearts of the people and places, the personalities
and landscapes she observes and portrays.

Certainly her intended readers are not the people of Latin American
or Cuba or Hawaii any more than they are the Navajos or the Pueblos or
the Apaches or Mexican Americans who are the subjects of her Southwestern writings. She presumably knew them better and closer, being a native
daughter to that region of the United States. No doubt Fergusson's books,
intimate and closely researched as they are, are not totally convincing or
impressive to rigorous cultural scholars of either the U.S. or Latin America
or to the native, citizen residents and readers of the cultures she interprets.
But as a popularizer, as a first impression, much past superficial or glib or
insincere misunderstanding or incomprehension, Fergusson, in her travels
south-west, offers an enjoyable introduction to new ways in new worlds,
even today when those worlds are often more virtually known and accessible as films, as television, as digitized data and disks than they are as real,
on-site experiences.

It is not difficult to ascribe relative merit to these books. Each reader
will find a favorite, determined in part by his or her affinity for each respective country and by current tides of historical and diplomatic events. In
this regard, Fergusson's books on Mexico and her fascinating tour of Cuba
perhaps hold most interest to American readers today. Assuredly her observations about Mexico and its celebrations—and then her later revisitation
to this close border neighbor—afford considerable insight. That insight
reveals to us the democratic and economic struggles of a country which
so very much influences the contemporary Southwest, our population, our
demographics, our travel agreements, and our pluralistic identity as both
Southwest and Aztlán, two sides, two dynamics of two reciprocal directions of immigration and cultural traffic.

If only for Fergusson's explanations of the celebrations of Cinco de
Mayo and Day of the Dead and of the powerful grasp of the Virgin of
Guadalupe and of Malinche (Anglos, often being either dazed or dazzled
by these celebrations as experienced through adoption and adaptation in
the Southwest), *Fiesta in Mexico* is timeless reading, much infused with
mythic understanding of Indian and mestizo Mexico. As such, it is still

rewarding as a handbook for persons sojourning in the Mexican Southwest as well as traveling to Mexico for either business or pleasure.

Guatemala, although in many ways the lesser of this group of books, affords considerable insight on Mexico's near neighbor and its causal influence on all of *el norte* as it extends all the way to the U.S. and throughout California, Arizona, New Mexico, and Texas. And *Venezuela* shines as a wonderful text on Simón Bolívar, the liberator, and Juan Vicente Gómez as Bolívar's and the country's powerful and tyrannical nemesis. And just as Bolívar stands tall and impressive, eponymic and charismatic, so too does Manuela Saenz, the woman who proved so important to both Bolívar and Venezuela.

Fergusson spends chapter after chapter, certainly more than equal time, on the heroines who have helped shape and determine Latin America, women with whom she identifies as a woman, as an intellectual, and women who serve as examples for all of Fergusson's readers—"new" women, rising in the long struggle of overall civility and equality, of suffrage and liberation from male domination.

Perhaps the most fascinating of the real—now become legendary— women who populate these books is Gabriela Mistral, the great Chilean poet and author whom Fergusson knew and much admired. Just as Bolívar registers in Fergusson's rendering of Venezuela and the broader spirit of South American liberation, Mistral pervades Fergusson's commendations of all Latin women who will, she feels confident, lead Chile to a fuller democracy. Seldom sycophantic or blindly worshipful of class or status, Fergusson's account of her visit with Mistral is compelling and indicative of the real force of change involved when kindred spirits convene in serious and fruitful discussion.

Fergusson's travel books need not be read in any special order—chronological or otherwise. As with most travel accounts—whether vacation, pilgrimage, exploration, recreation, or tourism—preparations, departures, and arrivals provide the general structure. And Fergusson's travel books generally follow suit and should be read both for these processes and for the greater understanding of the specific geographical locales and destinations. In this sense her Mexico books work to frame the others—Mexico's fiestas detailed initially and more broadly subsequently when she revisits Mexico twenty years later. Thus, the stop time of timeless myth and ritual is juxtaposed with commentary on the urbanization and social change wrought during those intervening years in a culture still very much tied to its indigenous Indian, Aztec, and Spanish influences. *Guatemala* functions as a segue or stepping-stone to her two main South American works, *Venezuela* and *Chile.* Her writings about the two islands, Cuba and Hawaii, then provide a wider, flanking perspective. In such an ordering her Hawaiian accounts stand something apart from the unity of her other works, all of them Hispanic and Latin in their cohesion.

Fiesta in Mexico is doubtlessly closest to her Southwestern writings, and its high points are her account of the Aztec culture with its pre-Cortesian ritualized human sacrifices and indigenous splendor and her linking those ancient blood ceremonies to a whole string of later-evolving rituals and fiestas, all modified by Catholicism and its rituals. Her account of Los Voladores, the flying men of Coxquihue is most vivid. This account, with all its linkage to ancient Aztec ritual, is presented in a fashion strikingly similar to Fergusson's accounts of American Indian dances in *Dancing Gods* and particularly to her fine account of the Shalako at Zuni.

All of *Fiesta in Mexico* is imprinted with techniques and themes found in *Dancing Gods*, and they are in many respects as much companion books as are *Fiesta in Mexico* and *Mexico Revisited*. The closeness of their composition and publication is reflected in their similarity of method.

Mexico Revisited (1955) is arranged according to the regions and directionality of the country—south, north, heartland, gulf, and center. A section of four chapters does resurrect some of Fergusson's earlier historical exposition and reasserts her interest in the Spanish conquest and its importance to Mexico and the American Southwest. But each region, as elaborated upon in *Fiesta*, is explained in terms of its special subcultural and subregional identity—from dances to linguistic idioms. Fergusson touts the liberators, of course—Zapata, Juárez, Pancho Villa—and is especially favorable to his widow Luz Corral, the woman who had shared in Villa's revolutionary zeal. Here, too, Fergusson's visit with Corral is at once charming and laudatory in its tribute to female forces and the role they play in the fate of nations and the determining of culture. William Randolph Hearst, Winfield Scott, Zachary Taylor, and the convergences which took Fray Marcos and Esteban in search of the golden cities of Cíbola again contribute to her linking of Mexico and the United States and the Southwest.

Guatemala takes its significance from Fergusson's fascination with the old Mayan empire, her accounts of the ruins of Copán, and an overview of archaeology in Central America. The modern Mayans she finds less friendly than Mexicans, but she exhibits considerable identification with the costumes, textiles, and especially the beauty of Antigua, the capital. Indian dances and ancient ritual again come to the forefront, but two most distinctive chapters are on "Coffee" and "Totonicapán," the essential, undefiled town of the republic. Of further interest, too, is Fergusson's impatience with American tourists generally—a bunch of spoiled softies in her estimation:

> Tourists take Guatemala timidly. Surely the world has never before produced as timorous, self-coddling, and jittery a specimen as the modern American tourist. Incredible that the grandchildren, even the children, of the hardy conquerors of a continent should be so scary. And what will come next? Of what earthly use will be these children who prattle of germs in their perambulators, who are trained to consider comfort above all gods, and who are so sheltered that they acquire no immunities, either to disease or to the least discomfort or inconvenience?[3]

Ever undaunted, Fergusson traipses all over the country, immune both to germs and discomfort—including bothersome tourists of lesser fortitude than she. But the chapter on coffee is a set piece, which, like Fergusson's accounts of key Mexican holidays and fiestas, stands alone as providing useful and fascinating background on a product which so very much affects people's lives around the world. Here, too, thanks to Fergusson's tough tourist tenure, strong or bad coffee, ironically part of the tourist's experience in both city and village, never fazes her—always accepting and curious of how such a product, like bananas or like cigars in Cuba, can typify—or stereotypify—so very much of a country's essential nature in a place where "all conversation . . . gets around sooner rather than later to the coffee crop and the world market" (*Guatemala*, 228).

When turning to Fergusson's accounts of islands, her Hawaiian writings, although informative, especially for wartime ambiance, pale in relation to her account of Cuba—a book where she truly hits her stride as a travel writer. Most unique, however, is her attempt to share her interest in cultural geography and heightening cultural relations with young readers—readers much in need, Fergusson felt, of knowledge and training to prevent them from becoming the stereotypical, fastidious American whiner abroad. In this respect her work of juvenilia, *Hawaiian Islands*, published in textbook format bears consideration. Published throughout the 1950s, Fergusson's young adult writing is clear and informative, stripped to essentials, but still conveying her common sense and good humor—her spunk and her sense of mission to spread the word that people must get to know people, all people, diverse people and places.

The intended audience is clearly travelers who, even if they do not take world tours, will find that the world will come to them, as it did on December 7, 1941, when the Japanese attacked Pearl Harbor. In a certain sense the many large photographs intrude rather than augment Fergusson's descriptions and explanations—especially when appearing in her books intended for adult travelers. But her choices are sound and her explanations full and, in the end, helpful to readers of all ages.

If the format were different her small book on Hawaii would make a fine carry-along, basic guide book. She talks of the geography and geology of the islands, tells of the races and their history, the missionaries (who, as a group, Fergusson consistently finds too intrusive and pervasive, and much inferior to live-and-let-live tourists), and the great assortment of produce —from sugar to pineapples to fish. Her descriptions of native crafts is again a characteristic component as is her effective chapter on the meaning and tradition of a luau and its accompanying music and dance. Much ahead of its time, Fergusson's chapter on multiracial and multicultural Hawaii anticipates much of today's concern with multicultural education. She closes with a typical, almost formulaic, chapter on Hawaii as a tourist wonderland.

In most ways, and impressive ways they are, Fergusson's best travel book outside of her Southwestern writings is *Cuba* (1946). One of the most intriguing of present-day travel books about Cuba is Tom Miller's *Trading with the Enemy: A Yankee Travels through Castro's Cuba* (1992). Author of many finely crafted and insightful travel books, Miller is much in the tradition of Fergusson—who as a Yankee traveling through pre-Castro Cuba found it alluring and glorious but in need of much liberation, too. As might be expected, Fergusson's hero, like the hero of many Cubans, is José Martí—a man whose preeminence Fergusson found in his personality, his spirit, and his talent as a great orator and writer (qualities held by Fergusson, too). And as might be expected, Fergusson's respect for Martí makes for one of the most compelling and memorable biographies in the book and evidences how biography can indeed determine history. Very much a book engaged with governmental forces in Cuban history, Fergusson's *Cuba* discusses colonial Cuba, its revolutionary tradition, and its close interrelation with the United States through both war and occupation—as well as trade.

Fergusson posits two Cubas—one sophisticated and one primitive— and both are dramatized in the most vivid ways. It is finally, however, the primitive Cuba which wins out in its inscrutable appeal, echoing Fergusson's continuing fascination with all strains, high and low, of exoticism and the white, Anglo tourist's alluring encounters with "dark and dusky" peoples. That such a genteel and civil woman as Fergusson could concern herself with witching, *brujería*, and *Naniguismo* points again to Fergusson's limitless curiosity and fascination with human behavior.

Admittedly, much of her knowledge comes from her own readings, but, again, her accounts of her own visits to a local *bruja* heighten the excitement connected with the subject and validate Fergusson's characteristic insistence on firsthand, person-to-person tourism. Always capable of writing about "sophisticated" elements and classes of any country and very much at home at those levels, Fergusson is, ironically, at her best when delving into the more magical and mystical and ritualistic aspects of culture and humanity. And this kind of juxtaposition puts just the right edge of shock and at times dark humor on what might otherwise be the one-sided, much sheltered, monotonous account of a lonely, aging "old maid," the "Miss Fergusson" side of her persona and personality. It transforms her into a heroine of her own occasions, very much a lone adventurer and courageous voyager offering us the observations and accounts of a vivacious and intelligent woman, a woman fully worthy of the appellation and the continuing, self-perpetuating mystique of a Beautiful Swift Fox.

Notes

. . . .

INSPIRATION: *TIERRA ENCANTADA*

1. Stanley Walker, "Long River, Long Book," *New Yorker,* Dec. 4, 1954, 229.

2. Leonard Lutwack, *The Role of Place in Literature.*

3. Lutwack, *Role of Place,* 2.

4. Rudolfo A. Anaya, "The Writer's Landscape: Epiphany in Landscape," *Latin American Literary Review* 5, no. 10 (Spring/Summer, 1977): 98–102.

5. Peggy Pond Church, "Return to a Landscape: For Mary MacArthur Bryan," unpublished typescript, Oct. 27, 1982–Mar. 2, 1983. Author's collection.

6. Anaya, "Writer's Landscape," 99.

7. Anaya, "Writer's Landscape," 100.

8. Anaya, "Writer's Landscape," 102. See also, William J. Mills, "Metaphorical Vision: Changes in Western Attitudes to the Environment," *Annals of the Association of American Geographers* 72, no. 2 (June, 1982): 237–53.

9. Marta Weigle and Kyle Fiore, *Santa Fe and Taos: The Writers Era, 1916–1941,* 11.

10. Emily Hahn, *Mabel: A Biography of Mabel Dodge Luhan,* 162.

11. Hahn, *Mabel,* 164.

12. See, for example, Peter Conrad, "Primitive America: D. H. Lawrence in New Mexico," 159–93.

13. See D. H. Lawrence, *Phoenix: The Posthumous Papers, 1936.*

14. Erna Fergusson, *Our Southwest,* 371. See also Glyne A. Griffith's "Travel Narrative as Cultural Critique: V. S. Naipaul's Travelling Theory," *Journal of Commonwealth Literature* 29, no. 2 (1993): 87–92. Griffith rightly contends: "Travel narrative participates in [a] complex power/knowledge nexus, and each literate/literary representation of a people and a culture may be seen for the most part as a consolidation of old stereotypes or alternately, as an examination and denaturalization of stereotype. The consolidated stereotype informs and is also informed by particular ways of seeing the world and the power relations in it" (88). Seen in this context, Lawrence's perceptions as traveler were power perceptions based on his own will to power perceptions about the "battle of the sexes," whether in indigenous or Anglo-European cultural or geographical settings.

15. D. H. Lawrence, *Studies in Classic American Literature,* 5–6.

16. D. H. Lawrence, "Taos," *Phoenix*, 100.

17. D. H. Lawrence, "New Mexico," *Phoenix*, 141–42.

18. Lawrence, "New Mexico," 142. See also Hahn, *Mabel*, 117–25.

19. Carl G. Jung, *Memories, Dreams, Reflections*, 247.

20. Jung, *Memories, Dreams, Reflections*, 248.

21. Jung, *Memories, Dreams, Reflections*, 249.

22. Jung, *Memories, Dreams, Reflections*, 252.

23. Jung, *Memories, Dreams, Reflections*, 253. For what amounts to an "anthology" of "enchantment" writers, see Tony Hillerman, ed. *The Spell of New Mexico*.

24. See Franz Huning, *Trader on the Santa Fe Trail: Memoirs of Franz Huning*, ed., with notes by his granddaughter, Lina Fergusson Browne; *Valencia News-Bulletin*, Mar. 22, 1982, 12; Joseph C. Winter, "Riddle of the Mysterious Rock," *Impact*, Jun. 12, 1984, 10.

25. See Erna Fergusson, *The Santa Fe New Mexican*, 12. See also Marc Simmons, *Albuquerque: A Narrative History*, 153–56, 164–65, 205–206, 217–20, 224–28, 236–37, 282–84.

26. Fergusson, *Santa Fe New Mexican*, 12. See also Irene Fisher, "Erna Fergusson," *Albuquerque Review*, Feb. 8, 1962, 8. Franz Huning's memoirs influenced both Erna and Harvey Fergusson in their self- and genealogical perceptions, and in their respective "historical" writings. In this respect, see Huning, *Trader*.

27. Hahn, *Mabel*, 191.

28. Dorothy Woodward, "Erna Fergusson," *New Mexico Quarterly* 22 (Spring, 1952), 88–89.

29. Fergusson, "Editorial Notes," *American Mercury* (Aug., 1931), xx.

30. See *Erna Fergusson's Albuquerque*, 23, 25–34, 37–44. Subsequent references to this source are given as *EFA* with page numbers. See also *Century Magazine* 113 (Nov., 1926), 23–31; and *Century Magazine* 113 (Dec., 1926), 199–207.

31. Remley, *Erna Fergusson*, 10–11.

32. Paul Horgan, "The Tribune Public Forum," *Albuquerque Tribune*, 1947.

33. Horgan, "Tribune Public Forum," 1947.

34. See Erna Fergusson, "Albuquerque: A Place to Live In," 151–78. See also *Encyclopaedia Britannica*, 1973 ed., s. v. "Albuquerque." She wrote several entries on both Albuquerque and the Southwest—early and late in her career, and reprinted in various editions—for both the *Encyclopaedia Britannica* and the *American Oxford Encyclopaedia*. The difficulties she went through, first in a rejection from Knopf, then in haggling with Dr. Paul A. F. Walker and Fred Harvey of the University of New Mexico Press, and then in deciding to underwrite the publication of the book herself with the help of a loan and the advice and assistance of Jim Threlkeld, an Albuquerque bookstore owner, and Merle Armitage, makes an interesting story in itself. Forced to make her living by her writing, she was a shrewd business woman in addition to her other roles. For example, she took on the 2,500-word *Encyclopedia Britannica* assignment from Kenneth Chapman for fifty dollars in part as "a lever if I wish to use [it] to push this UPress [*sic*] agreement on" (May 29, 1947, notes on "Talk with Dr. Paul A. F. Walker Jr.," Erna Fergusson Papers, University of New Mexico Zimmerman Library).

35. Joseph Addison, "The Pleasures of the Imagination," 2:178–79.

36. See John McPhee, "Annals of the Former World: Rising From the Plains—I," *New Yorker,* Feb. 24, 1986, 38–71. See Martin Price, "The Restoration and the Eighteenth Century," 1558–59. See also Frederick Turner, *Beyond Geography: The Western Spirit against the Wilderness;* "Literature Lost in the Thickets," *New York Times Book Review,* Feb. 15, 1987, 1–35.

37. *Encyclopaedia Britannica,* s. v. "Albuquerque," 16:533.

38. See box 7, no. 5, Fergusson Papers, University of New Mexico.

39. Erna Fergusson, "Bernalillo County," *New Mexico State Tribune,* Aug. 16, 1929.

40. Erna Fergusson, "Summary of a talk given at the Tourist School conducted by the New Mexico Dept. of Vocational Education in cooperation with the New Mexico State Tourist Bureau, the Public Schools, and the Chamber of Commerce," p. 2. Erna Fergusson file, Southwest Collection, Albuquerque Public Library.

41. Erna Fergusson, "The Jemez Mountains," *New Mexico State Tribune,* 1929, 6.

42. Fergusson, "The Jemez Mountains," 6.

43. Irene Fisher, interview with author, Albuquerque, New Mexico, July 9, 1981.

44. Fisher interview.

45. Keleher to Tingley, Jan. 3, 1955, box 8, no. 6, Fergusson Papers, University of New Mexico.

46. "Contract," Feb. 14, 1955, box 8, no. 6, Fergusson Papers, University of New Mexico. Of the proposed thirteen chapters, all are extant except chapter 2, which has been missing from Fergusson's papers since 1968. The proposed chapter title, "Alderman from the Bloody Second," makes the reason for the missing chapter all the more curious, if not mysterious.

TRAVEL: BEAUTIFUL SWIFT FOX

1. See Robert Scholes and Robert Kellogg, *The Nature of Narrative,* 3–81. See also Gaspar Pérez de Villagrá, *History of New Mexico;* Cabeza de Vaca, *Adventures in the Unknown Interior of America.*

2. Fergusson, *New Mexico: A Pageant of Three Peoples* (reprint, 1973), 161.

3. Earl Pomeroy, *In Search of the Golden West: The Tourist in Western America,* 233. For an excellent account of earlier nineteenth "literary travelers" on their way to California, see Stephen Fender, *Plotting the Golden West: American Literature and the Rhetoric of the California Trail.*

4. Pomeroy, *In Search of the Golden West,* 195.

5. John A. Jackle, *The Tourist: Travel In Twentieth-Century North America,* 231.

6. Jackle, *The Tourist,* 244.

7. See Janis P. Stout, *The Journey Narrative in American Literature: Patterns and Departures;* and Lutwack, *Role of Place.*

8. Stout, *Journey Narrative,* xi.

9. Stout, *Journey Narrative,* 15.

10. Lutwack, *Role of Place,* 138.

11. Lutwack, *Role of Place,* 142.

12. Leon Edel, "Biography and the Science of Man, *New Directions in Biography,* 2.

13. See Michel Butor, "Travel and Writing," *Mosaic* 8, no. 1 (Fall, 1974), 1–16.

14. Butor, "Travel and Writing," 1–13.

15. Butor, "Travel and Writing," 14.

16. Butor, "Travel and Writing," 15.

17. Butor, "Travel and Writing," 2.

18. Warner G. Rice, introduction to *Literature as a Mode of Travel*, 8. See also Donald R. Howard, *Writers and Pilgrims*, 104–27; Frans C. Amelinckx and Joyce N. Megay, eds., *Travel, Quest, and Pilgrimage as a Literary Theme;* Terry Tempest Williams, "The Erotic Landscape," *American Nature Writing, 1995,* 68–73; Donald Horne, *The Intelligent Tourist;* Marta Weigle, "On Coyotes and Crosses: That Which Is Wild and Wooden of the Twentieth-Century Southwest," *Essays on the Changing Images of the Southwest,* 72–104; Sylvia Rodríguez, "The Tourist Gaze, Gentrification, and the Commodification of Subjectivity in Taos," *Essays on the Changing Images of the Southwest,* 105–26.

19. See Wayne Franklin, "Speaking and Touching: The Problems of Inexpressibility in American Travel Books," *America: Exploration and Travel,* 18–38; and Fender, *Plotting the Golden West.* Subsequent references to Franklin's "Speaking and Touching" are given as "S&T" with page numbers.

20. Fender, *Plotting the Golden West,* 8.

21. Fender, *Plotting the Golden West,* 8–9.

22. Rodríguez, "Tourist Gaze," 112.

23. Rodríguez, "Tourist Gaze," 111.

24. Fender, *Plotting the Golden West,* 12.

25. Fergusson, "Editorial Notes," 20. See also D. H. Thomas, "The Who of It: The Couriers," 75–94. Thomas says about Fergusson, "She had many friends among the Indians, a friendship which allowed her unusual freedom of the pueblos and a chance to get *close* to the occupants" (75). See also Lesley Poling-Kempes, *The Harvey Girls: Women Who Opened the West:* "Erna Fergusson, a native New Mexican writer and successful business woman who had operated her own tour guide service in Santa Fe since 1921, was hired by Harvey to organize a courier corps of women to accompany Detour passengers on their jaunts into the Southwest. The Indian Detour Couriers were distinguished twenty-five-year-old women carefully screened and chosen to serve as hostesses and expert guides on the Harvey cars. The women had to be college graduates, and were given crash courses in southwestern art, geology, sociology, architecture, and history" (150–51). See also Judi Morris, *The Harvey Girls: The Women Who Civilized the West,* for an account, intended for young readers, of the Harvey Girls.

26. Fergusson, *The Koshare Book,* 1.

27. Louise Lowbar Cassidy, "Interesting Westerners: A 'Delight Maker,'" *Sunset Magazine* 54 (Jan., 1925), 38. D. H. Thomas stresses the contrast allowed by Fergusson's women guides: "Instead of rough sweaty cowboys, more often taciturn than talkative, the Koshare guides were expected to talk, long and knowledgeably, about the area" "The Who of It," 76.

28. Cassidy, "Interesting Westerners," 38.

29. Weigle, "On Coyotes and Crosses," 73.

30. Cassidy, "Interesting Westerners," 39.

31. Cassidy, "Interesting Westerners," 38.

32. Cassidy, "Interesting Westerners," 38.

33. T. M. Pearce to R. F. Gish, Sept. 26, 1981.

34. Harvey Fergusson, "New Mexico: An Old Land of New Delights," *The Koshare Tours*, 6. He also incorporates some of this knowledge of his sister's Koshare business into certain of his novels, such as *Hot Saturday* (1926) and *Footloose McGarnigal* (1930).

35. Harvey Fergusson, "New Mexico," 3. See also Harvey Fergusson, "The Cult of the Indian," *Scribner's Magazine* 87, no. 2 (Aug., 1930), 129–33; and "The Lure of the West," *American Motorist* (Dec., 1927), 10–11, 27, 32.

36. See Keith L. Bryant, Jr. *History of the Atchison, Topeka, and Santa Fe Railway*, 106–22.

37. Bryant, *Atchison, Topeka, and Santa Fe*, 106.

38. Bryant, *Atchison, Topeka, and Santa Fe*, 113. .

39. See Dorothy Townsend, "Harvey and His Girls Brought Elegance to the West," *Albuquerque Journal*, July 2, 1984, A6–A7. Many of the so-called Harvey Girls answered Harvey's ads to see a West that otherwise would be closed to them. Pearl Ramsey, who worked for Harvey in the 1930s, says, "So many of the girls, like I was, couldn't afford to travel and see the world, but we saw the West and parts of the country we would not have seen . . ." (A6). Also see D. H. Thomas, "The Who of It," 75–94.

40. Fergusson, *Our Southwest*, 205.

41. Richard H. Frost, "The Romantic Inflation of Pueblo Culture, *American West*, 17 (Jan.–Feb., 1980), 59–60.

42. "Booknotes," *New Republic* 69, no. 885 (Nov., 25, 1931), 52.

43. *New Republic* (Nov. 25, 1931), 52.

44. *New Republic* (Nov. 25, 1931), 52.

45. Leslie A. White, review of *Dancing Gods, American Journal of Sociology* 37, no. 5 (March, 1932): 843.

46. White, *American Journal of Sociology* (March, 1932) 842–43.

47. "The Flavor of New Mexico," *New Mexico Quarterly* 1, no. 4 (Nov., 1931), 422.

48. Fred T. Marsh, review of *Dancing Gods, Bookman* 74 (Oct., 1931), 215.

49. Maurice Fink, review of *Dancing Gods, Colorado Magazine* 35, no. 4 (Oct., 1958), 314.

50. Lawrence Clark Powell, *Southwest Classics*, 139.

51. Powell, *Southwest Classics*, 142.

52. Writings which anticipate or repeat in greater and lesser degrees and are inherent in *Dancing Gods* include the following: "Adobe or Not Adobe," *Country Life* 59 (Jan., 1931), 65–66; "Ceremonial Dances of the Pueblos," *Travel* 58 (Dec., 1931), 15–19; "From Redskins to Railroads," *Century Magazine* 113 (Nov., 1926), 23–31; "Senators Investigate Indians," *American Mercury* 23 (Aug., 1931), 464–68.

53. Edmund Wilson, "Zuni," in *Red, Black, Blond, and Olive*, 3–68.

54. Wilson, "Zuni," 68.

55. Wilson, "Zuni," 8–9.

56. Fergusson, *Dancing Gods*, xv. Subsequent references to this source are given as *DG* with page numbers.

57. Frances Drewry McMullen, "Ask Miss Fergusson: The Woman behind a Service of Girl Couriers in the Indian Country," *Woman's Citizen* 11 (Jan., 1927), 42.

58. Harvey Fergusson, *Footloose McGarnigal*, 103–104.

59. Harvey Fergusson, *Rio Grande*, 25.

60. William A. Keleher, "Erna Fergusson," in *Historical Society of New Mexico Hall of Fame Essays*, 34.

61. Robert Sayre, "The Proper Study: Autobiography in American Studies," in *The American Autobiography*, 21–22.

HISTORY: CLIO AT THE WHEEL

1. Joseph Miller and Henry G. Alsberg, eds. *New Mexico: A Guide to the Colorful State*.

2. Erna Fergusson, "Summary of a talk," 2.

3. See Fergusson, "Ceremonial Dances of the Pueblos," 15–19; and "Laughing Priests," *Theatre Arts Monthly* 17, no. 8 (Aug., 1933), 657–63.

4. Fergusson, "Ceremonial Dances of the Pueblo," 17.

5. Fergusson, "Laughing Priests," 661.

6. It should be noted that the original title for *Dancing Gods* was *Indian Dances*. Alfred A. Knopf issued Fergusson a contract on July 25, 1930, with an advance of $500 to be charged against earnings (box 10, folder 4, Fergusson Papers, University of New Mexico). Knopf met Erna Fergusson through his friendship with Witter Bynner, "always a very close friend," and it was at Bynner's house that Knopf remembered meeting Fergusson: "I went to the southwest in the winter of the early thirties. At that time Witter Bynner . . . was what one regarded as the active king of Santa Fe. I certainly attended at least one large party which he gave and I am sure it was at one such that I met Erna Fergusson. I had known Witter Bynner for many, many years" (letter from Knopf to R. F. Gish, Aug. 1, 1983). See also William A. Keleher, "Erna Fergusson," 45–46.

7. Lawrence Stone, "The Revival of Narrative: Reflections on a New Old History," *Past and Present*, no. 85 (Nov., 1979), 15.

8. Powell, *Southwest Classics*, 144.

9. Dudley Wynn, review of *Our Southwest*, *New Mexico Quarterly* 10, no. 2 (May, 1940), 122.

10. Katherine Woods, "A Colorful Panorama of the American Southwest," *New York Times Book Review*, May 5, 1940, 22.

11. Edgar C. McMechen, review of *Our Southwest*, *Colorado Magazine* 17, no. 4 (July, 1940), 156.

12. Stanley Walker, "The Real Southwest: A Semi-Desert Paradise," *New York Herald Tribune Weekly Book Review*, May 5, 1940, 3.

13. Remley, *Erna Fergusson*, 32. It bears noting here, too, that informants in *Our Southwest* simply remain anonymous like the more stereotypical "old Indian" or "old

Apache," which, although intended to protect confidentiality, ends up sounding contrived at the very least.

14. See Powell, *Southwest Classics,* 3–11.

15. Fergusson, *Our Southwest,* 20. Subsequent references to this source are given as *OS* with page numbers.

16. See, for example, Bradford Luckingham, *The Urban Southwest.*

17. See also Clayton R. Koppes, "From New Deal to Termination: Liberalism and Indian Policy, 1933–1953," *Pacific Historical Review* 46 (Nov., 1977): 543–66.

18. Erna Fergusson to J. Frank Dobie, San Antonio, Texas, Mar. 25, 1939, Humanities Research Center, University of Texas at Austin.

19. Fergusson to Dobie, Mar. 25, 1939.

20. Fergusson to Dobie, San Antonio, Texas, Mar. 30, 1939, Humanities Research Center, University of Texas at Austin. In addition to Dobie (and numerous others), Fergusson, in the writing of *Our Southwest,* relied on advice from her longtime family friend, Paul Horgan, sending him her chapters, most notably the chapters on "interpreters" and on the High Plains. More precisely, she asked Horgan for advice on the suitability of chapter titles and such pointed questions as the following: "1. What important phase of writing, or what important writers have I left out?; 2. Where do you think I have incorrectly placed the emphasis?; 3. I'm a little bit at sea in the whole matter of poetry. What poets out of the three states do you think I should mention?" (Fergusson to Horgan, Jan. 2, 1940, also Dec. 6, 1939; original letters in possession of Horgan's estate).

21. Harold Strauss, "Manuscript Record of Alfred A. Knopf, Inc.," July 27, 1939, Alfred A. Knopf Collection, Humanities Research Center, University of Texas at Austin.

22. Fergusson to Dobie, Albuquerque, New Mexico, June 2, 1940, Knopf Collection, University of Texas at Austin.

23. Fergusson to Knopf, June 22, 1959, Knopf Collection, University of Texas at Austin.

24. Fergusson to Knopf, June 30, 1959, Knopf Collection, University of Texas at Austin.

25. Fergusson to Knopf, June 30, 1959.

26. Fergusson to Knopf, Apr. 14, 1960, Knopf Collection, University of Texas at Austin.

27. Fergusson to J. J. Willett, Aug. 21, 1948, Fergusson Papers, University of New Mexico.

28. William A. Keleher, "Read This Book in Broad Daylight, Review Advises," *Albuquerque Tribune,* Dec. 23, 1948.

29. "The Criminal Record," *Saturday Review,* Jan. 22, 1949, 32.

30. Paul Horgan to Fergusson, Dec. 13, 1947, box 8, no. 5, Fergusson Papers, University of New Mexico.

31. James West Davidson and Mark Hamilton Lytle, *After the Fact: The Art of Historical Detection,* vi.

32. Stanley Walker, "Strange and Gory Doings across the Rio Grande," *New York Herald Tribune Weekly Book Review,* Jan. 2, 1949, 2.

33. Walker, "Strange and Gory Doings," 2.

34. Horgan to Fergusson, Dec. 13, 1947, Fergusson Papers, University of New Mexico.

35. Levette J. Davidson, review of *Murder and Mystery in New Mexico, New Mexico Historical Review* 24, no. 1 (Jan., 1949), 77.

36. Davidson, *New Mexico Historical Review,* 77.

37. Remley, *Erna Fergusson,* 34.

38. Erna Fergusson, *Murder and Mystery in New Mexico,* 13. Subsequent references to this source are given as *MMNM* with page numbers.

39. Fergusson to Merle Armitage, Mar. 31, 1948, Knopf Collection, University of Texas at Austin.

40. Horgan to Fergusson, May 24, 1940, Fergusson Papers, University of New Mexico Library; Fergusson to Horgan, n.d., letter in possession of Horgan's estate.

41. Fergusson to Armitage, n.d., Knopf Collection, University of Texas at Austin.

42. Fergusson to Armitage, June 19, 1948, Knopf Collection, University of Texas at Austin.

43. Fergusson to Herbert Weinstock, Sept. 23, 1948 and Oct. 13, 1948, Knopf Collection, University of Texas at Austin.

44. See Américo Paredes, *"With His Pistol in His Hand": A Border Ballad and Its Hero.* See also the motion picture, *The Ballad of Gregorio Cortez,* starring Edward James Olmos and produced by Michael Hausman in cooperation with the Sundance Institute.

45. For accounts of H. B. Fergusson's years in White Oaks, see his son's autobiography: Harvey Fergusson, *Home in the West: An Inquiry into My Origins;* 63–67; also see Simmons, *Albuquerque: A Narrative History,* 282.

ADVOCACY: PAGEANTRY AND PREJUDICE

1. Herbert Weinstock to Erna Fergusson, Dec. 22, 1947, Knopf Collection, University of Texas at Austin.

2. Weinstock to Fergusson, Dec. 22, 1947. Over the course of their correspondence about *New Mexico,* Weinstock issued some rather strong-sounding instructions to Fergusson about the scope of the book and what to emphasize. For example, "I do hope . . . that in your understandable eagerness to present the realities of present day New Mexico you will not forget that a large part of your possible audience will consist of tourists who will want to visit the state for its scenery, its Indians, and its wonderful remnants of various pasts—you will not, I am sure, dwell on the merely picturesque— but I don't want you to forget that it exists" (Feb. 21, 1949, box 10, folder 1, Fergusson Papers, University of New Mexico).

3. Fergusson to Weinstock, Jan. 5, 1948, Knopf Collection, University of Texas at Austin.

4. Fergusson to Weinstock, Jan. 5, 1948.

5. Fergusson to Weinstock, Jan. 15, 1949, Knopf Collection, University of Texas at Austin.

6. Fergusson to Weinstock, Jan. 15, 1949.

7. Fergusson to Carey McWilliams, Jan. 10, 1949, box. 1, folder 5, Fergusson Papers, University of New Mexico.

8. Fergusson to Weinstock, Jan. 15, 1949.

9. Fergusson to Weinstock, Feb. 1, 1949. Knopf Collection, University of Texas at Austin.

10. Fergusson to Weinstock, Feb. 1, 1949.

11. Plan to draw up contract, n.d., Knopf Collection, University of Texas at Austin.

12. Fergusson to Weinstock, Apr. 27, 1949, Knopf Collection, University of Texas at Austin. See also Erna Fergusson, "The New New Mexican," *New Mexico Quarterly Review* 19 (Winter, 1949), 417–26.

13. Fergusson to Weinstock, Apr. 27, 1949.

14. Fergusson to Weinstock, Apr. 27, 1949.

15. Weinstock to Fergusson, May 2, 1949, box 10, folder 2, Fergusson Papers, University of New Mexico.

16. Fergusson to Weinstock, June 29, 1950, Knopf Collection, University of Texas at Austin.

17. Fergusson to Weinstock, June 29, 1950.

18. Fergusson to Knopf, July 27, 1949, Knopf Collection, University of Texas at Austin.

19. Fergusson to Knopf, Jan. 30, 1952. Knopf Collection, Univ. of Texas at Austin.

20. Knopf to Fergusson, Feb. 1, 1952, Knopf Collection, University of Texas at Austin.

21. Harvey Fergusson to Erna Fergusson, July 9, 1951, box 1, folder 15, Fergusson Papers, University of New Mexico.

22. Harvey Fergusson to Erna Fergusson, July 20, 1951, box 1, folder 15, Fergusson Papers, University of New Mexico.

23. Weinstock to Fergusson, Aug. 9, 1951, box 10, folder 2, Fergusson Papers, University of New Mexico.

24. Fergusson to Weinstock, Aug. 13, 1951, box 10, folder 2, Fergusson Papers, University of New Mexico.

25. Fergusson to Weinstock, Sept. 4, 1956, Knopf Collection, University of Texas at Austin.

26. Fergusson, *New Mexico,* 394. Subsequent references to this source are given as *NM* with page numbers.

27. Fergusson admitted to Herbert Weinstock that the title for her third section "throws me." She told him: "Anglo, commonly used as opposed to Hispano or Spanish, I do not like; we are so much more everything else than English. *Gringo*, established as of ancient Spanish usage meaning foreigner or outlander, would be correct and reflects our diverse origin. But the word does carry a derogatory implication" (Fergusson to Weinstock, June 29, 1950, Knopf Collection, University of Texas at Austin. And on November 15, 1950, Fergusson informed Weinstock about her own editing choices: "As you will see, the Indian section uses a bit more than its fair third, as it is. But I am amputating from the Gringos—I don't like them as well anyhow—and may be able to

save enough space to restore the Santo Domingo bit" (Fergusson Papers, University of New Mexico).

28. See Erna Fergusson, "John Collier in New Mexico," *New Mexico Quarterly* 6 (Aug., 1936), 225–26; "The Coronado Cuarto Centennial," *New Mexico Quarterly* 10 (May, 1940), 67–71; "Navajos: Whose Problem?" *New Mexico Quarterly* 18 (Spring, 1948), 25–35; "The New New Mexican," *New Mexico Quarterly* 19 (Winter, 1949), 417–26; "Modern Apaches of New Mexico," *American Indian* 6 (Summer, 1951), 3–14; "New Mexico—State of Many Ages," *Think* 16 (Aug., 1950), 7–9, 24; "Crusade from Santa Fe," *North American Review* 242 (Winter, 1936–37), 376–87.

29. Fergusson, "New Mexico—State of Many Ages," 24.

30. Fergusson, "The Coronado Cuarto Centennial," 70.

31. Fergusson, "The New New Mexican," 417. Subsequent references to this source are given as "NNM" with page numbers.

32. See U.S. House of Representatives, *Congressional Record,* 55th Cong., 2nd sess. (Jan. 25–Feb. 22, 1898), 31, pt. 2:1374–96; (Mar. 8, 1898), 31, pt. 3:2613. H. B.'s February 2, 1898, speech before Congress includes elaborate detail about the probable dire consequences of withholding statehood from New Mexico. His purpose is twofold: to predispose members of the House to accept a bill in preparation (i.e., the Fergusson Act) which he intends to introduce and which advocates setting aside of public lands and, more generally, argues for the urgent need for statehood. He bases his argument on the probability that statehood would mean the relinquishment of public lands to the federal government and insists that if statehood is to be continually withheld, at least the granting of public lands should be allowed before they are taken up by private claims prior to official designation of statehood. In waging his argument he shrewdly assents to the closing of an "old," outstanding issue of statehood, or at least its postponement—then slips in what is essentially a restatement of the old issue. He appeals to the logic and sentiment of the congressmen who make up his primary audience, while speaking at the same time to the secondary audience of his constituency at home, especially the "Mexicans," and defending their rightful claims for statehood.

H. B. organizes his points around a historical, cause-and-effect approach (a pattern Erna Fergusson also adopts in "New Mexico's Mexicans" and "The New New Mexican") and explains how a Republican Congress, by establishing in 1891 a Court of Private Land Claims, adjudicated old Spanish and Mexican land grant claims and restored hundreds of thousands of acres to public domain. Ideally, those public lands would have been available for public schools and other institutions. He points out, further, that with the denial of statehood even more public lands will continue to be settled and taxed, and in the process the amount of land available for institutional use will diminish.

Throughout his argument he attributes the denial of statehood to partisan politics of the past. A master of paralipsis, or saying what he says he will not say, he complains about past Republican practices, while saying he does not intend to complain about those injustices so much as he hopes to look at the future and the happy resolution of the problem. He counters previous objections that the state is too sparsely populated, that the population is both uneducated and alien. He claims as his constituency and proudly defends the "pioneers" who have settled in New Mexico from other states on their way to the opportunities of the "great West," and he offers a personal testimonial to the loyalty of the "native" and "Spanish-American people of New Mexico." He is prepared to supplement his argument with population charts and data about Spanish American and "pioneer" citizens in the Territory.

33. See Harvey Fergusson, introduction to *El Gringo*, i–iii.

34. *Congressional Record*, Feb. 2, 1898, p. 1372. On March 8, 1898, H. B. continued his defense of the "brave and loyal soldiers" of New Mexico and his campaign for statehood. He inserted into the debate about the Spanish American War and appropriations of money for national defense that even though his constituency could not vote in national affairs, they were more than prepared to fight for the United States. His rhetoric rises to the occasion and builds to a crescendo of patriotism and defense of his region's native people: "They cannot vote in national affairs, as of right they ought to be entitled to do, but they can shoot in national defense; and if war with Spain is to come, they will shoot as they would vote, if they had a vote, in defense of American interest and for the honor, the dignity, and the glory of the American flag" (*Congressional Record*, Feb. 25, 1898–July 17, 1898).

35. Erna Fergusson, "New Mexico's Mexicans: The Picturesque Process of Americanization," *Century Magazine* 116 (Aug., 1928), 438. Subsequent references to this source are given as "NMM" with page numbers.

36. Fergusson, "Crusade from Santa Fe," 376–87. Subsequent references to this source are given as "CSF" with page numbers. See also Frederick E. Hoxie, "The Curious Story of Reformers and the American Indians," in *Indians in American History*, 205–28.

37. For a more detailed summary of the lobbying effort waged nationally against the Bursum Bill and for more biographical background on John Collier and especially on Collier's relationship with Stella Atwood and Mabel Dodge Luhan, see Kenneth R. Philp, *John Collier's Crusade for Indian Reform, 1920–1954*. See also Richard White, *It's Your Misfortune and None of My Own: A New History of the American West*, 491–94.

38. See "Justice for the Pueblo Indians," *Science* 56, no. 1458 (Dec. 8, 1922), 666.

39. Fergusson, "John Collier in New Mexico," 226.

40. La Farge to Fergusson, Jan. 30, 1951, Fergusson Papers, University of New Mexico.

41. Fergusson to La Farge, May 13, 1958, Knopf Collection, University of Texas at Austin.

42. "Book Reissue Angers Jicarilla Apaches," *Albuquerque Journal* (Oct. 14, 1973).

43. "Book Reissue."

44. Albert E. Stone, introduction to *Letters from an American Farmer*, 25.

FRIENDS: FIRST LADY OF LETTERS

1. Mabel Major and T. M. Pearce, *Southwest Heritage*, 169.

2. T. M. Pearce to R. F. Gish, Sept. 6, 1981.

3. Pearce to Gish.

4. Pearce to Gish. See also "U English Professor Lauds Miss Fergusson," *Albuquerque Tribune*, July 31, 1964.

5. Fergusson's transcript indicates that she majored in history and completed 121 hours of credit including: history, 37 hrs.; English, 33 hrs.; French, 29 hrs.; philosophy, psychology, logic, and ethics, 15 hrs.; Latin, 6 hrs.; and chemistry, 1 hr. Other sources indicate that she graduated from the Girls' Collegiate School in 1907, then traveled in Europe with her grandmother, returned to Albuquerque, where she enrolled in the university and graduated in 1912, then entered Columbia and received her M.A. in 1913. See Dorothy Woodward, "Erna Fergusson," *New Mexico Quarterly* 22 (Spring, 1952), 78.

6. "Tea Plans Announced By Alumnae," *Albuquerque Journal*, Aug. 15, 1965.

7. "Tributes Are Paid to Erna Fergusson," *Albuquerque Tribune*, Aug. 1, 1964. For an interesting account of Erna Fergusson's contribution to the publication of Peggy Pond Church's *The House at Otowi Bridge* by Fergusson's putting Peggy Pond Church "into the hands of her friend, Roland Dickey," see Peggy Pond Church, "On Building a Bridge," *New America* 3, no. 3 (Spring, 1979), 44–50.

8. W. A. Keleher, "Erna Mary Fergusson, 1888–1964," *New Mexico Historical Review*, 34, no. 4 (Oct., 1964), 345–50.

9. Keleher, "Erna Mary Fergusson," 350.

10. Paul Horgan, "Erna Fergusson and New Mexico: An Introduction," in *New Mexico: A Pageant of Three Peoples* (reprint, 1973), x.

11. Horgan, "Erna Fergusson and New Mexico," xi.

12. Erna Fergusson to Paul Horgan, Oct. 29 [1940], letter in possession of Horgan's estate. The typescript of *Our Hawaii* was received by Knopf June 16, 1941.

13. Paul Horgan, taped interview with R. F. Gish, Middletown Conn., Nov., 1981. See also *Nueva Granada: Paul Horgan and the Southwest* for full interviews conducted by Gish with Horgan.

14. Horgan interview.

15. Horgan interview.

16. Horgan interview.

17. Horgan interview.

18. Lawrence Clark Powell, "First Lady of Letters," *New Mexico* 40, no. 3 (March, 1962), 22–23; 37–39.

19. Powell, "First Lady of Letters," 23. See also Erna Fergusson, "A Writer's View of Southwest Libraries," in *Libraries of the Southwest: Their Growth, Strength, Needs*, 3–11.

20. Powell, "First Lady of Letters," 37.

21. Powell, "First Lady of Letters," 38.

22. Lawrence Clark Powell, "Southwest Classics Reread: Erna Fergusson and *Dancing Gods*," *Westways* (Mar., 1971), 13–17, 62.

23. Powell, "Southwest Classics Reread," 13.

24. Powell, "Southwest Classics Reread," 14.

25. Powell, "Southwest Classics Reread," 17.

26. Lawrence Clark Powell, interview with R. F. Gish, Tucson, Ariz., June 1, 1983.

27. Powell interview.

28. Powell interview.

29. Peggy Pond Church, interview with R. F. Gish, Santa Fe, New Mex., Jan. 9, 1984. See also "On Building a Bridge," *New America* 3, no. 3 (Spring, 1979), 44.

30. Church interview.

31. Church interview.

32. David Remley, *Erna Fergusson*, 2. Subsequent references to this source are given as *EF* with page numbers.

33. Frank Waters to R. F. Gish, Sept. 21, 1984.

34. Powell interview.

APPENDIX

1. Erna Fergusson, *Fiesta in Mexico,* (reprint, 1942), 258.

2. Erna Fergusson, *Chile,* 15. Subsequent references to this source are given as *Chile* with page numbers.

3. Erna Fergusson, *Guatemala,* 24. Subsequent references to this source are given as *Guatemala* with page numbers.

Bibliography

· ·

SPECIAL COLLECTIONS

Alfred A. Knopf Collection. Harry Ransom Humanities Research Center, University of Texas at Austin.

Erna Fergusson file. Southwest Collection, Albuquerque Public Library.

Erna Fergusson Papers. Coronado Room, Center for Southwest Research, University of New Mexico Zimmerman Library.

Franz Huning–H. B. Fergusson Collection. Coronado Room, Center for Southwest Research, University of New Mexico Zimmerman Library.

Southwestern Collection. University of Arizona Library.

WORKS BY ERNA FERGUSSON

"Acoma, the City of the Sky," *New Mexico Highway Journal* 1 (October, 1923), 4–5.

"Adobe or Not Adobe," *Country Life* 59 (January, 1931), 65–66.

"Albuquerque: A Place to Live In." In *Rocky Mountain Cities,* edited by Ray B. West, Jr., with an introduction by Carey McWilliams. New York: W. W. Norton and Co., 1949, 151–78.

"Americanism, My Definition—A Symposium," *New Mexico Quarterly* 6 (November, 1936), 295.

"Bernalillo County," *New Mexico State Tribune,* August 16, 1929. Other titles in this 1929 series, "See New Mexico First," include "Spilling the Beans on Fishing Places" and "The Jemez Mountains."

"Ceremonial Dances of the Pueblos," *Travel* 58 (December, 1931), 15–19.

Chile. New York: Alfred A. Knopf, 1943.

"Confessions of a Conformist," *Albuquerque Review,* June 7, 1961.

"The Coronado Cuarto Centennial," *New Mexico Quarterly* 10 (May, 1940), 67–71.

"Crusade from Santa Fe," *North American Review* 242 (Winter, 1936–37), 376–87.

Cuba. New York: Alfred A. Knopf, 1946.

Dancing Gods: Indian Ceremonials of New Mexico and Arizona. New York: Alfred A. Knopf, 1931. Reprint, Albuquerque: University of New Mexico Press, 1991.

Encyclopaedia Britannica, 1973 ed., s. v. "Albuquerque, s. v. "New Mexico." First published in 1962.

"Erna Fergusson." In *Mary Austin: A Memorial.* Santa Fe: Laboratory of Anthropology, September, 1944, 25–26.

Erna Fergusson's Albuquerque. Albuquerque: Merle Armitage Editions, 1947.

"Festival in Chalma," *Inter-American Monthly* 3 (August, 1944), 16–19.

Fiesta in Mexico. New York: Alfred A. Knopf, 1934. Reprint 1942.

"Flaming Arrow's People," *New Mexico Quarterly* 11, no. 4 (November, 1932), 352–53.

"From Redskins to Railroads," *Century Magazine* 113 (November, 1926), 23–31.

"From Rodeo to Rotary," *Century Magazine* 113 (December, 1926), 199–207.

"Gabriela Mistral," *Inter-American Monthly* 1 (August, 1942), 26–27.

Guatemala. New York: Alfred A. Knopf, 1937.

"Guatemala Is Swept and Garnished," *Country Life* 71 (November, 1936), 40–41, 105–106.

"Guatemala Journey," *House and Garden* 92 (November, 1947), 198–201.

Hawaii. Grand Rapids, Mich.: Fideler Co., 1950.

"Indians of Mexico and New Mexico," *New Mexico Quarterly* 4 (August, 1934), 169–73.

"The Individual's Role in the Pan American Program." In *Some Educational and Anthropological Aspects of Latin America.* Austin: University of Texas Press, 1948, 38–47.

"John Collier in New Mexico," *New Mexico Quarterly* 6 (August, 1936), 225–26.

"Justice as Interpreted," *New Mexico Quarterly* 3 (February, 1933), 3–8.

The Koshare Tours: Fascinating Motor Trips from Albuquerque; The Koshare Book about New Mexico and Albuquerque. Albuquerque: Albuquerque Chamber of Commerce and Koshare Tours, n.d. [1922?].

"Laughing Priests," *Theatre Arts Monthly* 17, no. 8 (August, 1933), 657–62.

Let's Read About Hawaiian Islands. Grand Rapids, Mich.: Fideler Co., 1950.

"The Merry Festival of the Dead," *Travel* 63 (June, 1934), 8–14, 53–54.

Mexican Cookbook. Santa Fe: Rydal Press, 1934. Rev. ed., 1940. Sixth printing, Albuquerque: University of New Mexico Press, 1945.

Mexico Revisited. New York: Alfred A. Knopf, 1955.

"Modern Apaches of New Mexico," *American Indian* 6 (Summer, 1951), 3–14.

Murder and Mystery in New Mexico. Albuquerque: Merle Armitage Editions, 1948.

"Navajos: Whose Problem?" *New Mexico Quarterly* 18 (Spring, 1948), 25–35.

New Mexico: A Pageant of Three Peoples. New York: Alfred A. Knopf, 1951. 2nd ed., rev., 1964. Reprint, Albuquerque: University of New Mexico Press, 1973.

"New Mexico's Mexicans: The Picturesque Process of Americanization," *Century Magazine* 116 (August, 1928), 437–44.

"New Mexico—State of Many Ages," *Think* 16 (August, 1950), 7–9, 24.

"The New New Mexican," *New Mexico Quarterly* 19 (Winter, 1949), 417–26.

Our Hawaii. New York: Alfred A. Knopf, 1942.

"Our Modern Indians," *New Mexico Quarterly* 29, no. 1 (Spring, 1959), 5–23.

Our Southwest. New York: Alfred A. Knopf, 1940.

"The Paradox of the Pueblo Veteran," *Southwest Review* 31, no. 3 (Summer, 1946), 229–31.

"Perpetual Pagans," *Scribner's Magazine* 92 (November, 1932), 293–95.

"The Sad Feast of Oaxaca," *American Mercury* 21 (January, 1934), 8–15.

"Senators Investigate Indians," *American Mercury* 23, no. 92 (August, 1931), 464–68.

"Taos Sketches," *Southwest Review* 17, no. 2 (January, 1932), 188–98.

"Tearing Down the West," *Yale Review* 25, no. 2 (December, 1935), 331–43.

Venezuela. New York: Alfred A. Knopf, 1939.

"What of Our Indian G. I.?" *Americas* 2 (July, 1950), 17–21, 46.

"A Writer's View of Southwest Libraries." In *Libraries in the Southwest: Their Growth, Strength, Needs.* Los Angeles: University of California Library, 1955, 3–11.

"You Yanquis," *New Mexico Quarterly* 12 (August, 1942), 261–71.

RELATED WORKS

Addison, Joseph. "The Pleasures of the Imagination." In *Oxford Anthology of English Literature.* Vol. 1. New York: Oxford University Press, 1973.

Amelinckx, Frans C.; and Joyce N. Megay, eds., *Travel, Quest, and Pilgrimage as a Literary Theme.* Ann Arbor: University Microfilms International, 1978.

Anaya, Rudolfo A. "The Writer's Landscape: Epiphany in Landscape," *Latin American Literary Review* 5, no. 10 (Spring/Summer, 1977): 98–102.

Bryant, Keith L. Jr. *History of the Atchison, Topeka, and Santa Fe Railway.* New York: Macmillan Publishing Co., Inc. 1974.

Butor, Michel. "Travel and Writing," *Mosaic* 8, no. 1 (Fall, 1974), 1–16.

Cassidy, Louise Lowber. "Interesting Westerners: A 'Delight Maker,'" *Sunset Magazine* 54 (January, 1925), 38–39.

Church, Peggy Pond. "On Building a Bridge," *New America* 3, no. 3 (Spring, 1979), 44–50.

———. *New and Selected Poems.* Boise: Ahsahta Press, 1976.

———. "Return to a Landscape: For Mary MacArthur Bryan," unpublished typescript, October 27, 1982–March 2, 1983.

Conrad, Peter. "Primitive America: D. H. Lawrence in New Mexico." In *Imagining America.* New York: Oxford University Press, 1980, 159–193.

"The Criminal Record," *Saturday Review,* January 22, 1949, 32.

Davidson, James West; and Mark Hamilton Lytle. *After the Fact: The Art of Historical Detection.* New York: Alfred A. Knopf, 1982.

Davidson, Levette J. Review of *Murder and Mystery in New Mexico, New Mexico Historical Review* 24, no. 1 (January, 1949), 77.

"Editorial Notes," *American Mercury* 23 (August, 1931), xx.

Fender, Stephen. *Plotting the Golden West: American Literature and the Rhetoric of the California Trail.* Cambridge: Cambridge University Press, 1981.

Fergusson, Harvey. "The Cult of the Indian," *Scribner's Magazine* 87, no. 2 (August, 1930), 129–33.

———. *Footloose McGarnigal.* New York: Alfred A. Knopf, 1930.

———. *Home in the West: An Inquiry into My Origins.* New York: Duell, Sloan, and Pearce, 1944.

———. Introduction to *El Gringo,* by W. W. H. Davis Santa Fe: Rydal Press, 1938

———. "The Lure of the West," *American Motorist* (December, 1927), 10–11, 27, 32.

———. *Rio Grande.* New York: Alfred A. Knopf, 1931.

Fisher, Irene. "Erna Fergusson," *Albuquerque Review* (February 8, 1962), 2.

Franklin, Wayne. "Speaking and Touching: The Problems of Inexpressibility in American Travel Books." In *America: Exploration and Travel,* edited by Steven E. Kagel. Bowling Green: Bowling Green State University Popular Press, 1979, 18–38.

Frost, Richard H. "The Romantic Inflation of Pueblo Culture, *American West* 17 (January–February, 1980), 5–9, 56–63.

Gish, Robert F. *Nueva Granada: Paul Horgan and the Southwest.* College Station: Texas A&M University, 1995.

Griffith, Glyne A. "Travel Narrative as Cultural Critique: V. S. Naipaul's Travelling Theory," *Journal of Commonwealth Literature* 29, no. 2 (Oxford: Hans Zell Publishers, 1993): 87–92.

Hahn, Emily. *Mabel: A Biography of Mabel Dodge Luhan.* Boston: Houghton Mifflin Co., 1977.

Hillerman, Tony, ed. *The Spell of New Mexico.* Albuquerque: University of New Mexico Press, 1976.

Horgan, Paul. "Erna Fergusson and New Mexico: An Introduction." In *New Mexico: A Pageant of Three Peoples.* Albuquerque: University of New Mexico Press, 1973, ix–xx.

Horne, Donald. *The Intelligent Tourist.* McMahons Point, NSW 2060: Margaret Gee Publishing, 1992.

Howard, Donald R. *Writers and Pilgrims.* Berkeley: University of California Press, 1980.

Hoxie, Frederick E. "The Curious Story of Reformers and the American Indians." In *Indians in American History.* Arlington Heights, Ill.: Harland Davidson, Inc., 1988, 205–28.

Huning, Franz. *Trader on the Santa Fe Trail: Memoirs of Franz Huning,* edited with notes by Lina Fergusson Browne. Albuquerque: University of Albuquerque in collaboration with Calvin Horn Publishing, Inc., 1973.

Jackle, John A. *The Tourist: Travel in Twentieth-Century North America.* Lincoln: University of Nebraska Press, 1985.

Jung, C. G. *Memories, Dreams, Reflections.* New York: Vintage Books, 1965.

Keleher, William A. "Erna Fergusson." In *Historical Society of New Mexico Hall of Fame Essays,* edited by Victor Westphall. Albuquerque: Historical Society of New Mexico, 1965, 27–54.

———. "Erna Mary Fergusson, 1888–1964," *New Mexico Historical Review* 34, no. 4 (October, 1964), 345–50.

Koppes, Clayton R. "From New Deal to Termination: Liberalism and Indian Policy, 1933–1953," *Pacific Historical Review* 46 (November, 1977), 543–66.

Lawrence, D. H. *Phoenix: The Posthumous Papers, 1936.* New York: Viking Press, 1936.

———. *Studies in Classic American Literature.* New York: Viking Press, 1964.

"Literature Lost in the Thickets," *New York Times Book Review,* February 15, 1987, 1–35.

Luckingham, Bradford. *The Urban Southwest.* El Paso: Texas Western Press, 1982.

Lutwack, Leonard. *The Role of Place in Literature.* Syracuse: Syracuse University Press, 1984.

McMechen, Edgar C. *Colorado Magazine* 17, no. 4 (July, 1940), 156.

McMullen, Frances Drewry. "Ask Miss Fergusson: The Woman behind a Service of Girl Couriers in the Indian Country," *Woman Citizen* 11 (January, 1927), 26–27, 41–42.

Major, Mabel; and T. M. Pearce. *Southwest Heritage.* Albuquerque: University of New Mexico Press, 1972.

Marsh, Fred T. Review of *Dancing Gods, Bookman* 74 (October, 1931), 215.

Miller, Joseph; and Henry G. Alsberg, eds. *New Mexico: A Guide to the Colorful State.* New York: Hastings House, 1962.

Mills, William J. "Metaphorical Vision: Changes in Western Attitudes to the Environment," *Annals of the Association of American Geographers* 72, no. 2 (June, 1982): 237–53.

Morris, Judy. *The Harvey Girls: The Women Who Civilized the West.* New York: Walker and Company, 1994.

Paredes, Américo. *"With His Pistol in His Hand": A Border Ballad and Its Hero.* Austin: University of Texas Press, 1958.

Philp, Kenneth R. *John Collier's Crusade for Indian Reform, 1920–1954.* Tucson: University of Arizona Press, 1977.

Poling-Kempes, Lesley. *The Harvey Girls: Women Who Opened the West.* New York: Paragon House, 1989.

Pomeroy, Earl. *In Search of the Golden West: The Tourist in Western America.* New York: Alfred A. Knopf, 1957.

Powell, Lawrence Clark. "First Lady of Letters," *New Mexico Magazine* 40, no. 3 (March, 1962), 22–23, 37–39.

———. *Southwest Classics.* Los Angeles: Ward Ritchie Press, 1974.

———. "Southwest Classics Reread: Erna Fergusson and *Dancing Gods*," *Westways* 63 (March, 1971), 13–17, 62.

———. "Western Books and Writers," *Westways* 56, no. 10 (October, 1964), 54; also 56, no. 11 (November, 1964), 52.

Price, Martin. "The Restoration and the Eighteenth Century." In *Oxford Anthology of English Literature.* Vol. 1. New York: Oxford University Press, 1973, 1558–59.

Remley, David. *Erna Fergusson.* Austin: Steck-Vaughn Co., 1969.

Rice, Warner G. Introduction to *Literature as a Mode of Travel.* New York: New York Public Library, 1963.

Rodríguez, Sylvia. "The Tourist Gaze, Gentrification, and Commodification of Subjectivity in Taos," *Essays on the Changing Images of the Southwest,* edited by Richard Francaviglia and David Narrett, with an introduction by David J. Weber. College Station: Texas A&M University Press, 1994, 105–26.

Sayre, Robert. "The Proper Study: Autobiography in American Studies." In *American Autobiography.* Englewood Cliffs, N. J.: Prentice Hall, Inc., 1981, 21–22.

Scholes, Robert; and Robert Kellogg. *The Nature of Narrative.* New York: Oxford University Press, 1966.

Simmons, Marc. *Albuquerque: A Narrative History.* Albuquerque: University of New Mexico Press, 1982.

Stone, Albert. Introduction to *Letters from an American Farmer.* New York: Penguin Books, 1981.

Stone, Lawrence. "The Revival of Narrative: Reflections on a New Old History," *Past and Present* no. 85 (November, 1979), 3–24.

Stout, Janis P. *The Journey Narrative in American Literature: Patterns and Departures.* Westport, Conn. Greenwood Press, 1983.

Thomas, D. H. "The Who of It: The Couriers." In *Southwestern Indian Detours: The Story of the Fred Harvey/Santa Fe Railway Experiment in Detourism.* Phoenix: Hunter Publishing Co., 1978, 75–94.

"Those Fabulous Fergussons," *El Palacio* 82, no. 2 (Summer, 1976), 42–47.

Turner, Frederick. *Beyond Geography: The Western Spirit against the Wilderness.* New York: Viking Press, 1980.

Vaca, Cabeza de. *Adventures in the Unknown Interior of America.* Translated by Cyclone Covey. Albuquerque: University of New Mexico Press, 1984.

Villagrá, Gaspar Pérez de. *History of New Mexico.* Translated by Gilberto Espinosa. Los Angeles: Quivira Society, 1933.

Walker, Stanley. *New Yorker,* December 4, 1954. 229.

———. *New York Herald Tribune Weekly Book Review,* May 5, 1940, 3.

Weigle, Marta. "On Coyotes and Crosses: That Which Is Wild and Wooden of the Twentieth-Century Southwest," *Essays on the Changing Images of the Southwest,* edited by Richard Francaviglia and David Narrett, with an introduction by David J. Weber. College Station: Texas A&M University Press, 1994, 72–104.

Weigle, Marta; and Fiore, Kyle. *Santa Fe and Taos: The Writers Era, 1916–1941.* Santa Fe: Ancient City Press, 1982.

———, eds. *New Mexico Artists and Writers: A Celebration, 1940.* Santa Fe: Ancient City Press, 1982.

White, Leslie A. Review of *Dancing Gods, American Journal of Sociology* 37, no. 5 (March, 1932): 843.

White, Richard. *It's Your Misfortune and None of My Own: A New History of the American Southwest.* Norman: University of Oklahoma Press, 1991.

Williams, Terry Tempest. "The Erotic Landscape," *American Nature Writing, 1995,* edited by John A. Murray. San Francisco: Sierra Club Books, 1995, 68–73.

Wilson, Edmund. "Zuni." In *Red, Black, Blond and Olive.* New York: Oxford University Press, 1956, 3–68.

Winter, Joseph C. "Riddle of the Mysterious Rock," *Impact,* June 12, 1984, 10.

Woods, Katherine. "A Colorful Panorama of the American Southwest," *New York Times Book Review,* May 5, 1940, 22.

Woodward, Dorothy. "Erna Fergusson," *New Mexico Quarterly* 22 (Spring, 1952), 75–89.

Wynn, Dudley. Review of *Our Southwest, New Mexico Quarterly* 10, no. 2 (May, 1940), 122.

Index

. . . .